Counting on the Latino Vote

LATINOS AS A NEW ELECTORATE

Race, Ethnicity, and Politics
Luis Fraga and Paula McClain

EDITORS

Louis DeSipio

Counting on the Latino Vote

LATINOS AS A NEW ELECTORATE

UNIVERSITY PRESS OF VIRGINIA

CHARLOTTESVILLE AND LONDON

THE UNIVERSITY PRESS OF VIRGINIA
Copyright © 1996 by the Rector and Visitors
of the University of Virginia
All rights reserved
PRINTED IN THE UNITED STATES OF AMERICA

First published 1996
First paperback edition 1998

The Library of Congress has cataloged the hardcover edition as follows:
LIBRARY OF CONGRESS CATALOGING-IN-PUBLICATION DATA

DeSipio, Louis.
    Counting on the Latino vote : Latinos as a new electorate / Louis
DeSipio.
       p.   cm—(Race and ethnicity in urban politics)
    Includes bibliographical references and index.
    ISBN 0-8139-1660-7 (cloth : alk. paper)
    ISBN 0-8139-1829-4 (paper : alk. paper)
    1. Hispanic Americans—Politics and government.   2. Voting—United
States.   I. Title. II. Series.
E184.S75D47   1996
323.1'168073—dc20   95-49230
                                              CIP

The cloth edition of this book was published in the series as originally titled,
Race and Ethnicity in Urban Politics.

♾ The paper used in this publication meets the minimum requirements of the
American National Standard for Information Sciences—Permanence of Paper
for Printed Library Materials, ANSI Z39.48-1984.

To Janet DiVincenzo
PARTNER AND FRIEND

Contents

Tables

Acknowledgments

A work such as this reflects the author's efforts and insights, but equally reflects the support of others. This is particularly true in the case of this research. At a fundamental level, it would not have been possible to conduct this analysis without the efforts of three individuals: Rodolfo O. de la Garza, William A. Díaz, and Harry P. Pachon.

The two surveys that provide the core of this research emerged from Harry and Rudy's efforts to improve the quality of the debate surrounding Latinos and American politics and to develop a research agenda concerning Latinos based on empirical findings. Their labors resulted in the National Latino Immigrant Survey and the Latino National Political Survey. These works offer baseline data about the demographic and political environments of Latinos and of the major Latino national-origin groups. Although these were separate studies, they shared two crucial similarities—financial support from the Ford Foundation and encouragement from Ford program officer Bill Díaz.

The support of these three individuals for my research goes far beyond merely offering me access to the data. Harry Pachon and the NALEO Educational Fund provided me a challenging applied research environment. Rudy de la Garza fulfilled the occasionally authoritarian role of the dissertation chair with a very light hand and offered me access to a series of fascinating research projects that prepared me well for teaching and independent research. Bill Díaz has encouraged and supported many of Harry and Rudy's research efforts. My work on these projects has offered me the opportunity to develop my own research skills. Finally, the Ford Foundation provided support for the research and writing of this manuscript.

Needless to say, these surveys reflect the efforts of many. Most important among these were the co-principal investigators of the Latino National Political Survey—F. Chris García, John A. García, and Angelo Falcón. I thank them for making these data available to me and including me in several aspects of their endeavor. I also thank the staff of the NALEO Educational Fund who contributed to making the National Latino Immigrant Survey a reality. I would particularly like to note the contribution of Survey Manager Eve Fielder.

My use of these data benefited from the insights of my dissertation committee. In addition to Rudy de la Garza and Harry Pachon, this committee included Walter Dean Burnham, Henry Dietz, Michael Hanchard, and Jeffrey Tulis. Each offered helpful insights and encouragement. I thank them for their help.

At the University of Texas, I would also like to thank Margo Gutiérrez and the Benson Latin American Collection. Their holdings on Latino politics never ceased to amaze me.

I would also like to thank Paula McClain and Luis Ricardo Fraga, the editors for the series on race and ethnicity in urban politics at the University Press of Virginia. Dick Holway at the press offered a steady and reassuring hand through the process of revising and preparing the manuscript for publication. My final thanks goes to the press' anonymous reviewer and again to Luis Fraga for thoughtful reviews of the manuscript.

Wellesley College and Mount Holyoke College have offered wonderful environments in which to learn to teach. Students at both institutions have forced me to defend many of the ideas presented here. As the manuscript was in its final stages of preparation, the University of Illinois at Urbana–Champaign offered me the home that I was seeking and the opportunity to further develop the ideas advanced here.

That said, my research would not have been possible without the support and encouragement of my partner, Janet DiVincenzo. She has the good sense to tell me when I have done enough for the day, and the good graces to edit my writing even after she has told me that I have done enough. To her, I dedicate this volume.

Counting on the Latino Vote

LATINOS AS A NEW ELECTORATE

CHAPTER I

New Americans and New Voters

As a nation of immigrants, the United States has had to face the continuing dilemma of how to incorporate politically and socially its newest members. Social incorporation has been left largely to individuals, local governments, and private institutions. The national government, however, developed a system for formal political incorporation—naturalization—that has remained virtually unchanged since 1790. The naturalization law passed by the first Congress, with only minor amendment, today offers immigrants with five years of legal residence access to all but one of the rights and privileges of the native-born: the naturalized may not serve as president.

Despite the relative ease of naturalizing, many immigrants do not make use of this privilege. Further, despite the formal openness of the system to many immigrant groups, some nationalities have been formally and informally excluded from naturalization during long periods of U.S. history. To the extent that this privilege for formal political inclusion is unexercised, whether through individual choice or legal prohibition, the fabric of the multiethnic society is torn (DeSipio and de la Garza 1992a).

With enough of these tears, the society runs the risk of overt ethnic acrimony and even rupture. To date, the United States has been more successful than other states in incorporating different peoples. For some, such as the early settlers and the Protestant Germans, the political incorporation took no more than one generation. For others, such as the original Chinese and Japanese immigrants, it took many generations. For the incorporation of the nation's involuntary migrant community, the African American, the outcome remains unclear today. Still others, southern and eastern Europeans for example, fall in-between these extremes, but few would argue that they are not today fully incorporated politically. In fact, political exclusion has been the exception in the American political system. Today, the excluded are only the newest immigrants and some of the descendants of those groups who historically faced formal exclusion.

Formal inclusion, however, does not guarantee equal levels of political participation. As a result, some racial and ethnic groups participate at much lower rates than others. This too presents a dilemma for a multiethnic state like the United States. Differential rates of participation lead to the potential that groups could claim they have been excluded and demand remedies. The introduction of this form of ethnic or racial demand making also threatens to induce ethnic acrimony.

In this study, I seek to examine how U.S. Latino populations have been incorporated into U.S. society. The experiences of Latinos offer useful insights into the question of how the United States politically incorporates its newest members. First, Latinos are a sizable component of the current immigration (both documented and undocumented) (U.S. Immigration and Naturalization Service [hereafter U.S. INS] 1992, table 3). Second, Latinos in general, but particularly Mexican immigrants, have long been a part of the migrant stream (Corwin 1978; DeSipio 1995a). Their experiences with incorporation have varied significantly in different historical periods (García and de la Garza 1977; de la Garza and DeSipio 1993). Related to this, the third insight that can be gained from the Latino experience is the long-term impact of de jure exclusion from political incorporation and participation and de facto marginalization. Mexican Americans and Puerto Ricans who faced this marginalization remain in the society but, in many cases, outside of the electorate. Arguably, the legacy of their exclusion does not end with them but instead extends to their children, who were raised in households with low levels of political socialization.

Finally, Latinos offer a fourth insight. Some Mexican Americans can trace their ancestry to the lands ceded to the United States at the conclusion of the Mexican American War. Although there were no more than 100,000 Mexican subjects in 1848 in what is now the southwestern United States, their presence offered their descendants treaty-based guarantees that assured them U.S. citizenship (Griswold del Castillo 1990; Gutiérrez 1995). Yet the local political culture prevented many from exercising this status freely (Pitt 1966; Weber 1973; Montejano 1987; Monroy 1990). At a more theoretical level, the root of the Mexican American experience in the Southwest ensures that a Mexican American and, perhaps, Latino ethnic claim can be based on a territorial claim. Hence, Mexican Americans are one of just two racial or ethnic groups in the continental United States who can claim to be territorially rooted; the other is the Native American (de la Garza, Kruszewski, and Arciniega 1973).

A study of this nature is timely for a second reason. For the first time, nationally representative studies of Latino political values, attitudes, and behaviors based on modern social science surveys exist. Two surveys of Latinos have been conducted, one of immigrants—the National Latino Immigrant Survey (NLIS)—and one of the three largest Latino national-origin groups (Latinos of Mexican, Puerto Rican, or Cuban ancestry)—the Latino National Political Survey (LNPS).

I use these survey data to examine a specific question about Latino political participation that relates to the broader question of political inclusion. Based on a finding that Latinos have lower than average levels of voting, I assess what the impact would be on the nation as a whole and in the states where they are concentrated if Latinos began to vote commensurate with their numbers. In order to make this exercise more concrete, I disaggregate Latino nonvoters into three categories: those who were registered but did not vote in 1988, those U.S. citizens who were not registered, and those who were not U.S. citizens. Within each of these categories, I find populations of Latino nonvoters that are likely to participate under the proper circumstances.

I label these potential segments of the Latino population *new electorates*. I select this term because it offers historical antecedents to the incorporation of previously excluded peoples in U.S. history. Later in this chapter, I discuss the experiences of these earlier efforts at inclusion in this century. Specifically, I examine the incorporation of immigrants— southern and eastern Europeans who immigrated after 1880 and began to participate in large numbers in the 1920s and 1930s—and of groups that required legislation (or constitutional amendment) to overcome previous exclusion—African Americans, women, and youth. I examine how their incorporation influenced the political alignments and partisan outcomes of the era. I use this discussion to suggest a continuum of the potential impact of the mobilization of Latinos as a new electorate.

I also examine the potential impact of the Latino vote on the national electorate. Specifically, I investigate whether Latinos will emerge as a realigning "new electorate," as southern and eastern European immigrants did during the New Deal (Anderson 1979; Gamm 1986; Erie 1988) and as African Americans have, to a lesser extent, over the past two decades. If Latinos do not follow the pattern of either of these two groups, I assess whether they reinforce existing patterns within the electorate, as have the two other new electorates of the twentieth century— women and youth.

I should note at the outset that Latinos may not form a new electorate along the lines of any of these previous new electorates. An alternative is a continuation of the current pattern—an increase in the number of

Latinos voting every four years with Latino mobilization following the class, education, and age characteristics of the population as a whole.

Before I get too deeply into the question of new electorates, however, I turn to the question of ethnicity and ethnic politics in the United States. The present and potential role of ethnicity underlies this discussion of Latinos as a potential new electorate because ethnicity offers a link between these populations that, under certain circumstances, can overcome other societal cleavages. As a result, as a background for the discussion that follows, I want to suggest possible directions that Latino ethnicity could take. I do not return to the discussion of ethnicity until the concluding chapter.

Ethnicity and the Multiethnic State

At a fundamental level, this analysis is a study of a form of ethnic politics. I am examining groups whose members may be linked politically by no more than ancestry (and, as Latinos, several ancestries at that). While the literature on ethnic politics is not very helpful in developing an understanding of the dynamics of the political incorporation of Latinos, it does offer some indicators of the potential outcomes of the political mobilization of Latinos as Latinos. This literature is most useful in highlighting the risks to the polity of a failed ethnic political incorporation.

Approaches to Ethnic Politics

The dominant paradigm of American ethnic politics focuses on the assimilation or acculturation of Europeans into the American amalgam (Handlin 1951; Higham 1955; Gordon 1964; Fuchs 1990). While there is an ongoing debate concerning the legacy of ethnicity for the second and subsequent generations, there is little evidence that ethnicity has produced significant long-term political conflict in the United States. Instead, ethnicity appears as one of several sociodemographic characteristics that sometimes influences political decision-making. In most analyses, European ethnicity is overshadowed by class and education and rarely proves the most salient factor in political decision-making.

While ethnicity rarely proves to be the determining factor in U.S. political outcomes (Waters 1990, 9), scholars continue to examine its possible legacies (Hansen [1937] 1987). Some scholars focus on "symbolic ethnicity" as a secondary predictor of political attitudes and behaviors. They argue that ethnicity shapes associational and occupational patterns that then shape political decisions (Parenti 1967; Greeley

1974; Alba 1990; for a criticism of this approach see Waters 1990, 164–68). Others look upon ethnicity, or its legacy, as a political tool that organizes voters much as an interest group coordinates common interests (Glazer and Moynihan 1963, 1975; Olzak 1983). These different approaches to ethnicity and its relation to U.S. politics are useful in demonstrating the fluidity of ethnicity and its ability to reshape itself from generation to generation. Yet for the most part, analysis of U.S. ethnic politics fails to find a routine ethnic impact on individual political behavior.

Most scholarly analysis of U.S. ethnic politics has focused on descendants of European immigrants. Several more recent studies guided by this scholarship, or by the notion of an assimilative or acculturative path for political incorporation, report concern that the country's newest immigrants, including Latinos, are not incorporating into U.S. politics as rapidly as did previous generations of immigrants (Novak 1971; Bouvier 1992). These critics argue that new immigrants are instead maintaining a culturally and, perhaps, politically distinct non-American, if not un-American identity.

These concerns about the Americanization of new immigrants have been applied to Latinos. Conservative critics of Latino elected officials and organizational leaders have charged that while Latino immigrants are willing to join the American polity, Latino leaders are pursuing an agenda that "racializes" Latinos and maintains Latino political distinctness (Chávez 1991; Skerry 1993). Other, less polemical, analysts raise a related concern that the changed opportunity structure in the post-New Deal state encourages national-origin groups to maintain an ethnic distinctness to use as political bargaining chips in an interest-group dominated political system (Glazer and Moynihan 1963; Fuchs 1990). This altered opportunity structure may change the resources available when today's immigrants decide to join the polity.

Comparative studies of international ethnic politics offer more confusion than clarity on the question of the role of ethnicity in U.S. politics. These comparativist studies tend to emphasize conflict over compromise (Horrowitz 1985; Olzak 1992). They also focus on the emergence of politically salient and inherently destabilizing ethnicity (Smith 1981; 1986) over ethnicity's relatively benign patterns and generation-by-generation decline in political salience, as has been the traditional U.S. model. The patterns of ethnic politics highlighted in these studies do not appear to characterize American ethnic politics in general or that of Latinos specifically (although Smith [1981] briefly discusses Puerto Ricans).

Comparativist studies analyze ethnicity in the developing world. The examples of contemporary immigrant-receiving countries in the first world offer yet another model. Canada and Australia, which along with the United States are the high-volume immigrant-receiving societies, have experimented with policies that allocate some state resources in specific programs on the basis of ethnicity (Foster and Stockley 1984; Betts 1988; Hawkins 1989; Richmond 1991). The effect of these policies is mixed. While they address the needs of the ethnic leaders who designed them and, perhaps, are suitable for the first wave of immigrants, they do not keep up with the changing dynamics of ethnicity in an immigrant-receiving society. As a result, the policies are under attack both from their supposed beneficiaries who perceive that they do not go far enough, and from opponents who believe that they cannot accomplish their goals of immigrant political incorporation. While these sorts of policies in Canada and Australia may motivate the Chávez and Skerry attacks on Latino leaders, there is little evidence that the United States will adopt policies similar to those of Canada or Australia or that Latino leaders are demanding such policies.

The literature on comparative racial politics is marginally more helpful. The distinction in U.S. politics between rigid racial barriers and fluid ethnic boundaries is useful (Omi and Winant 1986; 1994), but is not sufficiently complete when applied to Latinos. Some Latinos (particularly those of Mexican and Puerto Rican ancestry) have been treated as racial as well as ethnic minorities during lengthy periods in U.S. history. Further, a substantial minority identify themselves racially as distinct from whites and blacks. The federal government has also confused the applicability of racial politics to this community. It intentionally created a new nonracial category, Hispanic, to identify these peoples, but it has been inconsistent in the seriousness with which it collects data to understand this population better (Pachon and DeSipio 1987; de la Garza 1993).

The tension that exists in all analyses of ethnicity and politics is that the conditions for politically salient ethnicity to emerge are very fluid (Rothschild 1981). Ethnicity can disappear as a relevant political determinant, as it appears to have with the turn-of-the-century European immigrants (Hansen 1987 [1937]; Alba 1990, notwithstanding). But it can also reappear after long periods of dormancy (Isaacs 1975; Smith 1981). To date, the U.S. political system has been able to incorporate new members at a sufficiently rapid pace to ensure that the boundaries of ethnicity have not become rigid enough to reinforce other cleavages in the political culture. There have been few sustained demands for ethnic group–based resource allocation at the national level (such policies did occur informally in localities with political machines). At the national level, such practices are a relatively recent and ambiguous phenomenon and have resulted from efforts to remedy past exclusion.

This historical pattern does not guarantee that the political salience of ethnicity—specifically Latino or Mexican American, Puerto Rican, or Cuban American ethnicity—will not become a driving force in the future political order. Sustained exclusion of any group, whether formal or informal, presents a risk for a multiethnic state like the United States. As I indicate in chapter 5, the continual process of acculturation quickly separates new immigrants from the culture and politics of their countries of origin. Yet once immigrants are separated from the politics of their home countries, many do not formally join the U.S. polity. If immigrants are discouraged from naturalizing but cannot return to whence they came, their political awareness could come to be driven by their outsider, ethnic identity. Thus, their political understandings and their tools for organization could come to be shaped in ethnically distinct terms *against* the existing political order. As one group begins this process, others could make similar demands that could rip at the fabric of the American political culture. Were this unlikely scenario to unfold, the lessons and analysis of comparativist ethnic politics might be more useful in understanding its manifestation.

As I have indicated, with several specific and rather narrow exceptions, this sort of ethnic awareness and overtly ethnic politics has not occurred in the 220-year history of immigration to this country. In fact, the few exceptions have been led not by immigrants, but instead by "native" Americans who feared immigrants (for example, the Alien and Sedition Acts in the 1790s, the American or Know Nothing Party in the 1850s, and the red scare and restrictions placed on immigration after World War I).

Sustained exclusion of any group presents a second risk. Remedies designed to guarantee full and equal political inclusion for the formerly excluded generate demands by those who were not excluded (or their descendants) for equal benefits. The difficulties in retroactively incorporating the previously excluded suggest both risks that the polity runs in taking a laissez-faire approach to the process of political incorporation.

Among the excluded, the largest and most significant group, by far, are the African Americans. The retroactive grant of citizenship through the Fourteenth Amendment alone was not enough to ensure equal political access. Instead, after a wait of 100 years, the Voting Rights Act and activist federal intervention was necessary to guarantee unfettered black participation. The experience of slavery as well as the hundred-year history of exclusion once blacks received U.S. citizenship laid the groundwork for legitimate claims of redress.

The development of affirmative action programs to remedy past discrimination and, subsequently, discrimination against Mexican Americans and Puerto Ricans (or more broadly Hispanics) and Japanese Americans, Chinese Americans, and Filipino Americans (or more broadly Asians) have raised the salience of ethnicity and ethnic remedies to those who did not face past discrimination based on ethnicity. Recent immigrants form the largest group of these who did not face discrimination and who today have access to these protections designed to remedy past discrimination (de la Garza and DeSipio 1993). To the extent that these immigrants, or ethnic leaders speaking on their behalf, call for group-based protections based on the immigrant status that leaves them relatively disadvantaged compared to other, more established groups in the society, they have perverted the remedial intention of the affirmative action legislation. As I have suggested, these demands for targeted protections for immigrants run an even greater risk. By raising ethnic claims, they raise the general salience of ethnicity and the likelihood of calls for ethnic protections for older, more established groups in the society who face no objective disadvantage. Thus, just as the salience of ethnicity can arise from the initial exclusion, it can arise from progressive efforts to remedy past exclusion.

Latinos and Ethnic Politics

None of these studies of American or comparative ethnic politics or racial politics satisfactorily explain the dynamic of U.S. ethnic politics for Latinos or Latino national-origin groups. The dominant model for American ethnic politics, a relatively rapid political incorporation, was denied to the earliest Latinos, mostly Mexican Americans and Puerto Ricans (Pitt 1966; Weber 1973; Jennings and Rivera 1984; Montejano 1987; Monroy 1990; Sánchez Korrol 1994). Today, however, many of the barriers that prevented this incorporation have been eliminated, and many Latinos—both those previously excluded and new immigrants—acculturate at a rapid rate. The speed of this process creates the first tension in my analysis. A sufficiently large minority of Latinos may achieve a level of political acculturation such that they lose the potential to be *an* electorate (whether Latino– or national origin–based) before they can become a new electorate. In other words, ethnicity will come to play less of a role in their political decision-making than will other societal divisions. Thus, under these conditions of the declining salience of ethnicity, even if they join the electorate, they will have no distinct impact.

Because Latinos continue to immigrate at high levels and because of various forms of exclusion (naturalization barriers, the legacy of historical exclusion, or a new form of exclusion) an alternative scenario is possible: a move toward ethnic exclusivity. A strongly salient political ethnicity could be engendered that would preclude partisan compromise and the building of alliances with other groups. This is a second tension in this analysis. While Latinos or Mexicans, Puerto Ricans, Cubans, or Dominicans have been largely quiescent and desiring of political incorporation (and they could well continue to be until Latinos are fully incorporated into the political system), an ethnic movement could emerge under unique circumstances, either from within the community in response to the (believable) assertion of ethnic-based discrimination, or from without in response to a general increase in ethnic demand-making by other groups. The history of ethnicity in the United States suggests that these scenarios are unlikely, but the history of ethnicity in world politics argues that the possibility cannot be discounted.

The final tension results from the decision to focus on Latinos instead of exclusively on Mexican Americans, Puerto Ricans, Cuban Americans, or any of the other Latino national-origin groups. As I indicate in the subsequent analysis, Mexican Americans, Puerto Ricans, and Cuban Americans do not view themselves as having a panethnic political agenda. While there is evidence of partisan and policy commonalities and the emergence of some common panethnic identification among these national-origin groups, these national origins cannot today be viewed as an ethnicity. Recognizing these concerns about assuming a panethnic identity, I present the survey data disaggregated by national origin. Despite these differences, I believe it is valuable to compare their political experiences and to prognosticate about a political future that unites them. As I indicate, they share a common need for political incorporation.

The ultimate value of this approach will be determined only with time. Just as the outcomes of the other two tensions—the possible disappearance of politically salient ethnicity, and the development of ethnic exclusivity—cannot be anticipated, only time will tell whether Latinos develop a common political agenda.

Thus my research into the potential electoral impact of the Latino communities recognizes how fluid ethnicity can be as a political variable. While examining the role that Latinos could have as a new electorate, I recognize that the tendency of the U.S. political system to incorporate and acculturate newcomers may preclude any uniquely Latino electoral input before they coalesce sufficiently to increase their current impact. I recognize, on the other hand, that the meaning and salience of ethnicity in U.S. politics may change such that Latinos may come to act or be forced by the actions of others to shape their political views in terms that are exclusively or predominantly ethnic-based. For my prognostications to have any value, Latino political values and choices must remain sufficiently distinct so that they can be identified apart from the rest of the electorate. At the same time, they must behave as a part of the collective political environment.

I return to this theme of the salience of ethnicity, and more specifically Latino ethnicity, to U.S. politics in the final chapter. The assumption here is that Latino ethnicity is a complicated concept. Although some common issues unite the major Latino national-origin groups, few Latinos believe that there are common political bonds across the national-origin groups. Thus, while the conditions for a politically salient ethnicity based on exclusion may exist, factors internal to the Latino populations may prevent them from challenging the U.S. political system in ethnic terms.

New Electorates

Significant blocks of new voters entered the electorate four times in this century.[1] Three of these groups—women in the 1920s, African Americans in the 1960s and 18- to 20-year-olds (hereafter, youth) in the 1970s—entered the electorate on the basis of constitutional and statutory changes that expanded the franchise (the 19th Amendment, ratified in 1920; the 24th Amendment, ratified in 1964; the Voting Rights Act of 1965; and the 26th Amendment, ratified in 1971). A final new electorate—non–Anglo-Saxon European ethnics who mobilized and coalesced as an electorate in the 1920s and 1930s—did not require a constitutional amendment or statutory change to participate in American politics. Instead, around the time of the New Deal (roughly from the 1928 presidential election to the 1940 presidential election), some of these non–Anglo-Saxon Europeans significantly increased their level of participation and others shifted their allegiances to the Democratic Party on a state-by-state basis. By 1940, they constituted a new cohesive voting bloc of first-, second-, and, sometimes, third-generation European immigrants, and became a key component of the New Deal coalition. Although this new electorate included many first-generation immigrants, it included few recent immigrants.[2]

In order to develop models for what we might expect from Latinos over the next several decades, I discuss the entry of each of these previously excluded populations into the electorate. These histories include three factors that are of particular relevance to the role of Latinos as a new electorate. First, I look at the genesis of their gain or use of the franchise. Second, I assess the electoral impact of their having the franchise. Finally, I question whether the demand for the franchise emerged from within the population, whether the gain of the franchise was linked to demands for the votes of the newly empowered, and how the addition of the votes of the new electorate interacted with those of existing electorates. I summarize these characteristics in table 1.1.

TABLE 1.1. Theoretical dimensions of the new electorates of the twentieth century

	Women	Youth	African Americans	European ethnics
Factors necessary to create new electorate				
Constitutional change to ensure vote for new electorate	yes	yes	yes	no
Statutory change to ensure vote for new electorate	no	no	yes	no
Conditions of mobilization				
Premobilization vote in some states	yes	yes	yes	yes
Mobilization				
Generated from within new electorate	yes	yes	yes	yes
Generated from outside new electorate	some	no	yes	yes
Racial/Ethnic dimension	no	no	yes	yes
Electoral impact				
Immediate	no	no	yes	yes
Long-term	yes	no	yes	locally
Reinforcement of existing political alignments				
Initially	yes	no	no	no
Long-term	no	yes	no	yes
Creation of negative feelings in general population, initially	no	yes	regionally	no
Presence of cleavages within new electorate				
Initially	yes	yes	yes	no
Long-term	yes	yes	some	yes
Impact over time	increasing	decreasing	increasing	decreasing

New Electorates Created through Constitutional or Statutory Change: Women, Youth, and African Americans

The three forms of constitutional and statutory incorporation create different types of electorates. The entrance of women and youth into the electorate had little effect on electoral politics, at least in the short term. The incorporation of African Americans, on the other hand, has had a significant impact, particularly at the state and local level in areas with high concentrations of African American residents. The impact of their votes appeared immediately and continues today. By examining how these three groups joined the electorate, one sees a range of possible outcomes for the effect of political incorporation of new electorates, with blacks anchoring one end, and women and youth anchoring the other.

Women. The constitutional amendment that granted women the franchise emerged from mass and elite organization in its support. The leaders of this movement, however, were not broadly representative of women in 1910s society. Instead, they were mostly middle class, included few African Americans or southern and eastern Europeans, and emerged overwhelmingly from the Progressive movement. This leadership kept the movement narrowly focused and did not speak more broadly to women's status in the society.

Women's impact at the polls in the first few elections after the Nineteenth Amendment did not substantively alter the pattern of electoral outcomes. Campaigns, candidates, and political institutions did not make any special efforts to seek women's votes. Nor was there any effort to build on the organization that had gained the constitutional victory.

A study from the 1920s found that in addition to the traditional factors that keep people from the polls—class, education, age, and structural or procedural obstacles—two additional factors unique to women kept them from voting in large numbers. Lingering antisuffragist sentiment and husbands' objections explained why about 20 percent of the women did not vote (Merriam and Gosnell 1924, 109). Immigrant status and generation also distinguished women from men voters; younger women and immigrant women did not share the antisuffragist biases of the older native-born women. However, women in immigrant households voted at lower rates because their husbands objected more often than in native-born households.

By the 1930s, studies of political attitudes found women to be more conservative than men, specifically in their attitudes toward prohibition

(Tingsten 1963, 72–75). Although there were no national studies of voter registration and turnout by gender until the 1960s, Gamm's study of Boston suggests that voter registration rates for women remained low through the 1920s and increased to levels about 10 percent below those of men in the 1930s. Gamm also finds that women did not guide household political decisions: "women became Democrats after men had initiated the realignment" (Gamm 1986, 162). Although his discussion is not explicit, Gamm does present data that show a steady increase in registration among women through the 1920s, but he reports that women became mobilized only after the 1932 election (along with other segments of the electorate).

It should be noted that there are few studies of the political incorporation of women in the 1920s and 1930s. Absent specifics, it is reasonable to suggest that women were part of larger changes in the electorate. That is, women were included in the conversion of older non–Anglo-Saxon immigrants and African Americans to the Democratic Party, the mobilization of newer immigrants who had not previously participated around the New Deal coalition, and the increasing class division between Democrats and Republicans. I discuss these New Deal conversions and mobilizations later. The extent to which broader changes overshadowed gender in the electorate needs to be examined empirically.

By the 1970s, women voted at rates higher than men (U.S. Bureau of the Census 1989 [hereafter Census]). Increasingly, a "gender gap" began to emerge on some issues and in response to some candidates. Survey evidence indicates that more women than men were willing to support candidates irrespective of the candidate's gender. By 1987, women held 20 percent of elective offices nationwide (Census 1988). By this time, however, women were no longer a new electorate in the sense that I use the term here.

Youth. The 1960s and 1970s saw two new electorates emerge. One of these—youth—followed the pattern of women. A period of mobilization (somewhat shorter than that for women) led, in 1971, to constitutional change extending the franchise to 18- to 20-year-olds. The mobilization that led to the award of the franchise to youth was much shorter than the similar effort for women. The ethos of the age, particularly the draft for the Vietnam War, led to demands that youth be able to vote. The demand for the vote came as part of broader demands for societal change. As there was little debate over the granting of the franchise, however, it never became linked to other demands. Its advocates assumed that with the vote, the young would work within the system to promote their agenda. Unlike the experience of women, some candidates and parties did seek votes from youth almost immediately. These efforts were matched almost immediately by efforts to galvanize older voters against the demands of the new young voters. Also, similar to the women's vote, the youth vote was never cohesive. Instead, youth showed the same cleavages based on class, race, religion, region, and ideology of the dominant electorate.

Once eligible, young people did not take full advantage of the privilege. In the 1972 elections, for example, 49.6 percent of 18- to 24-year-olds voted compared to 70.8 percent of 45- to 64-year-olds (Census 1989, table A). By 1992, the gap widened with 40.4 percent of 18- to 20-year-olds voting compared to 70.0 percent of 45- to 64-year-olds (Census 1993a, table A).

Young voters have, on occasion, had an impact at the national level—for example, in the 1972 Democratic primaries. However, the perceived threat of a cohesive youth vote caused conservatives to mobilize against this threat; examples include the Nixon campaign's call to the Silent Majority and California Governor Ronald Reagan's marshaling of the middle class to oppose the student movement at the University of California at Berkeley. Further, the progressive political attitudes of student elites did not match the general ambivalence (and increasing conservatism) of youth as a whole. Over time, it became clear that young voters did not constitute a bloc and that their vote did not alter established electoral politics.

African Americans. The third new electorate created through constitutional and, in this case, statutory change was African Americans. The battle that led to the franchise for blacks was much more broad-based than that for either women or youth. While perhaps the most important element, the franchise was just one of many outcomes sought by the Civil Rights movement. Unlike the efforts that led to the women and youth votes, black leaders sought active and committed involvement from the mass of the black population.

Blacks, particularly in the North, were not completely disenfranchised before the Voting Rights Act of 1965 (Grimshaw 1992)[3] and did in fact participate in the mobilization and conversion associated with the New Deal (Weiss 1983) and the women's suffrage movement (Terborg-Penn 1977). Most blacks in the South and in parts of the North, however, did not have free access to the polls prior to 1965 (Branch 1988). With the ratification of the 24th Amendment and the passage of the Voting Rights Act of 1965, African Americans suddenly

gained near-universal access to the polls and encouragement to participate (Lawson 1976; Thernstrom 1987). It is this combination of nationwide mobilization to achieve the vote and encouragement to participate
(both from within the community and, initially, from without) that
many would argue separates the African American new electorate from
women and youth (Brown 1991).

The effect of African American enfranchisement was dramatic. According to Census Bureau estimates, the rate of black voter registration
increased to within 10 percent of the rate for whites by 1968 (Census
1989, table B). Although blacks continue to vote at lower levels than the
white population, black turnout levels exceed whites when class, youth,
and education are accounted for (Wolfinger and Rosenstone 1980).
Black and Black (1987) found that in the South, African American registration rates are particularly high in areas where blacks are not in the
majority. The number of black elected officials has also skyrocketed.
Although still small as a percentage of elected officials (between 1 and
2 percent), over 7,000 African Americans now hold elective office at the
federal, state, and local levels compared to less than 100 in 1965 (Joint
Center for Political and Economic Studies 1991).

The African American community also has distinct views from the
population as a whole on many public policy issues. While far from
monolithic, the political socialization and political attitudes of blacks
differ from those of the national political community. Blacks are overwhelmingly Democratic and strongly support civil rights, and economic
and social welfare agendas (Ornstein, Kohut, and McCarthy 1988).
These two trends—high levels of political participation and a progressive public policy agenda—crystallized in Jesse Jackson's presidential
campaigns in 1984 and 1988 (Reed 1986; Barker and Walters 1989).

While much study has focused on why blacks vote at high levels despite the barriers of class, education, and age, there has been no effort
to contrast African Americans with the two other twentieth-century
electorates created by constitutional change. The most important factors that explain such high participation are the legacy of the Civil
Rights movement, the continuing presence of discrimination, and a
sense of common fate (Brown 1991; Sigelman and Welch 1991; Verba
et al. 1993). Combined, these stimulated political participation. Implied
in these findings is that African Americans who came of age politically
before the mid-1960s are less likely to be politically active now.

Another measure of African American impact on the political process
is the backlash their franchise has caused among some nonblack voters.
Edsall and Edsall (1991) attribute the relative decline of the Democratic

Party in the 1970s and 1980s to the perception among southern white and ethnic white voters that the party had become too supportive of the black civil rights agenda and they were paying higher taxes to fund programs designed disproportionately to assist blacks (Huckfeldt and Kohfeld 1989). Assuming for a moment that this thesis is true, the black electorate's net impact on the system has been to mobilize blacks as liberal Democrats and convert some moderate white Democrats to the Republican Party.

The Continuum of New Electorates. Two ends of a continuum emerge from these electorates that were created through constitutional and statutory change. One end, which includes women and youth, constitutes a new electorate not significantly different from the established electorate that, at least initially, did not vote at equal levels. While these electorates may not agree internally on all issues—for example, women's support for prohibition or youth opposition to the Vietnam War—they largely fit into the existing electoral alignment and offer little challenge to the status quo. Further, at least initially, their votes were not sought in large numbers, and they voted at lower rates than did the rest of the population.

At the other end of the continuum is the African American community. The battle to gain the right to vote and other civil rights seems to have had a lasting impact on electoral participation and issue identification. Unlike (white) women and youth, blacks continue to challenge the national electoral alignment. If class and education factors are accounted for, blacks vote at rates higher than comparably situated whites. Their impact was sufficiently strong to spark a backlash that had an impact equal to, or perhaps greater than, their own impact on the electoral system. Mobilized black voters challenged the electoral system in programmatic as well as electoral ways. Yet their focus is not limited narrowly to black issues, but instead addresses the needs of many blacks and other disadvantaged citizens.

Conversion and Mobilization of an Ethnic Immigrant New Electorate during Realignment

The new electorate created by the New Deal in the late 1920s and 1930s was not the result of constitutional or statutory change. Instead, it was the outcome of first- and second-generation European immigrants who *mobilized*—that is, participated for the first time—and *converted*—that is, altered their partisan attachments. A second difference appears in the motive for the mobilization (and conversion). The primary cause was systemic. The political environment was going through a rapid change, and as a result, the participation of this new electorate was sought by existing political institutions. Undoubtedly, ethnic leaders took advantage of this systemic change to position their coethnics, to claim credit for new voters, and to demand rewards for that vote, but they were not the instigators. Instead, parties, machines, and candidates needing votes reached out to these immigrant, ethnic populations who had previously either not participated or had, but at much lower levels.

These immigrants and their children became a cohesive voting bloc between 1928 and 1936. Although these immigrants did not share a common ethnicity, they shared a common set of experiences in American politics. By the mid-1930s, these voters could reasonably be spoken of as a *bloc*, as they provided key support to the dominant Democratic Party coalition that lasted until the 1960s. Thus, despite the ethnic differences within, this New Deal new electorate offers a final model of the outcome of the incorporation of a new electorate. This model is of particular interest if the focus of political incorporation is immigrants.

The politics of the New Deal new electorate fits somewhere in the middle of the continuum that I have discussed. The national realignment that accompanied the New Deal was the tool for mobilizing this electorate that the Civil Rights movement was for blacks. Unlike blacks, however, the European ethnics did not share a set of issues to guarantee sustained cooperation. Instead, their common position in society allowed them to form an alliance that helped reshape the political system. Thus, in this model, the Depression led to a national upheaval that provided the spark to convert existing voters from one party to another and to mobilize previous nonvoters. Although this process occurred throughout the population, it had a particularly strong effect on the "new" immigrants from southern and eastern Europe and their children (Lubell 1952; Andersen 1979; Gamm 1986; Erie 1988; Cohen 1990).

Beginning in the 1950s, scholars began to examine the coalition that elected Roosevelt and reshaped the Democrats as the majority national party. According to one of the first students of this shift (Lubell 1952), Republicans became Democrats, but just as importantly nonvoters became active Democratic partisans. Lubell's insight initiated a stream of scholarship on the development of a new electorate during the New Deal realignment.

These studies have focused on both converting existing voters and mobilizing new voters. These two prongs of research are empirically related because, like today, many eligible voters did not participate in electoral politics 60 years ago (Gamm 1986, chapter 1). These non-voters consisted of recent immigrants including some who had naturalized and second-generation Italian, Irish, Jewish, and eastern European immigrants who shared with their parents no socialization into the American political system. Thus, mobilization in this period included naturalization, although many of the immigrants who began to vote around the New Deal had already naturalized (Ueda 1980). Instead, this mobilization required the capture of immigrants who had never fully socialized into American politics during the process of becoming American citizens.

Several city-level studies document the development of this new electorate. In Boston, Gamm (1986) finds that although it had become a bastion of Democratic support by the end of the New Deal, no single electoral realignment occurred. Through extensive precinct-by-precinct analysis, he argues that the realignment was built on an accumulation of small changes. Changes of this nature occur all the time, but the ferocity of politics between 1928 and 1936 compressed many changes into a short period.

A quick review of Boston's ethnic groups suggests the range of these small changes. At one extreme, the Irish had always voted at high levels and strongly Democratic, which they continued to do throughout the 1920s and 1930s. Like Boston's Irish, the Italians voted strongly Democratic in the 1920s. They continued to do so through the New Deal, but many more began to vote. Thus, Boston's Italian community responded to the New Deal by mobilizing at ever-greater levels. Jews, on the other hand, mobilized and converted to the Democrats. The conversion unified what had been a class-based division in partisan affiliation, with middle-class Jews converting from Republican to Democrat.

Black women who supported Roosevelt shifted the African American community from the Republicans. Finally, the old-line blue-collar Yankee population also shifted to the Democrats. Unlike the black and immigrant communities, however, Yankees became apathetic and demobilized. Thus, ethnic voters shifted to the Democratic Party at much higher rates than did the Yankee voters.

Studies of Chicago in the New Deal reinforce the picture painted by Gamm. In her study of Chicago factory workers, Cohen (1990) finds the twin effects of New Deal mobilization. First, the New Deal mobilized ethnic (what I have called first- and second-generation immigrants) and black voters. Second, it linked immigrant communities that had previously been insular with a common political and cultural community. Although the machine controlled and manipulated this newly formed community, the existence of the community ensured that class-based needs were articulated collectively. Cohen is not too precise about the timing of this process of conversion and mobilization. Allswang (1971), however, identifies 1928 as the key election year for Chicago's ethnic communities. Andersen (1979) suggests that the increase in Democratic voters among the newer immigrant groups (from southern and eastern Europe) resulted almost entirely from mobilization and not conversion.[4] This finding reflects the low numbers of voters from newer immigrant groups before 1920. Among older immigrant groups, however, conversion supplemented mobilization in making the Democratic Party *the* party of the Chicago ethnic.

Although limited to just two cities, these examinations of the electorate during the New Deal realignment establish a midpoint on the continuum for the incorporation of new electorates. National upheaval (in this case, economic and political) challenges existing political allegiances. The previously unmobilized immigrant community joined with earlier generations of immigrants to unify behind a national party and a national agenda. Thus, incorporation in this sense means not only access to the vote but also use of the vote to affirm new bonds to other, similar communities.

Summary

The experiences of the four twentieth-century new electorates indicate a continuum of possible outcomes when new electorates are incorporated into the U.S. political system. Anchoring one extreme is the experience of women and youth. Although grassroots mobilization succeeded in getting the franchise for women and youth, their votes were not actively solicited by parties or candidates and they did not have much of an electoral impact initially. Young voters have had little impact, and women began to act as a distinct voting bloc only 50 years after they won the franchise. As a result, neither of the new electorates' first generations can be said to have had an impact. This lack of impact reduced the likelihood that there would be a widespread incentive to participate. Furthermore, although their agendas differed in some policy areas from those of the broader electorate, neither youth nor women (until, perhaps, recently) have caused a shift in public policy.

Anchoring the other extreme is the experience of the African American population. Although some blacks voted prior to the mid-1960s, they voted in vastly larger numbers after the Civil Rights movement. Since that time, their votes have had an impact at all levels of the electoral system. At the local level, blacks have become the dominant electoral force in many cities and southern counties. At the national level, blacks have become key elements in many progressive candidacies for state and national office. Their vote has shifted the southern Democratic parties from racist to moderate, and their votes are necessary for most Democrats to win statewide office in the south. Their participation in the electoral system has caused a backlash among whites, expanding the number of Republicans, if not the diversity of the Republican Party.

Blacks have also shaped the debate on many domestic policy issues. Finally, black interest groups no longer battle just civil rights issues, but instead have become players across the domestic policy agenda. Thus, the new black electorate after 1965 saw an impact of its votes. Further, the process of winning the franchise had itself been an education that created an additional reward for participation. These factors combined to ensure both a short- and long-term impact for the black vote.

Between these extremes is the experience of the southern and eastern European ethnics who became an electoral force around the New Deal. Although their experiences varied by nationality, they shared a similar period of incorporation and were a key element of the Roosevelt New Deal coalition. Their incorporation was not preceded by a widespread social movement. Instead, local efforts at naturalization and the decay of the existing partisan alignment facilitated their incorporation. The collapse of the national economy and the change in the national political system ensured their political mobilization to an unprecedented degree. They seized a moment in American political history.

These three points on the continuum of new electorate incorporation offer comparisons for Latinos. That said, it is important to recognize that the experiences of women, youth, African Americans, and southern and eastern European ethnics are not the only possibilities. A final model that does not need extensive discussion is society's continued passive or active exclusion from the electoral system of the noncitizen or the citizen nonvoter. As I have argued, however, long-term exclusion of an identifiable group is a dangerous option for the polity and raises the likelihood of divisive ethnic politics. Historically, those who have been excluded make demands for remedies. Yet society has been ill-equipped to develop these remedies in a manner that is satisfactory to the descendants of both the excluded and the excluder.

Latinos share experiences with each of these new electorates. Table 1.1 summarizes the incorporative experiences and electoral outcomes of the four twentieth-century new electorates. In order to paint a picture of Latino inclusion and exclusion as it stands now and to prognosticate about future trajectories, my research examines extensive survey data about Latino political values, attitudes, behaviors, and, among noncitizens, attachment to the United States. The availability of these data distinguishes Latinos from previous new electorates. After a detailed discussion of Latino political attitudes and behaviors, I return, in chapter 7, to the discussion of new electorates to see what lessons can be learned from these cases of political inclusion of previously excluded or marginalized electorates.

Data Sources

The new research in this analysis will stem from two unique national studies of the Latino population. The first, the National Latino Immigrant Survey (NLIS), examines Latino immigrants' propensities to naturalize. The second, the Latino National Political Survey (LNPS), examines political attitudes and behaviors of the three largest Latino populations: those of Mexican, Cuban, and Puerto Rican ancestries. Both surveys are national in scope and have a sufficient number of respondents to allow for subgroup analysis. In appendix 1 I highlight the goals and methods of each survey, the common issues raised, and the ways in which their data lend themselves to my analysis of Latino political incorporation.

Here it is worthwhile to mention two important similarities between the studies. The surveys received funding from the same program officer (Dr. William A. Díaz) at the Ford Foundation. As a result, the foundation asked similar research questions of both survey teams. Although the NLIS was in the field first, the research teams that designed the two studies operated during the same period and shared problems and insights, such as the difficulties in developing an affordable sampling frame. In addition, one individual served on the advisory committee of both projects (Dr. Alejandro Portes of Johns Hopkins University). The second similarity is more idiosyncratic. I am the only person to have worked on both projects.[5]

Tables 1.2 through 1.5 offer sociodemographic profiles of the citizen and noncitizen respondents to each survey. In subsequent chapters, I return to these data to contrast these aggregate population profiles with the characteristics of subsets of the Latino population. These

TABLE I.2. Sociodemographics of naturalized U.S. citizen respondents to the NLIS

Characteristic	Mexican American (%)	Cuban American (%)	Dominican American (%)	Other Latino citizens (%)
Age, mean	41 years	49 years	39 years	43 years
Gender				
Male	46.9	36.1	11.7	36.9
Female	53.1	63.9	88.3	63.1
Education, mean	10 years	12 years	11 years	13 years
Household income, mean	$21,454	$23,543	$17,423	$24,004
Work status				
In labor force	65.0	59.2	62.8	61.8
In temporary labor force	4.2	6.5	9.3	1.3
Not in labor force	30.9	34.3	27.9	36.9
Home owner	69.0	69.3	14.2	50.3
Self-evaluated English language skills				
Does not speak well	20.9	12.6	32.7	6.9
Mixed language ability	37.0	47.4	47.4	47.6
Speaks well	42.0	40.0	19.9	45.5
Age at immigration, mean	17 years	25 years	20 years	23 years
Reason for immigration				
Family	47.1	11.3	22.9	28.2
Political	0.5	67.5	0.0	3.1
Economic	35.6	11.7	50.5	37.7
Other	16.8	9.5	26.6	31.0
Social milieu				
All Latino	11.9	13.7	15.9	5.9
Mixed	86.5	84.4	84.1	91.4
All Anglo	1.6	1.8	0.0	2.7
Citizenship milieu				
Mostly non-U.S. citizens	11.6	3.6	40.0	9.5
Mixed	40.7	44.8	21.8	64.7
Mostly U.S. citizens	47.7	51.6	38.1	25.8
n	159	230	29	135

SOURCE: National Latino Immigrant Survey.

subsets that I contrast with the aggregate data represent groupings of voters and nonvoters.

Terminology

Much of my discussion involves making ethnic and national-origin distinctions. As a result, it is important to be precise in the terminology used to identify the group being discussed. I use five national-origin–based terms for Latino populations: Mexican ancestry, Puerto Rican ancestry, Cuban ancestry, Dominican ancestry, and "other Latino." Those of Mexican ancestry, Cuban ancestry, and Dominican ancestry are residents of the United States who can trace their ancestry to Mexico, Cuba, or the Dominican Republic. Respondents of Puerto Rican ancestry are residents of the continental United States who trace their ancestry to

TABLE 1.3. Sociodemographics of non-U.S. citizen respondents to the NLIS

Characteristic	Mexican ancestry (%)	Cuban ancestry (%)	Dominican ancestry (%)	Other Latino ancestry (%)
Age, mean	40 years	47 years	41 years	38 years
Gender				
Male	44.6	44.9	34.4	47.1
Female	55.4	55.1	65.6	52.9
Education, mean	7 years	9 years	9 years	11 years
Household income, mean	$16,887	$18,261	$11,864	$20,634
Work status				
In labor force	52.6	48.3	51.9	65.4
In temporary labor force	11.3	10.6	22.3	6.7
Not in labor force	36.1	41.1	25.9	27.9
Home owner	54.9	58.2	17.1	34.2
Self-evaluated English language skills				
Does not speak well	50.3	40.9	51.0	20.0
Mixed language ability	34.5	35.1	42.1	47.5
Speaks well	15.2	24.1	6.9	32.5
Age at immigration, mean	22 years	33 years	28 years	24 years
Reason for immigration				
Family	37.0	12.7	34.3	26.8
Political	0.1	70.2	3.6	6.1
Economic	44.9	5.2	54.0	35.4
Other	18.0	11.8	8.0	31.8
Social milieu				
All Latino	26.0	15.1	11.9	4.3
Mixed	73.1	84.9	88.1	94.4
All Anglo	0.9	0.0	0.0	1.3
Citizenship milieu				
Mostly non-U.S. citizens	24.5	10.1	23.9	27.8
Mixed	48.0	39.6	47.5	50.6
Mostly U.S. citizens	27.5	50.3	28.6	21.6
n	537	197	82	238

SOURCE: National Latino Immigrant Survey.

TABLE 1.4. Demographics of U.S. citizen respondents to the LNPS

Characteristic	Mexican American (%)	Puerto Rican (%)	Cuban American (%)
Age, mean	39 years	38 years	45 years
Gender			
Male	46.3	44.3	44.9
Female	53.7	55.7	55.1
Race			
White	56.5	58.1	92.5
Black	0.2	4.2	3.7
Latino referent	43.3	37.7	3.8
Education, mean	11 years	10 years	12 years
Household income, mean	$27,439	$19,689	$34,755
Work status			
In labor force	60.2	50.0	68.6
Temporarily unemployed	11.9	12.1	6.2
Not in labor force	27.9	37.9	25.2
Home owner	49.0	13.3	48.4
Self-evaluated language skills			
English stronger	51.3	20.8	11.4
Bilingual	39.7	45.3	42.4
Spanish stronger	9.0	33.9	46.2
Identification			
National origin	63.5	75.9	65.2
Panethnic	28.0	15.1	18.2
American	8.5	9.1	16.7
Religion			
Catholic	73.7	65.1	74.8
Protestant	15.0	22.3	14.4
Other/No preference	11.3	12.5	10.8
Immigrant generation			
First	13.2	65.7	70.9
Second	21.2	25.4	22.4
Third	24.0	2.9	0.9
Fourth	41.6	6.0	5.8
Age at immigration (foreign born), mean	13 years	19 years	25 years
Social milieu			
Mostly Latino	24.5	31.4	33.8
Mixed Latino and Anglo	62.7	58.3	61.3
Mostly Anglo	12.8	10.4	4.9
n	878	587	312

SOURCE: Latino National Political Survey.

TABLE 1.5. Demographics of non-U.S. citizen respondents to the LNPS

Characteristic	Mexican ancestry (%)	Cuban ancestry (%)
Age, mean	34 years	48 years
Gender		
Male	60.0	52.5
Female	40.0	47.5
Race		
White	44.0	91.6
Black	0.3	2.9
Latino referent	55.7	5.5
Education, mean	7 years	9 years
Income, mean	$23,221	$20,293
Work status		
In labor force	71.5	54.7
Temporarily unemployed	9.6	7.7
Not in labor force	18.8	37.5
Home owner	26.3	24.7
Self-evaluated language skills		
English stronger	1.6	3.0
Bilingual	18.6	14.8
Spanish stronger	79.8	82.2
Identification		
National origin	87.8	88.5
Panethnic	12.0	8.9
American	0.3	2.7
Religion		
Catholic	82.3	80.2
Protestant	7.7	13.2
Other/No preference	10.1	6.6
Age at immigration, mean	21 years	34 years
Social milieu		
Mostly Latino	60.5	46.5
Mixed Latino and Anglo	37.3	47.5
Mostly Anglo	2.1	6.0
n	668	367

SOURCE: Latino National Political Survey.

Puerto Rico. The sampling frame of the LNPS excludes those Puerto Ricans residing in Puerto Rico. The "other Latino" category is a residual grouping of Latinos who trace their ancestry to parts of Latin America other than Mexico, Puerto Rico, Cuba, or the Dominican Republic. In using this category, I do not mean to imply homogeneity among these populations. In fact, I would hypothesize that just the opposite is more accurate (DeSipio et al. 1994). Instead, the categorization is a function of the absence of reliable data on the sociopolitical values, attitudes, and behaviors of, for example, Ecuadorians or Guatemalans. Although there has been some social science study of immigrants from other than the three major Latino sending countries, it is mostly impressionistic. With one exception (Gurak 1987 and related studies), the quantitative data on other Latinos is generated from small, nonrepresentative samples (Pessar 1987; Sassen-Koob 1987; Chávez and Flores 1988; Chávez, Flores, and Lopez-Garza 1990).

These five Latino national-origin terms—Mexican ancestry, Puerto Rican ancestry, Cuban ancestry, Dominican ancestry, and other Latino—do not distinguish between native and foreign-born or between generations of native-born. I am careful to identify whether I am discussing citizens or noncitizens and foreign-born or native-born. I use the ancestry terms for consistency and clarity to identify all individuals who can trace their ancestry to Mexico, Cuba, Puerto Rico, or the Dominican Republic.

When I use the more specific terms—Mexican American, Puerto Rican, Cuban American, or Dominican American—I am referring to the citizen components of the ancestry populations. Although the term is not as simple, I use the term "other Latino citizens" to identify the U.S. citizen populations among the other Latinos.

Clearly, the citizen and noncitizen populations overlap. Households, let alone neighborhoods, include citizens and noncitizens alike. Where precision about citizenship status is not possible, I will often use the more generic terms: Mexican American, Cuban American, Dominican American, and Puerto Rican.

I also use several panethnic terms. I use Latino and Hispanic interchangeably to refer to people in the United States who can trace their ancestry to Spanish-speaking areas of Latin America and the Caribbean. I use these terms selectively when I am referring to common characteristics of all of the Latino national-origin communities or to conscious efforts to unite the national-origin communities. Sometimes, however, data and secondary sources do not distinguish among national-origin groups and, for example, report on "Latinos in the Southwest." In cases such as this, I have used my best judgment as to whether to assume this means those of Mexican ancestry or to maintain the usage in the original.

I use several other panethnic or panracial terms. I use Anglos to refer to white non-Hispanics in the United States. As with my use of "other

Latino," I recognize the oversimplification implicit in this usage. The political values, attitudes, and behaviors of Italian Americans may significantly differ from Norwegian Americans, although both are Anglos in my usage. Since my purpose, however, is to contrast Latino communities with other groups in the society, I believe that this categorization can be justified. I also recognize that the term "Anglo" undervalues the contribution of southern and eastern Europeans to the white non-Hispanic population, but I have not found another term, other than the cumbersome "white non-Hispanic," that captures the population that I am seeking to identify. European American is inaccurate, as European is one of the three dominant elements (along with the black and indigenous populations) that make up the Latino population. Finally, I also use the panracial terms black or African American to identify the non-Hispanic black population in the United States.

CHAPTER 2

Myths and Realities

Latino Partisanship, Ideology, and Policy Preferences

DESPITE THEIR LONG history in the United States, Latinos have only recently become the focus of extensive and methodologically sophisticated scholarly analysis. The absence of comprehensive research has made it difficult to discuss in any depth the most basic characteristics of Latino politics. Basic traits such as partisanship, ideology, and policy preferences have been subject to debate. Often conflicting evidence could be marshaled to demonstrate that Mexican Americans, Puerto Ricans, Cuban Americans, and other Latinos held almost all types of political attitudes and beliefs.

My purpose in this chapter is twofold: First, I seek to review the academic literature on Latinos and politics to assess the conventional wisdoms on the building blocks of participatory politics—partisanship, ideology, and policy preferences. Second, I compare and contrast these conventional wisdoms to the picture of these communities presented in the NLIS and the LNPS.

The survey data demonstrate that the previously available picture presents only a partial canvas that neglects the complexity and diversity of the Latino communities. As will become evident, I cannot explore all dimensions of Latino political activity and interest. Instead, I develop a more complete sense of where the Latino adult population is today in terms of voting and policy preferences. This baseline picture serves as a backdrop for the discussion in subsequent chapters.

The Conventional Wisdom

As the Latino communities have grown in size, pundits' expectations for their political impact have increased as well. The proclamation of the 1980s as the "decade of the Hispanic" emerged from a perception that population growth alone ensured that candidates, political parties, and the media would seek Latino input and reward its participation. A growing body of literature demonstrates that sheer numbers alone do not ensure that the Latino communities will become central to the American political process (Wolfinger and Rosenstone 1980; de la Garza and DeSipio 1992; Nelson 1993; de la Garza, Menchaca, and DeSipio 1994; de la Garza and DeSipio 1996). Until recently, however, representative pictures of the communities were not available. Instead, analysts had to rely on data generated from poor national samples (de la Garza 1987; Calvo and Rosenstone 1989; García et al. 1989; de la Garza et al. 1992; Kosmin and Keysar 1992; Welch and Sigelman 1993). These data tended to homogenize Latino national-origin groups into a uniform whole that neglected to account for potential heterogeneity within the Latino populations. Overlooked were the different political concerns of the Latino national-origin groups or the differences between the foreign- and the native-born. Even though they are based on questionable assumptions, I review these conventional wisdoms as a point of departure for the surveys that form the basis of my study.

Partisanship

The notion of "Latino politics" stumbles as soon as the question of partisanship is raised. Mexican Americans and Puerto Ricans have traditionally shown strong levels of adherence to the Democratic Party (García and de la Garza 1977, 100–110; Jennings 1984b; Cain and Kiewiet 1987). Conversely, Cuban Americans are quite loyal to the Republican Party (Moreno and Rae 1992; Moreno and Warren 1992; Grenier et al. 1994). As with all populations, class plays an important role in Latino partisanship. Affluent Mexican Americans and Puerto Ricans are more likely than their poor coethnics to be Republican (Brischetto 1987). The Cuban community shows some partisan diversity as well, although it is less pronounced than among the Mexican Americans and Puerto Ricans. Cuban Americans who reside outside of South Florida are more likely to be Democrats than their South Florida coethnics.

Discussions such as this of Latino partisanship must be cautious. Opinion and exit polling of these communities is often flawed (de la Garza 1987). The difficulties are rife. Not all Latino communities are alike, and they are geographically concentrated in different regions of the country. Hence, a sample in the region of greatest Latino concentration—the Southwest—would exclude most Puerto Ricans, Cubans, and Latinos who trace their ancestry to other countries in Latin America. As

I show in chapter 3, Latinos, regardless of national origin, have more nonvoters as a share of the adult population than does any other major racial or ethnic group in U.S. society. Opinion polling, thus, has the additional burden of identifying likely Latino *voters* and not simply Latino *adults*. Samples must be drawn with particular care. Selecting high-concentration Latino sites weights the results in favor of the Democrats. Surveying in middle-class areas weights the results in favor of the Republicans. A telephone survey neglects some poor, presumably Democratic, respondents without phones. While opinion surveys and exit polls of the white and African American populations are sensitive to these issues, until recently there has not been sufficient baseline demographic and partisan information on Latinos to allow for accurate polling with small samples.

The impact of this imprecision can be seen in table 2.1, which compiles estimates of Mexican American (1960–76) and Latino (1976–92) support for the major parties' presidential candidates over the past 32 years. For the elections beginning in 1972 when there are multiple polls, this imprecision is particularly evident. Both estimates of the 1972 Mexican American vote gave George McGovern the majority of the votes. Yet one estimate was over 20 percent higher than the other. By 1992, the gap had narrowed. Yet the two major polls differed by 9 percent when discussing what was ostensibly the same population. This range was well outside either study's margin of error.

Despite the weakness of the electoral polling in these studies, two trends stand out. First, when Latino votes are aggregated, they show that the communities support the Democratic Party at rates higher than the population as a whole. Of the nine presidential races in table 2.1, Mexican Americans and Latinos supported the Democrats every time. The electorate as a whole voted Republican in five of these races. The second trend is that the level of Latino support for the Democrats is declining. From 1960 to 1976, Latino (mostly Mexican American) support for the Democrats averaged 84 percent. In the four elections between 1980 and 1992, Latino support for Democratic presidential candidates dropped to 63 percent. Part of this change is compositional. Over the years, increasing numbers of Cubans have joined the active electorate, and over this same period, they have shifted their allegiance from the Democrats to the Republicans (DeCew 1980; Craig 1991). Undoubtedly, some of the change between the 1960s and the 1980s can also be explained by more accurate polling techniques. Despite these changes, however, the data indicate that this second trend—toward greater, though far from majority support for the Republicans—is

TABLE 2.1. National Latino Voting Patterns, 1960–92

Year/Latino electorate	Democratic vote (%)	Republican vote (%)	Other vote (%)
1960			
Mexican Americans[a]	85	15	–
1964			
Mexican Americans[a]	90	10	–
1968			
Mexican Americans[a]	87	10	3
1972			
Mexican Americans[a]	64	36	–
Mexican Americans[b]	85	15	–
1976			
Mexican Americans[b]	92	8	–
Latinos[c]	82	18	–
1980			
Latinos[c]	56	37	7
1984			
Latinos (CBS)[d]	66	34	–
Latinos (NBC)[e]	68	32	–
Latinos (ABC)[e]	56	44	–
1988			
Latinos (CBS)[d]	70	30	–
Latinos (ABC)[f]	70	30	–
Latinos (NBC)[f]	69	31	–
Latinos (LA Times)[f]	62	38	–
1992			
Latinos (VRS)[g]	62	24	14
Latinos (LA Times)[h]	53	31	16

SOURCES: [a]García and de la Garza 1977, 101–103; [b]Gann and Duignan 1986, 210; [c]CBS News/*New York Times* exit poll in "Opinion Roundup" 1989, 24; [d]CBS News/*New York Times* exit poll in "Opinion Roundup" 1989, 25; [e]Balz 1987, 32; [f]"Opinion Roundup" 1989, 26; [g]Voter Research and Surveys exit poll (most of the networks and wire services used this exit poll in 1992); [h]*Los Angeles Times*, November 5, 1992.

slowly occurring and is not simply a function of changing electoral opportunities and more accurate polling strategies.

Ideology

Prior to the collection of the recent survey data on Latino political values and attitudes, even less was known about Latino ideology than was known about partisanship. This vacuum allowed scholars and advocates to make generalizations about Latino ideology that were hard to substantiate. Historical examples of Latinos and Latino organizations mobilizing around varying ideologies can be found to substantiate a wide range of positions on the ideological spectrum. Further, non-Latinos often describe Latino ideology as left, right, or apolitical on the basis of the ideological biases of the ascriber.

Reconstructing Latino ideology is an inexact process. Much of the discussion that follows generalizes from the activities of organizations and elected officials. I discuss the ideologies of leaders and organizations from different historical periods to gauge the ideological leanings of the communities.

Measuring the communities' ideologies through the activities of leaders and organizations is imprecise. Most of these organizations are elite-driven (or are at least not mass-based). Almost by definition, elected officials and community leaders are also elites (at least within the community). Yet no other measure exists of these communities' ideological leanings. As importantly, this discussion will demonstrate that the diversity of possible Latino ideologies depends both on the political values of the era and on the political opportunities open to Latinos.

Mexican Immigrant and Mexican American. The first example of a mass "Latino" politics was the participation, beginning in the 1880s, of Texas and New Mexico Mexican Americans in very conservative political machines that were sometimes, but not always, controlled by Anglos (Weeks 1930; Shelton 1946; Holmes 1967, chapter 2; Gutiérrez 1968, chapter 4; Anders 1979). Although Anglos often manipulated Mexican American voters in these political machines, some Mexican Americans did rise to leadership positions. Once in such roles, however, many Mexican American elected officials continued to represent the dominant conservative ideologies of their states and regions (Valdes y Tapia [1964] 1976, chapter 4; Anders 1979; García 1989, 114–16).

There were, however, exceptions to these patterns. In the late nineteenth and early twentieth centuries, some New Mexico elected officials emerged from the ferment caused by Las Gorras Blancas's efforts to reclaim, violently if necessary, the land owned by the Hispanos (the preferred identification term of New Mexico Hispanics) in northern New Mexico (Rosenbaum 1981, chapters 8 and 9; Gómez-Quiñones 1994). The International Workers of the World (IWW) was also active in organizing mineworkers in northern New Mexico and southern Colorado (as well as in Arizona) (Deutsch 1987, 110–12).

Colorado Mexican Americans were less important to statewide politics than their Texas and New Mexican coethnics. They also followed a different ideological path. Influenced by the radicalism of mineworkers' union organizing, Colorado Mexican American politics took on a more progressive form than in either Texas or New Mexico. As early as the mid-1920s, state Representative José Martínez mobilized voters around a demand for junior colleges so that "Americans of Spanish surnames can be educated" (Vigil 1976, 185).

An alternative model for Mexican American ideology appeared with the creation of the first wave of Mexican American civic organizations. The League of United Latin American Citizens (LULAC) was the first large-scale Mexican American organization to focus on the United States and not on Mexico (Weeks 1929; García 1989, chapter 2; Márquez 1993). Formed in Texas in 1929, it slowly expanded throughout the Southwest during the 1930s. Its agenda was assimilationist. It limited its membership to U.S. citizens, conducted its meetings in English, and sought "to develop . . . the best, purest and most perfect type of true and loyal citizen of the United States of America" (Montejano 1987, 232). Its membership, thus, was native-born and naturalized citizens who spoke English. These rules effectively limited its membership to the small Mexican American middle class. Yet its agenda called for fundamental, even radical, change, given the sociopolitical environment of the Southwest at the time. LULAC called for political socialization in the Mexican American communities, adaptation to American values, cultural pluralism, desegregation, and equal education (García 1989, chapter 2). For its first 30 years, LULAC was the driving force behind efforts to ensure equal education for Mexican Americans (San Miguel 1987).

The demand for equal treatment of the Mexican ancestry population was also heard from California in this era. The demand, however, emerged from a base in the trade union movement (Sanchez 1993, chapter 11). In April 1939, 136 union locals and Latino organizations formed the National Congress of Spanish Speaking Peoples (El Congreso). El Congreso was not limited to union organizing among Mexican Americans. It advocated programs to educate the general population about the contributions of Latinos in the Western Hemisphere, denounced theories of racial supremacy, and proposed bilingual education programs for Mexican American school children. It also advocated gender equality. Like LULAC, it called on noncitizens to naturalize and then to vote. El Congreso leaders ran unsuccessfully for local elective office.

Despite some similarities to LULAC, El Congreso spoke from a different ideological perspective. Trade union activity in this era, particularly in Los Angeles, guaranteed that it spoke from a much more ideologically leftist position. El Congreso had ties to the Communist Party as part of Popular Front efforts to organize U.S. racial minorities (Sanchez 1993, 245–46). Thus, in the same era, both the Mexican American middle and working classes were organizing to demand equal treatment, but were approaching the same demand from divergent ideological positions. El Congreso is notable for another reason. While its roots were in Los Angeles unions, it can be seen as the first "Latino" organization. Its 1939 organizing meeting included representatives from East Coast Puerto Rican and Cuban organizations.

The 1940s and 1950s saw the emergence of Mexican American organizations focused more on influencing political outcomes than LULAC or El Congreso had been. Like LULAC, these organizations were formed by the small Mexican American middle class. The first of these, the American G.I. Forum, emerged in the 1940s. It shared LULAC's focus on accommodation and integration of Mexican Americans as equals. It, however, developed links to organized labor that LULAC had never pursued (Allsup 1982; Calavita 1992, 48). While chapters of LULAC and the American G.I. Forum could be found throughout the Southwest, three other middle-class organizations of this era were more local: the Community Service Organization formed in Los Angeles in 1948, the Mexican American Political Association formed in Los Angeles in 1959, and the Political Association of Spanish-Speaking Organizations formed in Texas in 1960 (García and de la Garza 1977, 27–31).

The Chicano movement offers another ideological model for Mexican Americans. The movement, particularly Raza Unida, sprang from the same ground as the Mexican American machines and the middle-class Mexican American organizations. Its agenda, however, was not like the organizations that had preceded it. The movement did not articulate a single set of positions. At a minimum, however, it advanced an absolutist assertion of political and civil rights and, in its extreme form, ethnic autonomy or separatism (Gutiérrez 1968; Rosen 1975; Hamerback, Jensen, and Gutiérrez 1985; Muñoz 1989). While the assertion of ethnic autonomy can be seen as a fundamentally conservative position, neither the movement's leaders nor the country as a whole viewed autonomy in these terms. Instead, the movement was an active, though marginal, player in the ongoing societal change of the late 1960s and 1970s; as a movement of this era, it adopted the often confrontational rhetoric of the antiwar movement and the (African American) civil rights struggle.

Within the broader movement, however, lurked a very traditional element: Much of the Mexican American organizational activity in New Mexico focused on the assertion of rights to century-old land claims (Nabakov 1969; Cummings 1971; Hammerback, Jensen, and Gutiérrez 1985, chapter 1). These land claims were based on guarantees offered in the Treaty of Guadalupe Hidalgo (the treaty that ended the Mexican-American War and that had guaranteed citizenship and other rights to the former Mexican subjects) and were the focus of political organizational activity as early as the 1890s (Weber 1973, 234–38; Rosenbaum 1981, chapters 8–10).

With the decline of the Chicano movement and Raza Unida, the new Mexican American community organizations that emerged focused on regional and national issues (de la Garza 1984, table 2). In addition, each city with a sizable Mexican American population saw organizations emerge that focused on local issues. The most prominent of these post–Chicano movement organizations was the Southwest Voter Registration and Education Project (and the Southwest Voter Research Institute) formed in 1974 (Skerry 1993). Based in San Antonio, it has come to have a presence throughout the Southwest. It has also served as the model for voter registration efforts in the Puerto Rican community. As I indicate below, several post–Chicano movement Mexican American organizations have become national panethnic Latino organizations. The most notable of these are the National Council of La Raza (NCLR) and the Mexican American Legal Defense and Education Fund (MALDEF). Both organized as Mexican American organizations with a primary focus on the Southwest.

Among its other legacies, Raza Unida succeeded in ensuring that mainstream non–Mexican American political organizations in the Southwest began to include Mexican Americans, creating another impetus for local organization. The best example of this phenomenon is the Texas Democratic Party's creation of Mexican American Democrats (MAD). MAD endorsements have become essential symbols for progressive Anglo Democrats seeking statewide office. Further, with increased two-party competition in Texas, the Texas Democratic Party and statewide Democratic candidates cannot afford to exclude Mexican Americans or MAD.

In sum, the Mexican ancestry population and its organizations have been positioned across the ideological spectrum during different periods. They have served in conservative machines (both Democratic and Republican), been leaders of progressive elements in the Democratic parties, and been part of Popular Front organizations. They have joined organizations that foster American values and joined movements that promote cultural, if not political, autonomy in the Southwest.

Many Mexican Americans have also been nonideological. During periods of high immigration, Mexican Americans were active in immigrant and mutual aid societies. Such organizations have appeared in all immigrant communities. They seek to provide for the mutual benefit of the community while maintaining home country cultural and sometimes political ties. The viability of these organizations continues until the focus of the immigrants shifts from the home country to the United States. Yet as long as formal barriers to incorporation prevented Mexican Americans from participating in U.S. politics, these organizations survived. The formation of LULAC in the 1920s indicates that, at least for some Mexican Americans, the United States had become the focus of attention. By the 1950s, this perception of access was nearly universal, except, of course, among the newest immigrants.

If Mexican American ideology today is to be judged by the ideologies and issues of Mexican American (and Latino) leaders and organizations, it rests in the moderate to progressive wing of state Democratic parties in the Southwest and Illinois. Yet the true level of progressiveness of these parties varies considerably. One element that links all these periods, except perhaps the machine period, of Mexican American organization is the desire, if not the demand, for full and complete inclusion for U.S. citizens of Mexican origin. Over time, some have argued for extending this inclusion to non-U.S. citizens as well.

Puerto Rican. The Puerto Rican community has been more consistently on the statist side of the ideological spectrum than has the Mexican-ancestry community. This difference should be seen in terms of the opportunities available to Puerto Ricans in New York more than an intrinsic difference between the Mexican- and Puerto Rican-ancestry populations.

As with those of Mexican ancestry, the earliest political activities of Puerto Ricans focused more on Puerto Rico than on the United States (Sánchez Korrol 1983; 1994). By the 1930s, however, some Puerto Ricans began to participate in and organize around U.S. politics, particularly in New York (Falcón 1984). Until the 1970s, New York's enforcement of English literacy requirements for voting prevented many Puerto Ricans from participating in state and national politics. As a result, the common pattern of home-country focus among immigrants (or, in this case, migrants) may have lasted longer among Puerto Ricans than it would had New York State not discriminated against them (Baver 1984).

Despite this de facto exclusion and the continuing interest in island politics, Puerto Ricans began to participate in U.S politics on a large scale as early as the 1920s. Initial organizational efforts focused on local needs, particularly job-related needs. Union organization was much more common in this early era among Puerto Ricans than it was among Latinos of Mexican ancestry. The first Puerto Rican elected official, Oscar García Rivera, was elected jointly on Republican and American Labor Party tickets to the New York state assembly in 1937 (Jennings 1984a). Although linked to the communists, the American Labor Party was an active part of New York politics in the 1930s and early 1940s. The taint of communism remained with the community long after the local political influence of the party had dissolved.

Perhaps the greatest leader of the New York Puerto Rican community in this period was not himself Puerto Rican. Vito Marcantonio was an Italian American member of Congress during the 1930s and 1940s. Like Rivera, he received the American Labor Party nomination and, in various elections, the Democratic and Republican parties' nominations (Meyer 1989). After Marcantonio's defeat by a candidate jointly nominated by the Democrats and the Republicans, Puerto Rican partisanship shifted predominantly to the Democrats. The taint of communism upon Puerto Ricans remained, however. As late as 1959, the House Un-American Activities Committee warned of "the spread of communism in the Puerto Rican community" (Baver 1984, 45).

As early as the 1920s, Puerto Rican organizations reached out to organizations of what today would be called other Latino populations. New York has long been the home to immigrants from throughout the world, including those from Latin America and the Caribbean. Puerto Ricans were the largest of these populations and saw cultural connections as well as common political needs with these other Latinos (Sánchez Korrol 1983; 1994).

The 1950s and the 1960s saw a bifurcation of the Puerto Rican community's ideology. Some joined the conservative Democratic (Tammany) machine led by Carmine DeSapio. Others followed a more militant path, particularly in the 1960s (Baver 1984; Guzmán 1995). To the extent that the Puerto Rican leadership followed the machine, community-level organization focused on seeking support from federal and state government antipoverty programs. Groups using these funds often neglected community-level organizing (Gonzalez, with Gottlieb

1993). A more radical movement—the Young Lords—formed in the late 1960s. It can be seen as a Puerto Rican parallel to Raza Unida (Rodríguez, Sánchez Korrol, and Alers 1980).

Beginning in the 1970s, a leadership structure of Puerto Rican elected officials began to emerge. While Puerto Rican politics has been more consistently statist and politically left-leaning than the Mexican American community, it has not mobilized the community nor has it featured as much organizational activity.

Throughout this period of incorporation in New York politics and continuing to today, however, Puerto Ricans have maintained a relationship to Puerto Rico different from that maintained by those of Mexican ancestry to Mexico. Puerto Ricans in New York continue to participate actively in island politics and continue to expect a voice in its destiny (García Passalacqua 1993). The best available explanation for this difference is the unique status of Puerto Rico. It is a nation within a state. As the United States has structured the relationship, membership in the Puerto Rican nation and U.S. citizenship can coexist. As a result, the political bond has endured in a more lasting way than has the Mexican American bond to Mexico.

Cuban Immigrant and Cuban American. The vast majority of Cuban Americans trace their origins in the United States to migration after the 1959 Cuban revolution. The small pool of pre-1959 Cuban immigrants has a history that parallels the Puerto Ricans. A strong history of labor organization and union-oriented politics characterize these early Cuban immigrants. Their numbers were never large enough, however, to develop a "Cuban American politics" (Pérez 1978; Mormino and Pozzetta 1987; Portes and Stepik 1993, chapter 5).

The ideological position of the post-1959 Cuban immigrant population has been extensively studied. The driving factor is anticommunism and the desire to overthrow Fidel Castro (Pérez 1992, 94–99). As the community's focus has shifted from refugee to immigrant, however, the consistency of its ideological position has become less clear (Torres 1988; Moreno and Warren 1995). On domestic issues, its positions are often more progressive than the Florida Republican Party (of which it is a significant component). Cuban American leaders take positions in support of labor that make them the allies of the urban Florida Democrats (Grenier 1992; Grenier et al. 1994). The community's sole member of Congress until 1993, Ileana Ros-Lehtinen (a Republican) broke with President Bush on civil rights issues. Both Miami Cuban members of Congress broke with the Republican Congressional leadership to support Motor Voter legislation in 1993. This is not to suggest that the

Cuban American community is losing any of its conservatism on foreign policy. Instead, it suggests that the foreign policy conservatism has not steered the community toward a narrow range of ideological positions on other issues (Moreno 1994).

Emerging Latino Populations. The newest of the Latino communities includes immigrants from Latin American countries other than Mexico, Puerto Rico, and Cuba. These populations are much less studied than the more dominant Latino populations (NALEO 1993b). As their experiences vary widely, it is not possible to determine a single ideology or a single pattern of organizational development.

A study of the four largest of these populations in the areas of their greatest concentration—Colombians and Dominicans in New York and northern New Jersey and Guatemalans and Salvadorans in Los Angeles—indicates that these groups are developing political agendas similar to the dominant Latino populations (DeSipio et al. 1994). To the extent that they have organized, the most recent of these immigrant populations, Guatemalans, have focused on home town and country political needs through home town associations and fraternal, self-help organizations. Salvadorans have also focused on home country politics, on both sides of the ideological spectrum, and on mutual aid societies. They have also begun to develop a network of organizations focusing on U.S. political activities such as labor organization, church activity, and community organizing. The Salvadoran community in Los Angeles has also formed two multipurpose social service organizations that are able to tap both state and private funds to conduct projects to meet community needs.

Colombians and Dominicans have developed a more extensive organizational network that includes partisan political activity and city- and state-sponsored social service organizations. These more extensive networks reflect longer periods of residence in the United States as well as the political opportunity structure available in the New York area. Dominicans and, particularly, Colombians have organized to maintain home country relations in a manner unique to Latino populations. Their experience may come to be ever more common among immigrant-sending countries. The Colombians offer the best example of this new pattern. The Colombian government has sought to establish links to Colombian American and Colombian immigrant organizations. While facilitating cultural and political ties to Colombia, they encourage Colombians in the United States to naturalize. Thus, they seek to maintain ties to their emigrés while acknowledging the growing political attachment to the United States. Although it failed, the most recent set of proposed amendments to the Colombian constitution included a provision to grant representation in the Colombian legislature to Colombians abroad.

Thus, newer Latino immigrant communities would seem to be following the model established by the dominant Latino populations. They have, however, sped the process considerably. The initial pattern of political organization, which focuses on the country of origin and on mutual aid to fellow immigrants in the United States, quickly leads to organization to achieve more explicitly political goals, including the marshaling of state social service and social welfare funds for conationals. While this pattern is much more rapid among these emerging Latino populations than it was for Mexican Americans, Puerto Ricans, or Cuban Americans, the outcome in terms of community ideology is similar. Ideologically, emerging Latino populations seem to be developing an attachment to the U.S. political system at a rapid pace and place themselves broadly in the mainstream of a Great Society–style political agenda. While their political attachments and expectations are probably much less formed because of the recentness of their arrival, there is no evidence that they will offer a challenge to the current political alignment.

The Emergence of Latino Organizations. Since the decline of Raza Unida, the concerns of Mexican American and other Latino political organizations have been solidly within the bounds of the contemporary two-party debate and have been generally moderate to liberal in focus. National pan-Latino organizations have formed and sought to present a common national ethnic agenda on a series of issues that unite all Latinos (while recognizing, with less consistency, differences between Latino national-origin groups). Among the most important of these are two formed in the 1960s, originally as Mexican American organizations: the National Council of La Raza (originally the Southwest Council of La Raza) and the Mexican American Legal Defense and Education Fund. Although both of these organizations began in the Southwest as Mexican American organizations, I would argue that they have become pan-Latino in focus. They now ensure that their boards of directors include non–Mexican American Latinos, and they work on issues not narrowly limited to the needs of Mexican Americans. They seek to be actors in the national policymaking process. Both groups share a common genesis—an effort to develop alternatives to the radicalism of the Chicano movement—and a common source of initial support—the Ford Foundation (Sierra 1983; O'Connor and Epstein 1985). Despite its name, LULAC was almost entirely Mexican American, but also began to organize other than Mexican Americans and to expand outside of the Southwest in the 1970s.

The 1970s saw the creation of several other Latino organizations that shared the approach and the interest group-liberal ideology of MALDEF and NCLR; these were the Congressional Hispanic Caucus and the National Association of Latino Elected Officials (NALEO). To the extent that these are representative of the Latino communities, Latinos are centrist or left of center on domestic social and economic policy, and largely uninvolved in foreign policy.

The increasing diversity of the Latino communities has ensured that Latino organizations that do not fit within the rubric of the Democratic Party have either formed anew or, in the case of LULAC, reorganized. Among these are the National Hispanic Chamber of Commerce, the Republican National Hispanic Assembly, and, beginning in the late 1980s, LULAC. None of these has the prominence or the breadth of membership that characterize the groups associated with the Democratic Party agenda.

Ascriptions of Latino Ideology. As I have suggested, Latino communities have varying ideologies that have changed over time. Further, during most of the twentieth century a large component of the Latino population has been recent immigrants and others who are distanced from American political ideology. As a result, the question of Latino ideology has left a seemingly blank slate onto which the observer can ascribe values. Sometimes this ascription takes the form of ideologies similar to those of the person or organization doing the ascribing in order to build evidence of a broader movement. At other times, this ascription is used to distance Latinos from the ascriber's views in order to set Latinos apart from mainstream values. Although largely inaccurate in either case, these ascribed ideologies have occasionally entered the political debate as accurate representations of Latino ideology.

Perhaps the most common of these ascribed ideologies is the idea that Latinos distance themselves from or reject American politics. In the extreme, some analysts argue that Latinos or, at least, Mexican Americans, desire separatism (Nelson 1984; Butler 1986; de la Peña 1991). In its benign form, the assumption that Latinos are more interested in Mexican, Puerto Rican, or Cuban affairs than in U.S. politics is an oversimplification of the immigrant experience which sees immigrants more a part of the country of origin than of the United States (Bayes 1982). In this construction, immigrants are assumed to be sojourners, not permanent members of the society. There is no recognition of the transition from migrant to resident.

The charge that Mexican Americans, or Latinos in general, desire separatism continues to appear in the literature. Despite the fact that there is only one example of an organized effort at separatism by Mexican Americans (the 1915 Plan de San Diego, spawned in part by the tumult of the Mexican Revolution) and a huge pool of evidence of Mexican Americans working within the system, some analysts continue to present Mexican Americans as conquered Mexicans waiting to return to the homeland (Barrera 1988, chapter 9). The rhetoric of the Chicano movement offers convenient examples for these scholars, who fail to note that the movement itself was divided on this question and, more importantly, was never representative of more than a small minority of Mexican Americans.

The imputation of ideology is not limited to the question of attachment to the United States. The Republican Party has long claimed that Puerto Rican and Mexican American Democrats were proto-Republicans. Republicans base these claims on strong Latino family values, the concomitant conservatism on social policy, and strong support for the military and a strong defense (Skerry 1985, 255–56; Tarrance 1987; Weyr 1988, 119–23).

Many Democrats are similarly ascriptive when it comes to Latino ideology. They look to the low levels of formal education and relative poverty of many Latinos and assume an ideology and political agenda similar to the African American community. This sort of analysis fails to note differences between Latinos and blacks (Kamasaki and Yzaguirre 1991) and the great diversity within the Latino community in terms of nativity, citizenship, region, and demographics (Bean and Tienda 1990; DeSipio and Rocha 1992).

Within the Latino community, there is also an effort to categorize Latinos ideologically for various ends. Linda Chávez, initially with the Reagan White House and now a television pundit, has built a career around the notion that Latino leaders are out of touch with the Latino population. While Latinos simply want to assimilate like European immigrants did, she argues, its leadership follows a civil rights model based on entitlements that prevent full Latino incorporation (Chávez 1991).

Where Chávez seeks a cultureless Latino ethnicity that follows an assimilationist model, other Latinos seek an expanded role for culture within the Mexican American or Latino ethnicity. Mario Barrera, for example, notes that assimilation may be occurring among Mexican Americans and Mexican immigrants. He finds this trend "disturbing, because it reduces cultural diversity within the society, and because [he] feel[s] that Chicanos and others have not truly had a free choice in this matter" (1988, xi). His solution advocates an end to what he sees as forced assimilation. He believes that if this pressure to assimilate ends, Chicanos will move toward a form of regional autonomy.

Based on this review of Latino organizational and elected official activities and pundits' ascriptions, it is impossible to identify a single Latino ideology. Instead, Latinos have participated in organizations with left, center, and right ideological positions and have been described from without and within in several mutually exclusive ideological positions. Perhaps the best guess as to their current ideological position would be that of the several largest Latino organizations. Yet these organizations and their leaders are exactly the targets of Linda Chávez's attacks; moreover, these national organizations have an ambiguous relationship with Cuban immigrants and Cuban Americans, so this best guess may be just as inaccurate as previous efforts to categorize Latinos ideologically. Thus, until nationally representative survey data on Latinos were collected, it was not possible to answer even simple questions about ideology of the Latino communities.

Policy Concerns

Just as Latino partisanship and ideology have been unclear, the policy concerns of Latinos have not been evident. Perhaps more than partisanship and ideology, however, the question of policy concerns encouraged those outside the community to make "common sense" judgments about what must be of concern to Latinos. Again, these judgments failed to recognize the diversity of the Latino communities and their rootedness in U.S. politics. I identify three different sets of public policy issues that have been ascribed as the public policy focus of Latinos. The first is the most narrow; it pictures Latinos as immigrants who are primarily concerned about their countries of origin. As such, they are marginal members of U.S. society. The second set places Latinos broadly within the civil rights and domestic social welfare agenda. The third builds a Latino policy agenda around the issues and needs of the communities where their populations are concentrated. While these local issues and needs may have national ramifications, the interest and organization are both local. Although this third model does not necessarily contradict the second, it suggests that the Latino public policy agenda must not only protect rights and ensure access to federal programs, but also organize Latinos around community and state issues.

Within each of the national-origin groups, the first of the common-sense evaluations was that the true focus was not on the United States but on the country of origin. Prior to the presence of the national Latino organizations in the 1960s, this sojourner assumption dominated Anglo approaches to the public policy needs of Latino communities (Bogardus 1930; Altus 1949; Burma 1954; Rubel 1966). In this approach, Mexican Americans and other Latinos were assumed to be returning some day to Latin America or in any case to be so shaped by the culture of the country of origin that they could not become "true" Americans. Instead, these scholars presented Latinos' needs more in terms of pathologies that damned them as individuals and as victims of a Latin American culture that prevented their integration into U.S. society (Bayes 1992). These pathological explanations mirror "culture of poverty" analyses applied to African Americans and to the developing world (Paz 1961).

These analysts did not see immigrants' early community-level activities as "political"—perhaps accurately. As I have suggested, this first form of quasi-political activity often took place in intraethnic self-help or mutual aid societies. These mutual aid societies are the first recorded community organizations in the Puerto Rican and Mexican American communities; they exist today in the newer Central American immigrant communities (DeSipio et al. 1994). Despite the presence of these organizations, many of the proponents of this sojourner approach to Latino political behavior did not believe Latinos capable of working with others beyond the family.

Although contemporary analysts who adhere to an immigrant-driven Latino public policy agenda have moved beyond the narrow, deterministic focus of their predecessors, they continue to assume a narrow set of public policy concerns. These include some or all of the following: protecting high rates of immigration, ensuring immigrants' civil rights, establishing bilingual education (as a way to maintain Spanish language skills), ensuring access to welfare and other social benefit programs, acquiring rights to bilingual ballots, and more recently, enacting voting rights in U.S. elections for non-U.S. citizens (Chávez 1991; de la Garza and Trujillo 1991). Analysts who contend that these define the narrow public policy concerns of Latinos implicitly contend that Latinos deliberately remain outside of society and that the dominant society's concerns are marginal to Latinos.

The national-origin–focused and panethnic Latino organizations see the public policy needs of the Latino communities in a different light. Although the exact focus varies from one organization to another, these groups offer a second model for the public policy world of Latinos. Collectively, they fight for the protection of the civil rights of all Latinos, regardless of citizenship, and for the voting rights of Latino U.S. citizens. Increasingly, these groups are battling for economic access in addition to civil rights.

Highlighting the activity of several such organizations will indicate the range of public policy issues of concern to national Latino leaders. The Mexican American Legal Defense and Education Fund (MALDEF), for example, uses the courts to ensure Mexican American and Latino civil and voting rights. Initially, MALDEF's main concern was access to primary and secondary education and the implementation of transitional bilingual education programs. While they maintain this interest, MALDEF's focus has broadened to include higher education issues, workplace rights, and redistricting.

The National Council of La Raza (NCLR) lobbies Congress on a wide range of public policy issues including immigration, education, health care, voting rights, job training, and civil rights. NCLR also works to ensure that domestic social legislation accounts for the unique needs of Latinos. Recently, they have also begun to research the representation of Latinos in the media. Although their focus is national legislation, they maintain an active affiliate network that organizes around local issues.

The National Association of Latino Elected Officials (NALEO) coordinates a national network of immigrant and citizenship direct service agencies in order to ensure noncitizens access to naturalization. NALEO also battles to guarantee that government data sources include and publish data on the sociodemographic conditions of Latinos; the organization also offers training and technical assistance to newly elected Latinos.

The League of United Latin American Citizens and the Congressional Hispanic Caucus provide Washington internships to Latino college students. Each also conducts an annual conference or dinner that facilitates network development among Latino professionals and elected officials.

Recently, the Tomás Rivera Center (TRC) has undertaken an ambitious research agenda focusing on such diverse issues as Latino primary and secondary educational access, teacher training and certification, entrepreneurship in the Latino community, and Latino access to modern communications advances such as the internet. TRC, like many Latino research organizations, also provides direct services such as a program to assist Latino graduate students in completing their doctoral dissertations.

Other Latino organizations carry out public policy research on specific issues. ASPIRA and the Hispanic Association of Colleges and Universities examine educational access and educational programming.

The National Association for Bilingual Education monitors bilingual education strategies. The Labor Council for Latin American Advancement acts as an umbrella organization within the AFL-CIO to ensure that unions are aware of and respect the needs of their Latino members. The Latin American Manufacturing Association organizes to ensure that federal contracting goes to Latino-owned firms. SER-Jobs for Progress (a spin-off of LULAC) offers job training for Latinos. While this is only a partial list of Latino public policy research organizations and the issues they target, it should indicate the diversity of the public policy issues around which Latino elites organize.

None of these organizations are truly mass-based. As with all such organizations, it was unclear prior to the development of nationally representative survey data whether individual Latinos were similarly concerned with this broad range of issues. Regardless, the picture of Latino public policy activity evident in these diverse activities offers a stark contrast to the sojourner policy agenda presented in the initial model of Latino interests.

A third set of possible public policy issues of interest to the Latino communities is documented in a small but growing body of academic literature on the conduct of Latino politics (Browning, Marshall, and Tabb 1984; Hero 1987, 1992; Hero and Beatty 1989; Muñoz and Henry 1990; de la Garza, Menchaca, and DeSipio 1994). According to this model, Latinos are predominantly interested in local issues. These local issues are often idiosyncratic to the communities involved, varying from prisons in East Los Angeles to taxes in Miami (Pachon and Argüelles, with González 1994; Grenier et al. 1994). Some themes recur, like education, poverty, crime, drugs, gangs, and the responsiveness of electoral institutions (Villareal and Hernandez 1991; Moore and Pinderhughes 1993). It should be noted that this third model supplements more than contradicts the second. Local organizations and affiliates of the national organizations work around these community-specific issues.

National-Origin Group. Previous study has indicated that each Latino community has a distinct set of issues. Like the broader Latino issues discussed above, there is no real consensus on what constitutes a Mexican American, Puerto Rican, or Cuban American public policy issue.

Previous analysis is consistent in its assumption that each of the Latino national-origin groups is concerned about policies that affect the country of origin. The historical evidence suggests that this concern manifests itself in varying degrees. Miami Cubans, for example, have been driven from the beginning by the desire to overthrow Fidel Castro. While Cuban Americans have slowly begun to pay attention to domestic policy issues, their anticommunism remains central to their politics (Portes and Stepik 1993; Grenier et al. 1994; Moreno 1994).

Puerto Rican concern for island issues has varied. In 1950, island-based Puerto Ricans attempted to assassinate President Harry Truman and, in 1954, opened fire on the floor of the U.S. House of Representatives to call attention to their demand for Puerto Rican independence. Today, the focus of the status question has shifted to a debate between continued commonwealth status or statehood. Moreover, to the extent that the island's status is a concern for Puerto Ricans in the United States, the primary focus of concern in the continental United States was the right of Puerto Ricans not residing in Puerto Rico to vote in the plebiscite that determined Puerto Rico's future.

Mexican Americans' concerns about Mexico are more complicated than are Cuban Americans' about Cuba or Puerto Ricans' about Puerto Rico (de la Garza 1980). Almost from the beginning, the relationship was ambivalent. With the exception of remittances, the Mexican American community could offer little to Mexico for the first 120 years after the end of the Mexican-American War. Mexico did seek to repatriate some of its former nationals after the end of the war; this repatriation included the offer of land incentives to relocate (Griswold del Castillo 1990, 63–66). Few took advantage of these opportunities. As late as the 1930s, some Mexican Americans sought legal assistance from Mexican consuls when they faced discrimination in the United States (Sánchez 1993, chapter 5). With the emergence of Mexican American organizations such as LULAC and the American G.I. Forum, however, this tactical use of the Mexican government for ameliorating problems shifted. During the Chicano movement, some Mexican Americans again looked to Mexico, but the Mexico they sought was a romantic notion of Aztlán (the mythical place of Mexican and Mexican American origin), not Mexico as a nation-state.

Recently, the Mexican American community has had more to offer Mexico, and consequently, its support has been more actively sought. The Mexican government has deliberately reached out to the Mexican American (and Latino) communities (de la Garza 1989; de la Garza and Vargas 1992). Presumably, the government's goal is to create a potential force for lobbying the U.S. government on behalf of Mexico. This assumes what is not really the case from the historical evidence presented here—that Mexican Americans have a particularly strong public policy (as opposed to symbolic) attachment to Mexico.

In addition to the focus on the country of origin, the literature indicates that various issues are of particular regional or national-origin group importance (Pachon and DeSipio 1990, 1992a; NALEO unpublished data, 1993). Puerto Ricans, for example, became interested in housing and transportation issues in New York well before other Latinos were interested in them. Mexican Americans in the Southwest were concerned about the environment and water policy in the mid-1980s. The English-only movement galvanized Cubans in Florida before it caught the attention of Latinos in other states. Each of these issues, however, had statewide significance and was not necessarily uniquely important to Latinos.

This brief review of Latino policy concerns indicates that there is little universality as to what constitutes a Latino issue. I have discussed several models that attempt to establish the parameters of Latino public policy concerns. As with questions of Latino partisanship and ideology, however, only recently have concrete answers begun to emerge.

Latino Partisanship, Ideology, and Policy Preferences

The NLIS and the LNPS offer a new resource to examine the question of where to place the Latino electorates within the broader American political system. Future chapters distinguish between different elements of the Latino adult population. Here, I present aggregate data that distinguish only by national origin and citizenship to present a picture of contemporary Latino partisanship, ideology, and public policy concerns.

Partisanship

Among the three variables under study here—partisanship, ideology, and public policy preferences—partisanship has been the best understood. The findings of the two studies bear out previous analyses. Among U.S. citizens, approximately 66 percent of Mexican Americans and 70 percent of Puerto Ricans reported that they were Democrats. A comparable share of Cuban Americans were Republicans. Just 20 percent of the Mexican Americans and Puerto Ricans were Republican and approximately 25 percent of the Cuban Americans were Democrats (de la Garza et al. 1992, table 8.21).

The LNPS took great care to limit respondents placed in the independent category to those who reported no leanings to either of the parties (de la Garza et al. 1992, 205). The higher share of Mexican Americans and Puerto Ricans who reported that they were independent may reflect that the parties offered less to these groups than they did to either Cuban Americans or the Anglos.

I suggest another alternative, however. Some Latinos, particularly Mexican Americans and Puerto Ricans, are marginalized from the electoral process. Broadly, three categories of Latino voters are more likely to be marginalized: older Latinos, predominantly Mexican Americans, who were formally excluded from electoral participation prior to the Voting Rights Act; the children of these formally excluded Latinos; and the U.S.-born children of unnaturalized immigrants. The first of these groups faced a de jure denial of voting rights and had no opportunity to be socialized into voting. The second group of marginalized voters suffers the legacy of this denial. Like their parents, many have not been socialized as voters. The third category, the U.S.-citizen children of immigrants, have not been excluded, but they have not been incorporated either. These higher rates of independent partisanship among Mexican Americans and Puerto Ricans reflect distance from the electoral system more than rejection of the two dominant parties.

The non-U.S. citizens offered an indication of this absence of political socialization. Fully 70 percent of nonnaturalized Mexican and Dominican immigrants, nearly 55 percent of other Latino immigrants, and 40 percent of the Cuban immigrants reported that they were not attached to either of the parties (Pachon and DeSipio 1994, table 5.7). Only in the Cuban immigrant community, then, did partisan attachment exceed detachment from American partisan politics.

When the unaffiliated and small number feeling attachment to other parties are removed, the noncitizens showed the same partisanship patterns as their citizen coethnics. For nonnaturalized Mexican immigrants, however, the rates of Democratic partisanship were lower. Of those reporting partisanship, just 51 percent reported that they would be Democrats if they could vote. Of noncitizen Cuban immigrants, 85 percent reported that they would be Republicans.

Prior to the NLIS, little was known about Dominicans and other Latinos. Among the other Latino noncitizens, almost half would be Democrats and nearly one third would be Republicans. Approximately two thirds of noncitizen Dominican immigrants with partisan identifications reported that they would be Democrats.

These data also offer an indication of the likelihood of widespread partisan conversion among Latinos. Among the Republican U.S. citizens, approximately one quarter were former Democrats (de la Garza et al. 1992, table 8.25). Few Democrats were former Republicans.

These data indicated that the Republican Party claims that Latinos have been converting are accurate. Despite these conversions, however, the number of Latino Republicans remains small.

Ideology

Where the Latino communities follow the partisanship patterns predicted by previous analysis, their ideological leanings come as something of a surprise. Regardless of ancestry or citizenship status, Latinos were more likely to describe themselves as conservative than as liberal (de la Garza et al. 1992, tables 6.7 and 10.34). As the literature on Latino politics would predict, Cuban Americans were the most likely to be conservative. Surprisingly, however, Puerto Ricans were more likely than either Mexican Americans or Anglos to place themselves on the right side of the political spectrum. Nonnaturalized Mexican immigrants were more likely and Cuban immigrants less likely to be conservative than their U.S.-citizen coethnics (García, de la Garza, García, and Falcón 1991).

Policy Concerns

Despite conservative ideologies, the Latino communities' public policy concerns focused on social issues and an increased governmental role in domestic policy. Some of their policy positions did reflect their self-professed conservatism, as in their answers to questions about individual versus governmental responsibility for housing, jobs, and income. In addition, Latinos reported conservative attitudes on several specific issues: abortion, capital punishment, and some aspects of language and foreign policies. None of these specific issues, however, undermined what can be seen as a relatively liberal attitude toward the role and scope of government. Further, none of their positions reflected a population that was inordinately tied to the countries of origin or that was limited in its attachment to U.S. politics, as some analysts have suggested. As I will indicate, both the U.S. citizen and non-U.S. citizen Latino populations had public policy agendas that placed them solidly within the mainstream of U.S. politics. With a few notable exceptions, the issues they identified and the positions they took on these issues placed them under the rubric of a progressive, Great Society–type social agenda with one addition, a call for an immigrant settlement policy.

When asked to identify the most important problems facing the nation and the respondent's locality, respondents most frequently gave a social issue, such as fighting crime and controlling drugs, meeting the needs of the elderly, dependency versus self-sufficiency, and responding to prejudice and discrimination (de la Garza et al. 1992, tables 7.1 and 7.2). In terms of both national and local issues, Puerto Ricans were the most likely to mention social issues; Mexican Americans were the least likely. Economic issues, such as employment, were the second most likely national and local issues identified by each of the national-origin groups. The ranking of these issues and the rough proportion answering each was nearly identical among the non-U.S. citizens.

Few Latinos indicated that immigration or ethnic issues were the most important national or local issues. Measures such as these counter the contention that Latinos were driven by their desire to return to the countries of origin. They also contradict the notion that their U.S. political attitudes were driven by the desire to assist that country. Again, the non-U.S. citizens were equally unlikely to mention immigration or ethnic issues.

Also notable was the low salience of moral issues. Latinos reported much higher levels of Catholicism than did Anglos. Anecdotal evidence indicates that many Latinos who are recent converts to Protestantism have joined its more fundamentalist denominations. They also were more likely to report high levels of church attendance (de la Garza et al. 1992, tables 2.23, 2.25, and 2.26). Despite this religiosity, moral issues did not dominate their national and local political worlds, at least in terms of the *most* important public policy issue.

When asked to focus more narrowly on national-origin group concerns, respondents most often mentioned ethnic issues (de la Garza et al. 1992, table 9.16). This category included such items as the inability to work together on common problems and the absence of community-level leadership. Cuban Americans were more likely to see these ethnic items as problems than were Mexican Americans or Puerto Ricans. The Latino communities varied on the second-most frequently mentioned issue facing their coethnics. Cuban Americans identified political issues; Mexican Americans, education; and Puerto Ricans, social problems. Few Cuban Americans defined economic and social problems as their most important national-origin group concerns.

Latino concerns with social issues were accompanied by a willingness to pay more taxes to expand the government role in domestic public policy (de la Garza et al. 1992, table 7.3 and 10.40). Among U.S.-citizen Latinos, a majority were willing to pay more taxes for programs targeting crime control and drug prevention, public education, health care, child care services, and environmental protection. Majorities of the non-U.S. citizen respondents added to the list programs to help blacks, science and technology, and programs to help refugees and legal immigrants. When one considers that this survey was conducted in 1988, prior to the end of the Cold War, the opposition to increased spending on defense is quite revealing.

Although generally supportive of an expanded government role for domestic public policy programs, Latinos did not have a single perspective. Both national origin and citizenship divided the communities in regard to this topic. In general, Puerto Ricans were the most likely to call for an expanded government role and Cuban Americans the least likely. Noncitizens, regardless of national origin, were typically strong supporters of increased government programs to help refugees and legal immigrants, regardless of national origin. Citizens, on the other hand, were more likely to support expanded programs for African Americans than they were to support programs for refugees and legal immigrants.

The self-help ethos of immigrant communities also manifested itself in these data. Despite their greater poverty and lesser job skills, noncitizens were no more likely than citizens to advocate increased spending for public assistance and welfare. Among the nation-origin groups, a majority of only the Puerto Ricans advocated increased spending in this area.

Latino willingness to pay more taxes for these policy areas reflected a broader perception of government as an important problem solver in society. Regardless of national origin, Latinos overwhelmingly saw government as the proper vehicle to solve the national and local problems identified (de la Garza et al. 1992, table 6.8). More than 90 percent of each of the Latino national-origin groups and 86 percent of the Anglos saw government as the problem solver.

When asked about specific issues, Latinos were less clear on whether government or the individual should be the locus of the solution (de la Garza et al. 1992, tables 6.9–6.11 and 10.35–10.37). The majority of Puerto Ricans believed that government should provide jobs, a belief opposed by the plurality of Mexican American and Cuban American U.S. citizens and the majority of Anglos. Pluralities of each of the Latino national-origin groups believed that government should provide housing. Anglos were evenly divided on the role of government in this area, however. Pluralities of the Latino national-origin groups and Anglos believed that individuals should provide for their minimum incomes. On each of the issues, non-U.S. citizens were more likely to see a government role than their were U.S.-citizen coethnics.

On a range of other issues, Latinos took positions sometimes distinct from Anglos on public policy issues facing the country. As I have indicated, these positions were within the mainstream debate. On language policy, for example, the majority of Latinos, regardless of national origin, opposed making English the official language of the United States (see tables 2.2 and 2.3). Between 33 and 49 percent, however, supported official language status for English. Despite this broad acceptance, Latinos demonstrated more sensitivity to the needs of the non–

TABLE 2.2. Public policy perspectives among U.S. citizens
(by national origin)

Policy area	Mexican American (%)	Puerto Rican (%)	Cuban American (%)	Anglo (%)
Language policy				
English should be the official language	44.4[a]	48.9	40.0	79.3
Public services should be provided in Spanish	90.2	93.7	94.5	70.6
Immigration policy				
Preference should be given to Latin American immigrants	37.9	37.1	29.6	NA[b]
There are too many immigrants	75.2	79.4	65.5	NA
U.S. citizens should be hired over noncitizens	54.7	55.0	42.0	51.5
Foreign policy				
More concerned with U.S. politics	89.5	55.4	76.5	NA
The United States should establish relations with Cuba	43.7	40.3	33.5	50.9
Puerto Rico should remain a commonwealth	55.4	69.4	60.7	47.9
The cause of Mexico's problems is internal corruption	85.1	82.5	92.2	86.4
The United States should be more involved in Central America	38.7	57.1	70.7	NA
The cause of Central America's problems is poverty and lack of human rights	69.0	55.8	41.8	NA
Other issues				
Support for quotas for jobs/college admission	31.3	33.9	18.2	6.4
Support for capital punishment for murderers	65.4	53.1	69.7	NA
Abortion should never be permitted	20.2	22.3	11.7	NA

SOURCE: The Latino National Political Survey.
[a]Percentage who agree or strongly agree; [b]NA, not asked.

TABLE 2.3. Public policy perspectives among non-U.S. citizens
(by national origin)

Policy area	Mexican ancestry (%)	Cuban ancestry (%)
Language policy		
English should be the official language	45.1[a]	34.1
Public services should be provided in Spanish	90.2	93.7
Immigration policy		
Preference should be given to Latin American immigrants	96.2	96.0
There are too many immigrants	83.6	72.7
U.S. citizens should be hired over noncitizens	32.0	36.2
Foreign policy		
More concerned with U.S. politics	37.6	51.6
The United States should establish relations with Cuba	55.4	34.5
Puerto Rico should remain a commonwealth	67.2	69.6
The cause of Mexico's problems is internal corruption	82.8	93.5
The United States should be more involved in Central America	40.9	79.7
The cause of Central America's problems is poverty and lack of human rights	65.5	25.4
Other issues		
Support for government quotas for jobs and college admission	32.8	23.6
Support for capital punishment for murderers	43.3	63.6
Abortion should never be permitted	28.5	17.7

SOURCE: The Latino National Political Survey.
[a] Percentage who agree or strongly agree.

English speakers than did Anglos. More than nine in ten, again regardless of national origin, advocated that public services be offered in
Spanish.

Citizen and non-U.S.-citizen Latinos differed on some aspects of immigration policy. U.S.-citizen Latinos opposed the notion that preference should be given to Latin American immigrants. Majorities of
noncitizens overwhelmingly supported this proposition. U.S.-citizen
Mexican Americans and Puerto Ricans supported the proposition that
citizens should be hired over noncitizens. The majority of Mexican and

Cuban immigrants, regardless of citizenship status, opposed this proposition. Majorities of both citizens and noncitizens reported that there were too many immigrants in the United States.

The foreign policy positions of these populations did not indicate that they are a fifth column for their countries of origin, as some conservative critics suggest. On at least one issue—relations with Cuba—they advocated a more conservative position than did the Anglo population.

In terms of specific foreign policy issues, U.S.-citizen Latinos opposed extending diplomatic relations to Cuba. A narrow majority of Anglos reported that the United States should recognize Havana. The majority of Latino citizens and noncitizens supported maintaining Puerto Rico as a commonwealth. Again, the majority of Anglos opposed this position.

The Latino communities did not have similar positions on all foreign policy issues. Cuban Americans believed that the United States should be more involved in Central America. Mexican Americans, on the other hand, called for less U.S. involvement. The majority of Mexican Americans saw poverty and lack of human rights as being at the root of Central America's problems. Cuban Americans attributed Central America's problems to other causes. On both these questions, Puerto Ricans fell between the Cuban American and Mexican American positions.

On a range of other public policy issues, Latinos took moderate positions that showed some, but not a great deal of, variation across national-origin groups. Approximately one third of Mexican Americans and Puerto Ricans supported government quotas for jobs and college admission. Among Cuban Americans, approximately 20 percent supported quotas. Each of these rates was above the approximately 6 percent of Anglos who supported quotas. Majorities of Latino citizens and Cuban ancestry non-U.S. citizens supported capital punishment for murderers. Latino national-origin groups also varied in their opposition to abortion. Just 12 percent of Cuban American U.S. citizens categorically opposed it. As many as 29 percent of Mexican-ancestry non-U.S. citizens rejected abortion in all cases.

Thus, contrary to much of the previous analysis of Latinos and public policy, the evidence from the Latino National Political Survey indicates that Latinos are concerned about a broad range of public policy issues. Their positions on these issues are broadly within the mainstream two-party debate at the time of the surveys; in more cases than not, their positions are moderately progressive. The progressive impulse is particularly evident in questions about the scope of government activity.

Latinos see a need for a broad expansion of governmental services in domestic policy, and they are willing to pay increased taxes to provide these services.

Conclusions

This chapter has shown where our understandings of Latino politics have come from and how they agree with and differ from the picture presented through survey research on these populations. Its goal has been to indicate that many of the "commonsense" understandings of Latino partisanship, ideology, and policy concerns neglect the diversity of these populations and of their continuing adaptation to the political environments and opportunity structures available in different historical periods. These data indicate diversity based on both national origin and nativity.

Although the experiences of Mexican Americans, Puerto Ricans, and Cuban Americans clearly vary, several common experiences shape these communities and influence our understanding of their political development. The most important of these is immigration (or, in the case of Puerto Ricans, migration). With the exception of a small number of descendants of the residents of the Southwest prior to 1848, all Latinos are immigrants, migrants, or their descendants (Gutiérrez 1995). Concomitant with the immigration experience that these national-origin groups share is the impact and the legacy of the acculturation experience.

In addition to immigration and acculturation, Latinos, particularly Mexican Americans and Puerto Ricans, have experienced political and social exclusion. Until the extension of the Voting Rights Act to the "Spanish-language minority" in 1975, many Latinos were excluded from the polls. Those who could participate faced intimidation and manipulation when they sought to exercise this right (de la Garza and DeSipio 1993). This widespread de jure and de facto exclusion from competitive electoral politics limited the political options of many Latinos and reduced the level of political socialization in the communities such that many immigrants and their descendants did not become regular participants in the U.S. electoral system.

This legacy of the impacts of immigration and exclusion appears in more than just low voting rates. These communities are often neglected or misunderstood by those who seek to analyze and explain U.S. politics. Taking what opportunities were offered by the electoral and social systems in different eras, Mexican Americans and, later, Puerto Ricans and Cuban Americans assumed various partisan and ideological positions and have been concerned about a range of public policy issues. Further, the continuing high rates of immigration through much of this century have guaranteed that the Latino population always included recent immigrants who are distant from American politics. The diversity of this experience has allowed serious scholars, as well as ideologues and nativists, to make of Latinos what they want and to ascribe positions and values.

The newly collected national survey data offer a baseline against which future claims about the communities must be measured. In sum, these data indicate that Latinos follow the anticipated partisan patterns; Mexican Americans and Puerto Ricans are solidly Democratic, and Cuban Americans are solidly Republican. Dominicans and other Latinos, about whom little was known prior to the NLIS, lean to the Democrats. Further, these surveys find a self-professed conservatism among Latinos, regardless of national origin or nativity. The primary policy concerns of these communities focus on social issues to the exclusion of economic, moral, foreign policy, or ethnic issues.

When asked about policy issues facing the country, Latinos report positions solidly within the mainstream of political debate in the United States, sometimes more liberal and sometimes more conservative, but never outside of the current debate. Regardless of national origin, they call for an expansion of government services in a range of policy areas, even at the cost of added taxes. In sum, on the basis of these data, I would argue that Latinos are within the existing boundaries of the political discourse and share the concerns of the non-Latinos. As I will indicate in the next chapter, however, their ability to influence electoral outcomes and to shape national and local policy is muted by low levels of electoral participation.

CHAPTER 3

The Latino Electorates:
Current and Potential

IN THE PREVIOUS chapter, I reviewed the myths that have shaped academic analysis of Latino politics as well as the new insights available about Latino partisanship, ideology, and policy preferences derived from survey data in order to contrast these conventional wisdoms to the more concrete findings available from the survey data. This discussion begged an important question. Many in the Latino community cannot or do not participate in electoral politics. As a result, the positions and opinions of these nonparticipants do not have a way to influence policy through the ballot box.[1] For the communities as a whole, the large numbers of those who do not or cannot participate limit the ability of the Latino population to translate its numerical strength into commensurate numbers of elected officials who are either Latino themselves or sympathetic to Latino community needs. Certainly, electoral nonparticipation characterizes all racial and ethnic communities. The impact is particularly strong, however, among Latinos (see table 3.1).

In this chapter, I have four goals. First, I disaggregate the Latino voters from the nonvoters and categorize the nonvoters by reason of nonparticipation. Second, I examine the partisan, ideological, and public policy preferences of the voters to see how they differ from the broader population of U.S. citizen Latinos. Third, I examine the states in which these Latino voters can have an electoral impact. Finally, I examine the possibility of partisan conversion among Latino Democratic and Republican voters. I find that, at present levels, Latinos can make an electoral difference in state and local elections. Further, though their votes can offer the key difference for either party, traditional levels of Democratic Party adherence for Mexican Americans and Puerto Ricans and Republican Party adherence for Cuban Americans remain strong. Finally, among existing voters, I find little evidence of widespread partisan conversion. My discussion is designed to establish a foundation with

58

which I can assess the possible impact and influence of the new Latino electorates discussed in subsequent chapters.

Latino Voters and Nonvoters

In the 1992 election, approximately 4.2 million Latinos went to the polls, constituting 3.7 percent of the national electorate (Census 1993a, table 1).[2] These 4.2 million voters represent a record high for the number of Latino voters and a 14.2 percent increase in Latino turnout compared to the 1988 election. This increase among Latino voters exceeded the 11.4 percent increase in turnout for the U.S. population as a whole between 1988 and 1992 (de la Garza and DeSipio 1996).[3]

These relative increases, however, are misleading. For the electorate as a whole, 1992 saw the highest turnout percentage since 1972 (61.3 percent) and the most rapid percentage increase in the raw number of voters since the Census Bureau began to collect voting data in 1964. For Latinos, on the other hand, the increase in the raw number of voters that had been evident through the 1980s slowed. The percentage increase in Latino voters (14.2 percent) was lower than the increases between 1980 and 1984 (20.0 percent) and 1984 and 1988 (26.0 percent). Finally, because of the rapid increase in U.S.-citizen adult Latinos, turnout did increase over 1988 levels (to 48.3 percent), but just barely returned to the levels achieved in 1984. These voter registration and turnout data are of *eligible* adults; I exclude non-U.S. citizens from the pool of adults (NALEO 1992). In sum, among all adult citizens, the trend toward decline in the percentage voting reversed and the actual number voting increased dramatically; among Latinos, conversely, turnout returned to 1984 levels and the steady increase in those turning out slowed.

Further, the number of Latino adults who did not go to the polls also increased over 1988 levels. In 1992, 10,450,000 adult Latinos (citizens and noncitizens) did not go to the polls, increasing from 9,183,000 in 1988, an addition of 13.8 percent. Another way of looking at this phenomenon is that while Latinos constitute 3.7 percent of voters, they make up 14.6 percent of the nonvoters.

Why is this the case? Like all populations, Latino adults include individuals who report that they were registered but did not vote; who were eligible to, but did not register; and who were not U.S. citizens (plus a category of individuals who did not vote but who were not sure in which of these three categories of nonvoting they belonged).[4] As is

TABLE 3.1. Voting and nonvoting patterns in the 1992 elections (by race and ethnic group)

Race or ethnicity	Adult population, 1992 (,000)	Voted in 1992 (,000)	Turnout (%)
White	157,837	100,405	63.6
Black	21,039	11,371	54.0
Latino	14,688	4,238	28.8
Asian/Pacific Islander	5,129	1,402	27.3
All populations	185,684	113,866	61.3

		Nonvoting categories, 1992		
Race or ethnicity	Total not voting (,000)	Registered, not voting (,000)	Not registered (,000)	Not a U.S. citizen (,000)	Other (,000)
---	---	---	---	---	---
White	57,432	10,279 (17.9%)[a]	30,580 (53.2%)	8,284 (14.4%)	8,289 (14.4%)
Black	9,668	2,070 (21.4%)	4,684 (48.4%)	1,044 (10.8%)	1,870 (19.3%)
Latino	10,450	899 (8.6%)	2,646 (25.3%)	5,910 (56.6%)	995 (9.5%)
Asian/Pacific Islander	3,726	200 (5.4%)	869 (23.5%)	2,319 (62.2%)	338 (9.1%)
Total population	71,818	12,712 (17.7%)	36,568 (50.9%)	11,900 (16.6%)	10,638 (14.8%)

SOURCE: U.S. Bureau of the Census 1993a: tables 1 and 17.
NOTE: These calculations are based on the Current Population Survey estimates of voter registration and turnout in the 1992 elections. They should be used with some caution for three reasons. First, they overestimate 1992 voting by approximately 9.1 percent (Census 1993a: table D). Second, although there is no study of the accuracy of Latino self-reported registration and voting, analysts have found that African Americans and poor people have higher than average rates of overreporting. Finally, Current Population Survey data collected through early 1993 are based on a sampling frame developed from the 1980 census of population that contained an undercount of the Latino and African American populations (Census 1990; Passel 1990).
[a] Percentage of nonvoters.

indicated in table 3.1, Latinos are much more likely than whites, blacks, or the population as a whole to have a large share in the non-U.S.-citizen category of nonvoting.

The impact of non-U.S. citizenship on Latino nonvoting is evident when Latinos are compared to whites and blacks. More than one half of Latino nonvoters are noncitizens, as compared to just 11 percent of African Americans and 15 percent of whites. These white and black noncitizenship rates include Latinos, who can be of any race and who, as a result, appear in both the Latino and the racial categories. Assuming that approximately 90 percent of Latinos are white, then the noncitizenship as a share of nonvoting rate for (non-Hispanic) whites drops to 5.7 percent and for (non-Hispanic) blacks to 5.0 percent. Clearly, before non-U.S. citizens can move to the voting rolls, an intermediate step—naturalization—must occur.

Although numerically smaller, the registered nonvoter and nonregistered citizen categories also reflect the unique characteristics of Latinos, regardless of national origin. Extensive analysis of different populations within the U.S. political system has demonstrated the relationship between three demographic characteristics—age, education, and income—and the propensity to vote and to participate in other forms of politics (Campbell et al. 1960; Verba and Nie 1972; Wolfinger and Rosenstone 1980; Bobo 1990; Tate 1993).

For each of these three characteristics, Latinos are more likely to have large components of the population with characteristics that predict high levels of nonvoting: relative youth, low levels of income, and low levels of formal education (Bean and Tienda 1990; DeSipio and Rocha 1992). In order to move these U.S.-citizen nonvoters into voting, then, some form of community mobilization must overcome the effects of these demographic characteristics.

Several studies of the impact of age, education, income, and citizenship have examined the combined effect of these characteristics on participation by Latinos. Wolfinger and Rosenstone (1980) examined Mexican American and Puerto Rican voting based on Current Population Survey data from 1974. They reported that "other demographic factors being held constant, we find that Chicanos are *more* likely to vote than the rest of the population" (1980, 92; emphasis in the original). Concerning Puerto Ricans, they found that if other demographic characteristics are held constant, Puerto Ricans were 7 percent less likely than the rest of the population to vote in 1974 (1980, 93). The authors cautioned that the significance of their finding of increased likelihood of voting among Mexican Americans is "substantively and statistically" close to zero. Nevertheless, their analysis indicates that were it not for demographic and citizenship constraints, Mexican Americans would have voted at the same rates as the rest of the population in 1974.

Focusing just on California in the 1984 election, Uhlaner, Cain, and Kiewiet found that for Latinos "once one compares [U.S. citizens] of similar socioeconomic position, differences in participation evaporate" (1989, 210). They noted that the participatory patterns of Latinos follow the patterns of blacks in this regard.[5]

A study of Cuban American participation in Miami between 1955 and 1985 indicates that, beginning in 1973, Cuban Americans were more likely to vote in local elections than were non-Hispanic whites (Stowers 1990). This higher level of voting occurred despite a lower average socioeconomic status among the Miami Cuban Americans. Ethnicity, however, has not replaced the role of class in Miami Cuban American politics. Among Cuban Americans, Stowers finds that those with higher class status were more likely to vote than those with lower class status.

A study of political resources that includes a valid sample of Latinos demonstrates that there was no independent impact of ethnicity on the likelihood of participation in a wide range of modes of political participation (Verba et al. 1993). Instead, differences in participation between Latinos and Anglos can be explained solely by differences in the political skills that individuals bring to the political process. These political resources are developed in part through education and in the workplace.

Although these four studies ask somewhat different questions and use very different methodologies, they offer a consistent picture of Latino participation. Among Latino U.S. citizens, and individually among Mexican Americans, Puerto Ricans, and Cuban Americans, lower levels of participation are a function of socioeconomic factors and not a cultural trait.

None of these studies or others that examine participation patterns distinguish between the characteristics of those who registered and did not vote, and those who were eligible but did not register. In the chapters that follow, I examine each of these distinct elements of the Latino voting and nonvoting populations in order to explain the disparate reasons for participation and nonparticipation (see table 3.2). I begin in this chapter by examining the voters in terms of their partisanship, ideology, and policy positions. Based on these current levels of participation and the existing political beliefs, I discuss the likelihood of Latino impact on electoral outcomes in today's political system. In other words, I establish a baseline for Latino participation without the addition of any of the new electorates. I conclude the discussion of the current Latino electorate in this chapter by assessing the likelihood that Latinos will convert from their present partisan positions. These potential converts comprise "new electorate number 1."

In subsequent chapters, I study the characteristics and levels of political activity of the three groups of nonvoters. The first of these is the registered nonvoter whom I call the "Reticents." I evaluate their partisan-

TABLE 3.2. Characteristics and estimated size of Latino new electorates

New electorate 1	Current Latino voters and the potential for partisan conversion Estimated size in 1992: 4,238,000 Analyzed in chapter 3
New electorate 2 ("Reticents")	U.S. citizens who were registered to vote in 1988 but did not vote Estimated size in 1992: 899,000 Analyzed in chapter 4
New electorate 3 ("Reluctants")	U.S. citizens who were not registered to vote in 1988 Estimated size in 1992: 2,646,000 Analyzed in chapter 4

New electorate 4 ("Recruits")	Non-U.S. citizens, many of whom were eligible to naturalize in 1988
	Estimated size in 1992:
	    All Latino non-U.S. citizens: 5,910,000
	    Latino immigrants eligible for
	        U.S. citizenship: 2,500,000–3,000,000
	Analyzed in chapters 5 and 6

ship, ideology, and policy preferences and likelihood of their voting. These Reticents comprise "new electorate number 2."

"New electorate number 3" consists of U.S. citizens not registered to vote; I call them the "Reluctants." This new electorate has been the major focus of individual-level political organization in the Latino community over the past 15 years.

Finally, the fourth potential new electorate is the noncitizen adult— the "Recruits." I disaggregate the Recruits into three groups of noncitizens who could be targeted to become citizens and voters: those who are eligible for and interested in citizenship; those who are or have been involved in political activity; and those who have been active in community and school-based activities.

Latino Voters

As I have indicated, the current pool of Latino voters numbers around 4 million. These voters represent approximately one quarter of Latino adults nationwide (and almost one half of the U.S.-citizen adults). In this section, I describe the demographic characteristics and partisanship, ideology, and policy preferences of these Latino voters. These data should be contrasted with the comparable data for all U.S. citizens (and to a lesser degree non-U.S. citizens) presented in chapters 1 and 2. Since the voters make up almost half of the U.S. citizen respondents, their opinions tend to drive the overall composition of citizen policy preferences. The impact of the voters is enhanced by the fact that the voters are much less likely to take neutral positions on issues or to fail to answer questions.

The link between higher socioeconomic status and likelihood of voting appears in these data (see table 3.3). In aggregate, Latino voters were three to five years older than Latino U.S. citizens as a whole. Mexican Americans and Puerto Ricans had annual household incomes of $2,500 to $3,500 more than their U.S.-citizen coethnics. For each of the national-origin groups, education levels did not vary between voters and the broader U.S. citizen population.

Latino voters also differed on several other sociodemographic characteristics introduced in chapter 1. Regardless of national origin, Latino voters were more likely to own homes than their nonvoter coethnics. Home ownership is potentially important, as it indicates residential and community stability, a characteristic associated with higher electoral participation.

Greater differences appear in Latino voter partisanship and ideology. As might be expected, voters were less likely than Latino U.S. citizens to be independents. Among Mexican Americans and Cuban Americans, voters were also more likely to identify with the Democratic and Republican parties, respectively. The result is a more highly partisan group than the already highly partisan Latino U.S. citizen population. Among Mexican American and Puerto Rican voters, 78 and 76 percent, respectively, identified themselves as Democrats, whereas among Cuban Americans 74 percent identified themselves as Republicans.

Among all three national-origin groups, the voters were more likely to report that they were on the conservative side of the ideological spectrum. Despite the strong Democratic partisanship among Mexican American and Puerto Rican voters, both national-origin groups were slightly more conservative than their citizen coethnics who do not vote. Only Mexican American voters included more moderates than conservatives. Although many Puerto Ricans and Mexican Americans reported that they were conservative, this conservatism was more moderate than was the Cuban American conservatism.

In terms of policy positions, voting citizens did not differ significantly from nonvoting citizens. Considering the very minor variations in partisanship and ideology between the voters and the broader group of U.S. citizens, this is not surprising. In terms of specific issues, Latino voters

TABLE 3.3. Sociodemographics of 1988 voters

Characteristic	Mexican American	Puerto Rican	Cuban American
Age, mean	44 years	41 years	49 years
Gender			
Male	46.1%	45.2%	44.6%
Female	53.9%	54.8%	55.4%
Race			
White	56.2%	58.4%	92.2%
Black	0.0%	4.0%	5.5%
Latino referent	43.8%	37.6%	2.4%
Education, mean	11 years	10 years	12 years
Household income, mean	$31,036	$22,344	$34,824
Work status			
In labor force	62.2%	54.1%	68.8%
In temporary labor force	7.7%	9.5%	2.9%
Unemployed	30.1%	36.4%	28.2%
Home owner	65.0%	22.0%	55.9%
Self-evaluated language skills			
English stronger	51.2%	20.3%	12.0%
Bilingual	40.2%	47.1%	35.7%
Spanish stronger	8.6%	32.6%	52.3%
Identification			
National origin	63.8%	71.1%	66.6%
Panethnic	26.9%	17.1%	16.7%
American	9.4%	11.9%	16.7%
Religion			
Catholic	80.1%	66.1%	77.0%
Protestant	11.2%	24.7%	14.7%
Other/no preference	8.6%	9.2%	8.4%
Immigration generation			
First	12.2%	71.1%	76.1%
Second	25.2%	20.9%	16.5%
Third	24.6%	0.9%	1.1%
Fourth	38.0%	7.1%	6.3%
Age at immigration (foreign born), mean	12 years	18 years	27 years
Social milieu			
Mostly Latino	22.8%	28.0%	32.4%
Mixed Latino and Anglo	64.8%	61.2%	62.6%
Mostly Anglo	12.3%	10.7%	5.0%

SOURCE: Latino National Political Survey.

and nonvoters, regardless of national origin, supported increasing the government's role in five of the ten policy areas: education, the environment, child services, crime and drugs, and health care. Again, for all of the national-origin groups, but particularly for Cuban Americans, these positions of advocating expansion of the government role defied their self-reported conservatism. Regardless of national origin, the majority of Latino voters and nonvoters opposed new government activity in three of the policy areas: science and technology, welfare, and defense.

The majority of Puerto Ricans supported expanded government services for refugees in contrast to Mexican Americans and Cuban Americans. Cuban Americans also differed on support for programs to assist blacks. While majorities of the Mexican American and Puerto Rican voters reported that they would be willing to pay more taxes to expand these types of programs, only a minority of Cubans would expand them. Despite these differences on these three policy areas, it should be noted that Latinos, regardless of national origin, took relatively similar positions across the ten issues.

On language, immigration, and foreign policy, Mexican American and Cuban American voters tended to take more absolute positions than did nonvoting U.S. citizens. For example, they opposed the enactment of English as the official language and the proposition that Latin Americans should be given preference in the immigration system (see table 3.4). When Puerto Rican voters differed from Puerto Rican nonvoters, on the other hand, the voters were more likely to move to the center. Regardless of national origin, voters were more likely to be more concerned with U.S. politics than country-of-origin politics (or to be equally concerned with both). As I have suggested, however, the differences between citizen voters and nonvoters are quite narrow. The patterns that I highlight here are consistent across specific policy issues.

Latino voters, then, were more likely to reflect the dominant partisanship of their national-origin group than were the nonvoters. Concerning positions on policy issues, voters did not differ significantly from U.S. citizens. Yet these findings are noteworthy for two other, somewhat contradictory, reasons. First, in terms of partisanship and policy preferences, the voters are a representative group. If these nonvoters were to enter the electorate, the partisan, ideological, and policy positions of the Latino community would not shift dramatically. Second, the demographic differences between voters and nonvoters exist and follow the anticipated patterns, with the poorer, the less educated, and the younger participating less (this is discussed in greater depth in the next chapter). In other racial and ethnic populations, demographic

TABLE 3.4. Public policy perspectives of voters (by national origin)

Policy area	Mexican American (%)	Puerto Rican (%)	Cuban American (%)	Anglo (%)
Language policy				
English should be the official language	42.1[a]	50.2	37.6	79.5
Public services should be provided in Spanish	89.8	92.8	94.2	69.3
Immigration policy				
Preference should be given to Latin American immigrants	36.9	39.6	29.4	NA[b]
There are too many immigrants	78.7	77.9	65.4	73.3
U.S. citizens should be hired over noncitizens	60.8	56.7	43.1	50.8
Foreign policy				
More concerned with U.S. politics	89.8	57.5	78.2	NA
The United States should establish relations with Cuba	41.4	36.8	28.7	49.1
Puerto Rico should remain a commonwealth	50.3	67.6	62.6	45.2
The cause of Mexico's problems is internal corruption	84.2	79.1	94.8	86.8
The United States should be more involved in Central America	35.6	57.9	73.4	NA
The cause of Central America's problems is poverty and lack of human rights	71.3	55.3	34.4	NA
Other issues				
Support for government quotas for jobs and college admission	29.9	30.9	20.1	6.0
Support for capital punishment for murderers	62.5	56.8	67.6	NA
Abortion should never be permitted	20.5	18.3	12.7	NA

SOURCE: Latino National Political Survey.
[a]Percentage who agree or strongly agree; [b]NA, not asked.

differences manifest themselves in partisan and policy differences. Among Latinos, however, partisanship and, particularly, policy positions are relatively consistent within national-origin groups, hinting that ethnicity may be playing a stronger role than demographics.

Demographics, however, play a key role in levels of Latino participation. Thus, inclusion of U.S.-citizen nonvoters as voters requires mobilization to overcome the antiparticipatory impacts of youth, low levels of formal education, limited incomes, and other sociodemographic characteristics that disproportionately influence Latino voting.

Latino Votes Count

Earlier in this chapter, I indicated that the Latino share of the national vote was 3.7 percent in 1992. While accurate, this figure is misleading because of the way that elections are conducted in the United States. First, Latinos are not evenly distributed throughout the country. Eighty-six percent of Latinos are concentrated in nine states—Arizona, California, Colorado, Florida, Illinois, New Jersey, New Mexico, New York, and Texas. This leaves few Latinos in the remaining 41 states (Census 1991*a*, 4–5). The concentration of the Latino vote in nine states ensures that it is a sizable share of the statewide vote. Second, within these states, Latinos are unevenly distributed. For races that are not statewide, some areas have large concentrations of Latinos and other areas have few. Only a relative handful of districts are, in fact, statewide. These include a state's senators, its governor, and other statewide officials, and the electoral votes for the presidential election.

In this section, I examine various scenarios in which existing Latino voters influence electoral outcomes. Despite the fact that they constitute a very small share of the total electoral races, I focus primarily on general elections for statewide races. This focus results from the fact that campaigns for these offices are the most studied. As a result, I can compare the Latino influence both across states and between elections. While local level offices may be of greater relevance to many Latino voters, there is insufficient data to develop objective measures of Latino influence. In the discussion that follows, I develop a comprehensive strategy for viewing Latino influence in statewide races. I then discuss in more general terms ways in which Latinos influence electoral outcomes in other types of electoral races. When more data become available, Latino influence on these other levels of office and types of races, such as in party primaries and in local races, can be examined more comprehensively.

Estimating the Latino Share of Statewide Voting

The concentration of Latinos in nine states ensures that they have the *potential* to play a role not only in statewide elections in these states, but also in the presidential race which, because of the electoral college, is a series of 50 state-level races in which the largest vote-getter receives all the state's electoral votes. In terms of the electoral college, Latino

TABLE 3.5. Latino share of the 1992 statewide vote in selected states

State	Total vote	Latino vote	% Latino of statewide vote
Arizona	1,728,000	156,000	9.0
California	11,789,000	1,135,000	9.6
Colorado	1,688,000	136,000	8.1
Florida	5,772,000	411,000	7.1
Illinois	5,650,000	171,000	3.0
New Jersey	3,572,000	173,000	4.8
New Mexico	675,000	172,000	25.5
New York	7,613,000	382,000	5.0
Texas	6,817,000	927,000	13.6

SOURCE: U.S. Bureau of the Census 1993a, table 4.

votes are not distributed evenly. Despite being only 4 percent of the voting population, Latinos are cohesive voting blocs in states with 75 percent of the votes needed to carry the presidency. Their cohesiveness appears in their strong partisan registration patterns, to the Democrats in eight of the states and to the Republicans in one.

In the nine states, the Latino share of the 1992 vote ranged from a low of 3.0 percent in Illinois to a high of 25.5 percent in New Mexico (see table 3.5). This Latino share of the statewide vote reflects two factors: Latino voting and the statewide vote. The levels are generally representative of the minimum share of the Latino vote that we can anticipate for presidential elections in the current political environment. The nature of the 1992 election was such that the pool of statewide votes (the denominator in the equation to measure the Latino share of the vote) might have been inflated above levels that will be reached in future elections. If this hypothesis is accurate, then the true Latino share of the statewide vote will be higher in future elections even if the Latino vote does not grow. I discuss each of these factors—the raw Latino vote and the statewide vote—in turn.

With three exceptions, the statewide Latino vote recorded in the 1992 elections is at approximately the level that would be predicted by Latino electoral participation in the 1980s, allowing for routine increases in the number of Latino voters between elections. I base this "routine" level of increase on the average change in the raw number of Latino votes in each state between the 1980 and 1984 elections and the 1984 and 1988 elections. The three exceptions are Colorado, New York, and California. Unexpectedly, the 1992 Latino voter turnout rates in New York and Colorado declined from 1988 levels (by 7.1 and

0.7 percent, respectively). Trends from the 1980s would suggest that a more realistic measure of the Latino share of the statewide votes is slightly higher, perhaps 10 percent for Colorado Latinos and 7 percent for New York Latinos.[6] Equally unexpectedly, in California, the reported level of Latino electoral turnout increased by more than 37 percent, a figure that must be viewed as inflated. Based on the 1980, 1984, and 1988 elections, a more realistic estimate for California would be slightly in excess of 1 million voters or about 9 percent of the 1992 statewide vote.

It should be noted that New Mexico's and, to a lesser extent, Colorado's Latino populations (and Latino vote) are higher than those reported. The Current Population Survey's "Latinos" are self-reported based on either self-identification or descent from an immigrant from Latin America or the Caribbean. Many New Mexican and some Colorado Latinos do not self-identify as Latino (or a variant) and trace their ancestry to Spanish colonists who lived in New Mexico prior to Mexican independence. Traditionally some of these "other Hispanics" do not appear in Current Population Survey (CPS) voting data. I cannot develop an estimate of this population's impact except to speculate that they could add as much as several percent to the Latino share of the New Mexico vote. Their impact would be less in Colorado.

The second element that influences the calculation of the Latino share of the statewide vote is the state's total vote. In the nine states with sizable Latino populations, the total vote increased over 1988 levels at rates of between 4 and 29 percent. In five of the states, the percentage increase in the total vote exceeded the increase in the Latino vote. These patterns reverse longstanding declines or stagnation in non-Latino voting. Clearly, 1992 could be the beginning of a new era in American politics. If this is the case, the Latino share of the statewide votes in these states may stagnate at current levels or grow very slowly while the non-Latino vote continues to increase. On the other hand, 1992 may have been an exception to the decades-long pattern of slow growth in the total Latino vote and slow decline in the percentage of non-Latinos turning out.

This second pattern is probably more valid. It assumes that Latinos were largely left out of the mobilization and conversion that accompanied Ross Perot's candidacy and Bill Clinton's outreach to young voters (de la Garza and DeSipio 1996). If this is the case, then, the Latino vote in future elections will return to the pattern of the 1980s and increase much more rapidly than the total vote. Thus, in future elections without

Perot or an equivalent figure to mobilize and convert non-Latino voters, the Latino share of the vote will reflect Latino voting increases, particularly in the nine states with concentrated Latino populations. This increasing share of the vote will occur even if the new electorates discussed here do not enter the electorate.

Though necessarily imprecise, the estimates of the Latino share of the vote in the nine states offer a baseline with which to measure Latino electoral influence in general elections at the state level. My comfort with these estimates reflects the assumption that while the 1992 election mobilized many new voters, particularly non-Hispanic whites, the Latino community did not experience a strong mobilization of new voters who would not otherwise have joined the electorate. The California data indicate that a widespread mobilization of new voters might have happened there. Since there was no effort to mobilize California Latinos and the Clinton and Bush campaigns stopped competing for any votes early in the race, however, I believe that these CPS estimates are flawed. With the exception of California, then, while it would be inaccurate to develop an estimate of the Latino vote based solely on 1992 results, it is increasingly safe when the results of the 1992 elections are compared to those of 1980, 1984, and 1988.

Latino Impact in Statewide General Elections

The question of what impact this number of votes can have has been actively debated in discussions of Latino politics (Pachon and DeSipio 1988; de la Garza and DeSipio 1992, particularly Fraga 1992; Guerra 1992; Saiz 1992). The minimum qualification for the Latino vote to make a difference is that the gap between the winning and losing candidate must be no larger than the gap in the partisan split of the Latino vote. Since the Latino share of the vote in most of these nine states is less than 10 percent and the partisan gap is between 4 and 6 percent, this condition requires that the margin of victory be quite small. When this condition is met, Latinos can mathematically influence the winning margin.

Despite the small relative size of the Latino electorate in some of these states, strong levels of partisanship enhance their potential impact. In all but Florida where Republican Latinos dominate, Democrats prevail. "Prevail," in this case, signifies more than the simple majority or plurality that occurs in the non-Hispanic white population. In New Mexico, for example, 90 percent of Latinos reported that they are Democrats (see table 3.6). With the exception of New Jersey, all of the Latino

TABLE 3.6. Partisanship (by state)

State	Democrat (%)	Independent (%)	Republican (%)	n
Arizona	—[a]			
California	80.6	3.1	16.3	217
Colorado	—[a]			
Florida	26.7	3.1	70.2	59
Illinois	81.1	1.4	17.5	57
New Jersey	63.0	3.1	34.0	41
New Mexico	90.6	0.4	9.0	79
New York	82.9	3.8	13.3	66
Texas	73.8	7.1	19.2	182
Other states	71.1	5.4	23.5	150

SOURCE: Latino National Political Survey.
[a] Small sample sizes prevent presenting state-level partisanship data on Arizona and Colorado. In both cases, the small samples indicate strong Democratic partisanship comparable to California, New Mexico, or Texas.

Democratic states had majorities supporting that party in excess of 74 percent versus 20 percent support for the Republicans. In Florida, the Republican majority was 70 versus 27 percent.

Once the mathematical threshold is reached for potential influence, Latinos can claim partial credit for the victory when a discernible and cohesive bloc of Latinos votes for a winning candidate who has a sufficiently narrow victory margin that he or she needed those Latino votes to win. The specific level of this threshold varies from state to state and, within each state, by the size and partisan split of the non-Latino vote. I develop these estimates later in this chapter for the 1992 presidential election.

While the strong Democratic partisanship in eight of the nine states increases the possibility that this needed boost will come from Democratic Latinos, a sufficiently narrow Republican (or Democratic, in the case of Florida) victory margin can also invoke this credit claiming. The necessary margin in this latter case would have to be particularly narrow, as little as the 20 to 25 percent of the statewide Latino vote that can realistically be said to vote for the minority party. Prior to 1992, this second scenario—Latinos being integral to the victory of a Republican candidate—seemed unlikely. Yet as I will suggest, it appears to have occurred in two 1992 races.

A final caveat is necessary. It is important here to note that I am discussing the regular, or *core*, Latino vote in each of the states (DeSipio and de la Garza 1992*b*). I am not discussing the impact of new voters mobilized for a specific candidate or election or of a swing vote converted from its traditional partisan voting patterns. Some of the increase in the non-Latino vote in 1992 may be just this sort of "impact" electorate, either irregular- or nonvoters mobilized by Ross Perot or young voters mobilized for the first time by Bill Clinton and Music Television's (MTV's) "Rock the Vote" campaign (Ceaser and Busch 1993, chapter 4; Frankovic 1993, 129; Pomper 1993, 142).

Although it did not happen in 1992, Latino voters and potential voters have been mobilized by issues or candidates to serve as an impact electorate. In 1994, California Latinos turned out in record numbers for an off-year election (Tomás Rivera Center 1995). Here the impetus was opposition to Proposition 187. The impact of their record turnout was muted, however, by the fact that the non-Hispanic white electorate was also mobilized around 187, in the opposite direction.

The slowing level of increase in Latino voting in 1992 and the decline in turnout among eligible adults in 1988 indicate that the Latino vote did not feature a unique or exceptional mobilization in either 1992 or 1988. Hence, when I use Latino voting data from 1992 or the survey data based on the 1988 election, I would argue that this represents the core, or regular, Latino vote, the approximate magnitude of which can be reliably expected to participate in future elections (with some increase—between 10 and 20 percent every four years—to reflect the natural growth in the number of Latinos who vote). Thus, the potential levels of influence indicated here are minimums for future elections regardless of whether new Latino electorates are mobilized.

If new Latino mobilization occurs (and the non-Latino electorate does not grow commensurately), the gap in the non-Latino vote can be larger and Latinos can continue to have an impact. With these increases, the opportunities for Latinos to influence electoral outcomes and to claim credit for electoral outcomes will also grow. Thus, to restate the point, the potential Latino influence demonstrated here is the minimum level for the present that can only increase in the future.

Close Statewide Races and the Margin for Latino Impact

As I have indicated, the first condition necessary for the core Latino vote to have a statewide impact is a close race. This raises two questions: how close and how often do such races occur? In some cases, particularly in Illinois and New Jersey, Latino influence requires very narrow races. In the case of Illinois, for example, using the vote totals from the 1992 race, the Latino vote could make a difference only if the range between the winning candidate and the losing candidate is no wider than 51.0 percent to 49.0 percent in a Democratic victory and 50.5 to 49.5 in a Republican victory (assuming a two-person race). These varying rates that depend on the partisanship of the victor reflect the fact that the Democrats can realistically rely on no more than 65 to 70 percent of the Illinois Latino vote and the Republicans 25 to 30 percent. At the other extreme, Latino voters can be said to have influenced New Mexico electoral outcomes in any race with a margin narrower than 67.2 percent versus 32.8 percent for the Democrats and 56.4 percent versus 43.6 percent for the Republicans (using 67.5 percent for the Democrats and 25 percent for the Republicans).

Most states are closer to the Illinois rather than New Mexico end of this continuum. When one considers the narrowness of these margins, can Latinos realistically expect to claim credit for influencing statewide and national electoral outcomes? Surprisingly, the answer is a cautious yes. A study of the range of electoral margins in statewide races in the nine states with large Latino populations in 1988 and 1990 demonstrates that some races were sufficiently close (NALEO 1992, 16–17). Of the nine gubernatorial races in this period, two had two-point ranges between the winner and loser (Arizona and Texas in 1990) and two had three-point margins (California and Illinois in 1990). Among the 12 Senate races, one had a two-point or less margin (Florida in 1988), and one other had a three-point spread (New Jersey in 1990). Extending this analysis through the 1992 Senate elections finds that just one of the seven races had a winning margin of two points or less (New York). None of the states with large Latino populations had gubernatorial races in 1992. Thus, of the 28 races for statewide office between 1988 and 1992, four had margins of two points or less and three had three-point margins between the winner and the loser. If these examples are representative, Latinos voting at current rates can reasonably expect to be in a position to influence statewide general election outcomes between 15 and 25 percent of the time in those nine states in which they are concentrated.

Unlike races for Senate and governor, presidential races show more consistency in margins across states. In 1988, for example, of the nine states with concentrated Latino populations, one state had a 2 percent margin (Illinois) and one other had a 3 percent margin (California). In both cases, George Bush carried these states and probably could have even if no Latino Republican voted. Had the states shifted to the Democrats, Bush would have still won the electoral college handily. At the other extreme, Bush beat Dukakis by 10 percent or more in four of the

states with large Latino populations. Further, Latinos supported the losing candidate in all but two of the nine states; the margin in one of these
two (Florida) was larger than the total Latino vote, leaving just one state
where Latinos could claim that they influenced the outcome of the 1992
presidential race (New York). As a result, DeSipio and Rocha (1992,
18) find that had no Latinos voted for president in 1988 in all states but
New York, the election would have turned out no differently. To have
an impact in New York, one third of the Latino Democratic vote would
have had to shift to the Republicans, an unlikely event.

The 1992 election, on the other hand, saw more close contests and a
role for both Latino Democrats and Republicans. Two states had victory margins of 2 percent or less (Arizona and Florida), one had a margin of less than 3 percent (New Jersey), and one (Texas) had a margin of
3.5 percent. Equally important for Latino voters, the Democrats carried
six of the eight states with majorities of Latino Democrats and the Republicans carried the state in which Latino, mostly Cuban, Republicans
dominate the Latino vote.

Because of the combination of Democratic victories and close races,
Latino votes were influential in six of the nine states (see table 3.7). In
the remaining three states (California, Illinois, and New York), the
Democratic margin of victory was larger than the entire Latino vote.
Thus, while Latinos undoubtedly contributed to this margin, the out-
come would have been no different if no Latinos had voted.

In three states (Colorado, New Jersey, and New Mexico), Latino voters were integral to narrow Democratic victories. Had, for example, less
than 49.1 percent of Colorado's Latinos, less than 45.9 percent of New
Jersey's Latinos, or less than 28.4 percent of New Mexico's Latinos
voted Democratic, the Republicans would have carried these states. Traditional patterns of Latino Democratic adherence in these states as well
as 1992 exit polls indicate that the Democratic ticket did get at least
these levels of Latino support in these states. Thus, the core Latino
Democratic vote proved integral to three Democratic victories. Two of
these victories were in small states, and the third was in a middle-sized
state. Hence, their impact on the Clinton electoral college victory margin was minimal. Had the Bush campaign been able to eke out a victory
in these states, the Clinton majority in the electoral college would have
shown a still sizable 342 to 196 edge.

Republican Latinos also played a role in three states—two in a non-
traditional manner. In Florida, the narrow Republican victory required
at least 24.4 percent of the Florida Latino vote. Again, both traditional
Florida Latino partisanship patterns and exit polling demonstrate that

TABLE 3.7. Latino influence in the 1992 elections

A. Margin between Bush and Clinton in selected states

State	Clinton vote	Bush vote	Clinton victory margin[a]	Absolute difference as % of state vote
AZ	543,050	572,086	−29,006	2.0[b]
CA	5,121,325	3,630,575	+1,490,750	13.5
CO	629,681	562,850	+66,831	4.3
FL	2,071,651	2,171,781	−100,130	1.9
IL	2,453,350	1,734,096	+719,354	14.3
NJ	1,436,206	1,356,865	+79,371	2.4
NM	261,617	212,824	+48,793	8.6
NY	3,444,450	2,346,649	+1,097,801	16.0
TX	2,281,815	2,496,071	−214,256	3.5

B. Latino votes as a share of the winning margin in selected states

State	Winning candidate	Latino vote for winning candidate	Winner's margin if no Latino had voted for winner	Impact
AZ	Bush	40,560[c]	−11,474	Clinton victory
CA	Clinton	737,750	+753,000	No change
CO	Clinton	106,080	+39,249	Bush victory
FL	Bush	304,140	−204,010	Clinton victory
IL	Clinton	104,310	+615,044	No change
NJ	Clinton	86,500	−7,129	Bush victory
NM	Clinton	110,080	−61,287	Bush victory
NY	Clinton	240,660	+857,141	No change
TX	Bush	222,480	−8,224	Clinton victory

SOURCES: Voter Research and Surveys exit polls; Pomper 1993: 136–137, based on *Congressional Quarterly Weekly Report 51* (January 23, 1993); U.S. Bureau of the Census 1993a, table 4.
[a] For ease of presentation, I represent the margin as the Clinton vote minus the Bush vote. Thus, a plus represents a Clinton victory and a minus a Bush victory. [b] State vote includes Perot totals. Because electoral college delegates are awarded on the basis of winning a plurality of votes, however, the margin between the first- and second-place candidates is the significant margin. [c] These Latino vote totals for the winning candidates are derived from U.S. Bureau of the Census Current Population Survey data, which overestimate turnout, and from Voter Research and Surveys exit polls. See the methodological note to table 3.1.

the Republicans received at least this much support. Interestingly, the Latino Republican minorities in Arizona and Texas may also have played a role in Republican victories in those states. To ensure their statewide victories, the Republicans needed at least 18.6 percent of the Arizona Latino vote and 23.1 percent of the Texas Latino vote. These levels of support are reasonable expectations for Republicans in two-person races. The three-person race in 1992 changed the equation.

These rates are on the high but still possible end of what Republicans could expect. Nonetheless, Republican Latinos were integral to at least one and as many as three Republican state victories. These three states awarded the Bush campaign 65 of its 168 electoral votes. Had he lost all three, his defeat would have been of the magnitude of Michael Dukakis's 1988 defeat.

These findings indicate that although opportunities for influence in general elections are infrequent, Latinos can influence the outcome of statewide elections in the nine states where they are concentrated. For their influence to be felt, the margin of the non-Latino vote must be narrow and the party that wins must earn a sufficient share of Latino votes to bridge this margin. As the Latino vote grows, whether through the slow ongoing expansion of the Latino vote or through the inclusion of new electorates 2, 3, or 4, the non-Latino electoral margins that can be bridged will become ever wider.

Other Opportunities for Latino Electoral Influence

Latino electoral influence can also be exercised in party primaries and in local races. This influence can appear throughout a campaign. The anticipation of Latino votes can drive potential candidates to enter the race. In the 1988 Democratic primaries, for example, Michael Dukakis, Jesse Jackson, and Bruce Babbitt entered the race for the Democratic presidential nomination in part because they assumed that Latino votes could distinguish them from their fellow candidates in key primary states (DeSipio and Rocha 1992).

Primary elections in the nine states with large Latino populations also offer an opportunity for Latinos to exercise political influence. Because of the disproportionate Democratic registration advantage in eight of these states, the most likely venue for primary influence is in the Democratic Party in all states but Florida. There has been little study of the role of Latinos in primary elections, but there are several examples of Latino electorates proving to be integral to the outcomes. In the 1988 Texas Democratic presidential primaries, Mexican Americans gave a majority of their votes to Michael Dukakis. These votes, joined with a plurality of the non–Mexican American Democratic votes, assured Dukakis of a somewhat unexpected win in Texas, and allowed him to claim a Super Tuesday victory that solidified his front-runner status (de la Garza 1992).

Primaries for statewide races also offer Latino Democrats (and Republicans in Florida) the opportunity to influence outcomes. Latinos in

Colorado proved essential for Ben Nighthorse Campbell's victory in the 1992 Colorado primary over the favorite, former Governor Richard Lamm, who had alienated many Latinos with anti-immigrant rhetoric (Hero 1996). With Campbell's 1995 conversion to the Republican Party, it will be interesting to see if Colorado's Latinos follow.

Similar opportunities appear in city-wide races in cities with non-Latino majorities (Polinard et al. 1994). Hero and Beatty (1989) find that Denver Latino voters were critical to Federico Peña's election as Mayor. After two terms in the mayoralty and some private practice, Peña moved to national politics in 1993 as the Secretary of Transportation in the Clinton administration. Latinos played an equally critical role in Harold Washington's first mayoral victory in Chicago. Influence in city-wide races may be the exception, but it is not a new phenomenon. In the late 1950s, Raymond Telles won the mayoralty of El Paso in large part because of the mobilization of Mexican American votes (García 1989, chapter 5).

Increasingly, Latino votes can also be heard in districts that are designed to increase the likelihood of electing a Latino to office. Congress extended Voting Rights Act coverage to Latinos in 1975. After 1982, Congress mandated that where possible, electoral districts be drawn to ensure that minority voters could elect the candidate of their choosing. Although not stated explicitly, this ability to elect a candidate of their own choosing came to be interpreted by the courts as electing a black, Latino, Asian, or Native American (de la Garza and DeSipio 1993; Davidson and Grofman 1994). The impact of these more favorable districting rules was felt immediately. Between 1984 and 1992, the number of Latino elected officials increased by between 3 and 5 percent annually (NALEO 1993a). The growth rates exceeded both Latino population growth in these states and changes in the pool of elective offices (Pachon and DeSipio 1992b). Despite these rapid rates of increase in the number of Latinos elected to office, the traditional socioeconomic barriers to Latino participation remain. A recent study of five core Latino barrios during the 1990 general elections found that in four of the communities there was little effort by candidates, campaigns, or electoral institutions to mobilize Latino voters. In two of the communities, there was not even any effort by community organizations (de la Garza, Menchaca, and DeSipio 1994). Thus, Latinos are making local-level gains; yet these gains are not necessarily the result of increased community mobilization.

Thus, Latino electoral influence can be felt in a variety of ways. The most easily studied is statewide and presidential races. In these elections, the Latino vote is more cohesive than the non-Latino vote, ensuring that its impact can be felt in close races. The existing pool of Latino voters can also influence electoral outcomes in party primaries and in local races. Again, the races must be close, but in areas of high Latino voter concentration they have greater opportunities to be the deciding vote. Despite this potential for influence, the high levels of noncitizenship and the lower-than-average socioeconomic traits among the citizens reduce the likelihood that candidates and campaigns will reach out to Latino voters and seek their votes.

New Electorate Number 1:
Partisan Conversion of Latino Voters

The first of the potential new Latino electorates exists within the pool of current voters. To the extent that Latino Democrats might shift their allegiance to the Republicans or that the much smaller pool of Latino Republicans might emerge as a new Democratic vote, conversion offers the potential for a new electorate. I offer three measures of the conversion potential of the current Latino electorates. First, I highlight some of the areas of potential cleavage between Latino partisans and their current parties. Then, I return to a quantitative discussion based on survey findings to see if this conversion has happened and if there is any evidence that conversion might occur in the future. I discuss the proportion of the current electorates built on partisan conversion and examine the loyalty of current partisans to see if more will shift in the future. In both cases, I contrast any evidence of partisan conversion with self-perceived partisan loyalty.

Issue Cleavage between the Parties and
Their Latino Partisans

Republican strategists perceive a potential for conversion among Latino Democrats. They think that moral and family issues, support for a strong defense, and concerns about affirmative action remedies push Latinos and Mexicans Americans, in particular, to the Republicans. Democrats have not made similar claims about converting Latino, particularly Cuban American, Republicans. Instead, when they address the topic at all, they assert that the Democratic Party meets the needs of communities, like Latinos, that seek to overcome discrimination and achieve a more equitable distribution of societal resources through a more interventionist state. Often, though, the Democratic message is confused and seems to many to be pandering (Baker 1993, 62; de la Garza and DeSipio 1996). As should be suggested from the data presented so far, the actual issue concerns of the Latino communities have been far more complex than these simple images. As a result, the possibilities for partisan alignment between Latinos and the present party structure are quite varied.

Republican claims are reinforced by Latinos' self-professed conservative ideology that places them squarely in the Republican camp. The Republican focus on family and moral values, opposition to homosexuality, support for a strong defense, and resistance to affirmative action reinforces this potential for an ideological realignment. Also, Latinos have larger families and reported a high level of school- and children-focused activities. They were intolerant of homosexuals and ambivalent about affirmative action. Pluralities adopted the national belief in job and educational allocation based on merit (de la Garza et al. 1992, tables 2.7, 6.5, 6.9–6.11, 7.39, and 8.12).

As the Republicans argue, Latinos are strongly patriotic. Despite this patriotism, however, Latinos did not see a need for added defense expenditures (even though these data were collected before the end of the Cold War). Patriotism, then, may be confused by some Republican strategists as a call for a Republican foreign policy (de la Garza et al. 1992, tables 6.1, 7.3, and 7.32).

The Republican picture of Latinos as proto-Republicans neglects the overwhelming Democratic registration rates among Mexican Americans and Puerto Ricans. It also neglects elements of the Latino policy world as well as some elements of the Republican Party. In terms of Latino policy focus, at both the national and local levels, Latinos express concern about social issues (de la Garza et al. 1992, tables 7.1 and 7.2). Despite George Bush's rhetoric in 1988 of a kinder, gentler America, issues such as these are more frequently addressed both by national Democratic campaigns and candidates and by local elected officials than they are by Republicans. These local elected officials tend more often than not to be Democrats or holders of nonpartisan offices in areas where there are high Latino population concentrations (except, of course, in South Florida).

Further, Latino policy positions conflict with the preferences of more established factions within the Republican Party. In terms of immigration policy, Latinos and vocal elements of the Republican coalition oppose immigration. The majority of Latinos, however, advocate protections for the civil rights of immigrants and expanded government programs to assist immigrants and refugees (de la Garza et al. 1992, tables 7.23–7.25). On language policy, there is a similar pattern. Republicans and Latinos believe that residents of the United States should learn English. Latinos also believe in protecting the rights of Spanish speakers, funding bilingual education programs, and limiting the ability of the private sector to restrict use of the Spanish language in the workforce (de la Garza et al. 1992, tables 7.15–7.22). While many Republicans undoubtedly could tolerate and even endorse these positions, very vocal elements of the party, including party leaders such as California Governor Pete Wilson and columnist Patrick Buchanan and his followers, could not.

Conflicting with macho stereotypes among Latinos (NALEO 1992), LNPS respondents took progressive positions on gender issues, believing that women are as qualified as men and, in some cases, more qualified, and that women are better off if they are in the workforce (de la Garza et al. 1992, tables 7.33–7.35). Again, these positions mesh with those of many Republicans. Yet they also conflict with vocal and entrenched elements of the party.

This discussion should not suggest that Latinos and Democrats are necessarily permanent allies. Despite the advocacy among all Latino national-origin groups for an expansion of government services in a wide range of issues, Latinos took fundamentally conservative positions on several contentious issues that are at odds with key segments of the Democratic Party, including abortion (which the majority of Mexican Americans and Puerto Ricans oppose), the death penalty (which the majority of Latinos support), and diplomatic relations with Cuba (which Latinos narrowly oppose). The last two are certainly topics of debate within the party, but are more likely than not to be advocated by Democrats. Puerto Ricans and Cuban Americans also advocated an increased role for the United States in Central America (de la Garza et al. 1992, tables 7.3, 7.27, 7.30, 7.37, and 7.38).

Further, while Latinos perceived societal discrimination against their coethnics and other Latinos (as well as against blacks), the majority did not perceive that they have been targets themselves. Thus, Democratic Party rhetoric must be sensitive to the distinction that many Latinos must be making between societal and individual discrimination. The caution, particularly among Mexican Americans and Puerto Ricans, over the issue of merit- or quota-based job and educational opportunities reflects this conflict between societal and individual issues (de la Garza et al. 1992, tables 7.5, 7.8–7.14, and 7.36).

The purpose of this discussion is to indicate that current alliances between the Latino communities and either of the political parties could change. The history of predominant Democratic allegiance is important but by no means determines future partisanship. As I have indicated, both parties appeal to certain Latino values, and either party could attract elements of the Latino vote. Yet the costs for the Republicans are higher because they would have to do this at the expense of other, more established, party factions. It would take a wide-ranging reorganization of the Republican coalition to incorporate Mexican American and Puerto Rican interests and to respond to their public policy needs without coming into conflict with other elements of the party. To the extent that Cuba could diminish as an issue (after Fidel Castro falls), Cuban Americans could increasingly find a home in the Florida and national Democratic parties with little dislocation of the existing Democratic coalition. Limited evidence indicates that this realignment may be beginning to occur on a campaign-by-campaign basis for some statewide and local offices (Moreno and Warren 1996).

Existing Levels of Conversion

As indicated in chapter 2, approximately one quarter of U.S.-citizen Latino Republicans and as many as one third of Mexican American Republicans are former Democrats. Among the voters, the pattern holds, and for Mexican American Republican voters, it intensifies. Although the number of Mexican American Republicans was small, almost half were former Democrats. While this might indicate significant levels of conversion, I would contend instead that it reflects the small number of older Mexican Americans who were socialized as Republicans; among Mexican Americans and Puerto Ricans, few lifelong Republicans were 35 years of age or older. Even with these conversions, Mexican American Democrats outnumbered the Republicans by a ratio of six to one such that these converted Democrats accounted for just 8 percent of the Mexican American vote. The likelihood among Puerto Rican and Cuban Republican voters of being former Democrats was smaller than among the Mexican American voters.

While small in absolute numbers, converted Democrats outnumbered converted Republicans. This finding suggests, at a minimum, that the pattern of Republican ascendancy evident in the general population is also evident among Latinos. With the exception of the Cuban American community, however, the Republicans started with fewer adherents, and their overall appeal seems to be less strong.

The permanence of this conversion is open to question. Almost three quarters of the Mexican Americans and over half the Puerto Rican former Democrats reported that they are "not strong" Republicans. Cubans and Anglos who had converted, on the other hand, overwhelmingly reported that they are strong Republicans.

What does this existing level of partisan conversion indicate for the future? Since the numbers are so small, it is difficult to provide other than impressionistic interpretations. The most important of these is that the converted Democrats were not evenly dispersed across the country. More than half of the former Democratic Mexican Americans resided in Texas, suggesting that the Texas (and not the national) Democratic Party structure is at fault. This finding is interesting because many of the claims of a potential swing vote emerged from Texas Republicans. Unexpectedly, the converted Republicans were about the same age, had approximately the same level of formal education, and had lower family incomes than the average Mexican American voter. Again, though, small sample sizes make these findings very impressionistic.

Despite Republican claims to the contrary, these data indicate that a large-scale Latino partisan conversion has yet to occur. Even in Texas, where there was the most evidence, Democratic Latinos outnumbered Republican Latinos by three to one. Admittedly, that ratio would have increased had the Democrats not lost the adherence of the new Republicans. Nevertheless, conversion of a much larger scale must occur before Democrats, even in Texas, face genuine competition for the majority of Latino votes.

Conversion Potential

Prior to formal partisan conversion, voters may go through a period of experimenting with support of the other party's candidates. Among Latinos, a significant minority of voters in 1988 fled the Democratic Party to vote for George Bush. Few Republican Latinos reversed this trend and voted for Michael Dukakis. As I have only one data point, 1988, I cannot determine whether these "Bush Democrats" represent a trend or an anomaly. I would caution, however, that the Dukakis campaign did not mobilize the Latino electorates during the general election and limited most of its Latino outreach to the last weeks of the campaign when victory seemed remote (de la Garza and DeSipio 1992).

Nearly half of Cuban American Democrats, more than one third of Puerto Rican Democrats, and almost one quarter of Mexican American Democrats voted for George Bush. As a result of the relatively small number of Mexican American and Puerto Rican Republicans, these crossover voters created the anomalous situation in which the majority of George Bush's support in these communities came from Democrats. Specifically, 51.2 percent of his Mexican American supporters and

56.9 percent of his Puerto Rican supporters were Democrats. Despite this relatively large-scale defection by traditional Latino Democrats, strong Democratic partisanship ensured that Dukakis carried the Mexican American vote by a margin of 62 to 37 percent and that he only narrowly lost the Puerto Rican vote, by a 51 to 47 percent margin. When Mexican American, Puerto Rican, and Cuban American votes are collapsed into a single "Latino" vote and weighted relative to their share of the national population, Dukakis carried these votes by a 55 to 44 percent margin.

The volume of these 1988 defectors raises the possibility that a relatively large number of Mexican Americans and particularly Puerto Ricans will convert to the Republicans. Undermining this possibility, however, is the composition of these Bush voters. Half reported that they were strong Democrats. As their total numbers are small, it is again necessary to report on their demographic characteristics impressionistically. The Mexican American Bush Democrats were considerably older than average; the Puerto Rican Bush Democrats had lower than average levels of education. Both Mexican American and Puerto Rican Bush Democrats had lower than average levels of family income.

These characteristics suggest an alternative hypothesis to the contention that these Bush Democrats were ripe for Republican conversion. They may instead reflect three aspects of the 1988 campaign. First, the Dukakis campaign made little outreach to Latinos. Second, Bush was able to tap into the Reagan legacy which had induced the highest levels of Mexican American support for the Republicans ever recorded (see table 2.1; also Flores and Brischetto 1992). Finally, the LNPS collected the voting data between eight and 18 months after the election. These findings may, then, reflect people's faulty memories of a campaign that did little to mobilize Latinos.

In sum, although high levels of support from Democrats doubled the Bush Mexican American and Puerto Rican vote, it is not yet possible to determine if these levels of support for Republicans are permanent or were idiosyncratic to the 1988 race. One bit of impressionistic evidence is available from the comparison of the 1992 and 1988 exit polls. If the Perot vote is eliminated from the 1992 poll leaving a two-person race, Clinton exceeded Dukakis's level of Latino support. This is all the more remarkable in that he was able to do this despite the relative non-competitive nature of the race in four of the nine states with large Latino populations (California, Illinois, New York, and, for Democrats, Texas).

It would be inappropriate, however, to dismiss these 1988 results. I think they offer a useful indicator of the minimum levels of Democratic support with the current pool of voters and their present partisan allegiances. Clearly this could change if these Latino Bush Democrats begin to see themselves as and behave as Republicans (new electorate number 1) or if new categories of Latino voters enter the electorate (new electorates 2, 3, and 4).

Conclusions

This chapter has sought to accomplish four goals. First, I indicated why the Latino adult population includes so many nonparticipants. In addition to voters, there are registered nonvoters, nonregistered U.S. citizens, and non–U.S. citizens. The last of these categories accounted for more than half of nonvoting Latinos in the 1992 elections, a rate 10 times that of the non-Latino white and black populations.

My second purpose was to delineate the partisanship, ideology, and policy positions of the Latino voters. I found that with the exception of partisanship, they do not differ greatly from nonvoting Latino U.S. citizens on these matters and that the voters drive the positions held by the U.S. citizens in these areas. In the next chapter, I distinguish the demographic characteristics of the citizen nonvoters.

Third, I examined the impact that existing Latino voters can have. I sought to establish a baseline for changes that could come if any of the new electorates begin to participate in significant numbers. In close statewide elections, Latinos can influence electoral outcomes. Senatorial and gubernatorial races between 1988 and 1992 indicate that 15 to 25 percent of elections are close enough that Latinos could influence the outcomes. Based on the experiences of recent presidential elections, I find that the close races occur in many states. Existing Latino voters can also influence the pool of candidates, primary outcomes, and general elections for state and local races. This potential rises as the concentration of Latinos in the electoral district increases.

Finally, I examined the possibility that Latinos will experience a partisan conversion—the first of the possible new electorates. I ascertain that the small partisan conversion that has taken place to date has not reduced overwhelming Democratic dominance in seven of the eight Democratic-dominant states. Further, the Republicans have faced almost no loss to the Democrats. Despite this low level of formal conversion, the 1988 election saw a much more substantial experimentation with Republican voting. While these "Bush Democrats" may indicate a future migration (and not just experimentation), I offer explanations for this voting that fall short of future conversion. At a minimum, however, I argue that these data offer an indication of the minimum levels of Latino support that the Democrats can anticipate in two-person races.

CHAPTER 4

The Reticents and the Reluctants

What Keeps U.S.-Citizen Latinos
from the Polls?

SINCE THE EXTENSION of the Voting Rights Act to Latino communities in 1975, the vast majority of efforts to increase electoral turnout have focused on new electorate number 3, the Reluctant—the nonregistered citizen—and to a lesser, though still significant degree, on new electorate number 2, the Reticent—the registered nonvoter. The most common form of this outreach is the voter registration drive. Drives, or at least the promise of large-scale voter registration efforts, have become nearly ubiquitous in high-density Latino areas prior to key elections (Rodríguez et al. 1994; Valadez 1994).

If perfectly effective and universally implemented, these strategies could have added as many as 899,000 registered nonvoters and 3,621,000 nonregistered citizens to the 1992 vote (Census 1993a). If they were sufficiently effective only to achieve the more realistic goal of raising Latino citizen registration and voting rates to the levels of the population as a whole, 5,749,690 Latinos would have gone to the polls in 1992, a difference of 36 percent from the actual turnout of 4,238,000.

While this many nonvoters would seem to offer a rich pool for Latino empowerment, under present conditions it is unrealistic to expect that many of these current nonvoters can be induced to join the electorate. This less-than-optimistic prediction stems from several considerations that I develop in this chapter. First, the demographic characteristics of these nonvoting communities are those of populations least likely to vote. These demographic limitations can be overcome, but they require something other than conventional registration drives.

Second, extensive resources have been expended in seeking to register and mobilize these nonvoters. Even so, the registration efforts have not reached a majority of Latino citizen adults. These resources, moreover, are declining; thus, there is little reason to expect that additional registration campaigns can make voters out of these nonvoters.

Finally, developing estimates of complete voter registration and turnout is unrealistic for any community, no matter how mobilized. As a result, I develop lower and more realistic estimates for potential mobilization of new electorates 2 and 3. Increased voting even at these lower levels could have a significant impact in several of the states during close elections.

I would also like to add three notes of caution. First, these data are based on Latinos and the 1988 election. For all electorates, but particularly for Latinos, 1988 was not a high salience election (de la Garza and DeSipio 1992). Through much of the general election, Vice President Bush had a commanding lead over Massachusetts Governor Michael Dukakis. The Dukakis campaign was not able to develop a clear and consistent message that mobilized the ambivalent. In part, voter turnout—a record low for the twentieth century—reflected this halting campaign. This malaise also affected Latinos. As a result, I think it fair to suggest that the data on 1988 reflect a baseline for potential Latino influence. The 1988 Latino voters were core voters, who reliably turn out in state and national elections (DeSipio and de la Garza 1992*b*).

The second caution is a function of survey data. These findings about voter turnout and candidate preferences should be interpreted with some caution. All respondents answered these questions between eight and 18 months after the election and there is undoubtedly some misreporting. This misreporting is probably highest among the Reluctants, who were asked who they would have voted for had they voted. As the Reluctants are probably more marginalized from the election process, their memories may be clouded.

Finally, I focus on the process of voter registration. The recent passage of "Motor Voter" legislation may reduce the need for traditional voter registration efforts. By easing the costs of registration, its advocates anticipate that more people will register. They further assume that registration will lead to voting. Their first assumption seems correct; if it is, the need for organized voter registration efforts will be reduced considerably (Piven and Cloward 1988; Teixeira 1992). But the second assumption—that registration leads to voting—may be flawed, at least for Latinos. Registration without accompanying mobilization to overcome the impact of class, education, and age may simply increase the share of the citizen population who are registered, not the share who vote.

In this chapter, then, I examine the relative size of new electorates 2 and 3 in each of the nine states. In order to offer a partial explanation of the nonvoting behavior, I explore the demographics of these nonvoters. I then examine the extent to which Latinos in each of the states have experienced voter registration drives and some indicators of the successes and failures of this voter empowerment strategy. I then return to the question of what impact these nonvoters could have were they to begin to participate. Finally, I conclude with a discussion of strategy. Specifically, I look at why the voter registration model discussed in this chapter can have only limited utility among Latinos.

The Reticents and the Reluctants

All communities have populations that do not vote. In nonimmigrant communities, most of these nonvoters are U.S. citizens. Among Latinos, on the other hand, the majority are not U.S. citizens. As a result, among Latino adults, the share of the registered who did not turn out on election day and of the citizens who were not registered is smaller than among other racial or national-origin groups. These lower rates of Reticents and Reluctants are not a strength, however, as they reflect the size of the noncitizen adult population.

In order to compare Latinos to whites and blacks more accurately, I calculated registration and turnout rates just for the U.S. citizens. Among citizens, Latinos had a lower share of the registered who turned out and lower shares of citizen adults who registered (see table 4.1).

The combined impact of these lower than average registration and turnout levels is that for every 1,000 citizen adults, just 484 Latinos

TABLE 4.1. Turnout as a share of registration and registration as a share of citizen adults, 1992 (by race and national origin)

Race/ National origin	Turnout/ Registration (%)	Registration/ Adult U.S. citizens (%)	Voters per 1,000 U.S. citizen adults
White	90.7	74.0	671.2
Black	84.6	67.2	568.5
Asian	87.5	57.0	498.8
Latino	82.5	58.7	484.3
Total population	90.0	72.8	655.2

SOURCE: U.S. Bureau of the Census 1993a, tables 2 and 17.
NOTE: These data are based on self-reporting up to two weeks after the election and overreport actual registration and turnout. There is no evidence that overreporting varies for different racial or ethnic groups.

went to the polls. For whites and blacks, the numbers voting were 671 and 569, respectively. These findings raise three questions. First, what is the impact of these citizen nonvoters? Is this impact concentrated in some of the nine states with significant Latino populations, both for statewide elections and for electoral college votes? And, do these citizen nonvoters follow the demographic patterns of whites and blacks who do not vote? I reserve the question for later in the chapter of what the partisan and electoral impact of these Latino nonvoters would be. Here, I want to look just at voter turnout.

State-Level Impact

The share of Latino citizens who did not vote varies considerably from state to state (see table 4.2). In Colorado, for example, a complete mobilization of all citizen nonvoters would have increased Latino turnout statewide by 50 percent. The Latino share of the Colorado vote would have increased to approximately 12 percent from the current level of 8 percent. In Texas, on the other hand, mobilization of all of the

TABLE 4.2. Nonvoting among U.S. citizen Latinos, 1992 (by state)

State	Reticents (registered nonvoters)	Reluctants (nonregistered U.S. citizens)	Voters
Arizona	41,000 (12.6)[a]	129,000 (39.6)	156,000 (47.9)
California	249,000 (10.1)	1,084,000 (43.9)	1,135,000 (46.0)
Colorado	9,000 (4.3)	62,000 (30.0)	136,000 (65.7)
Florida	61,000 (8.4)	256,000 (35.2)	411,000 (56.5)
Illinois	52,000 (14.1)	147,000 (39.7)	171,000 (46.2)
New Jersey	34,000 (10.0)	132,000 (38.9)	173,000 (51.0)
New Mexico	18,000 (6.2)	99,000 (34.3)	172,000 (59.5)
New York	67,000 (8.2)	372,000 (45.3)	382,000 (46.5)
Texas	276,000 (13.5)	839,000 (41.9)	927,000 (45.4)

SOURCE: U.S. Bureau of the Census 1993c.
[a]Percentage of citizen adults is given in parentheses.

nonparticipating U.S. citizens would have more than doubled the state-wide Latino turnout; in this case, Latinos would have cast as many as one quarter of the state's votes (assuming the unlikely circumstance that a new mobilization of this magnitude among Latinos had no impact on non-Latino turnout). Four other states—Arizona, California, Illinois, and New York—would also have seen their Latino votes more than double.

These data on citizen nonvoting offer a second and more refined indicator for strategists. The type of mobilization needed varies by state. To use Colorado as an example, again, almost all of the Latino registered voters go to the polls, leaving few Reticents available to mobilize. Texas and Illinois, on the other hand, see three times the percentage of registered voters not going to the polls as Colorado, suggesting the need for get-out-the-vote strategies in these states.

In the three largest states, the Reluctants are more than 40 percent of the adult Latino population. Almost a quarter of a million nonregistered citizens lived in California, New York, and Texas alone. These states have high percentages of both Reticents and Reluctants.[1]

Electoral strategies cannot be based on raw numbers alone, however. If the goal is to see the Reluctants through to voting, a registration-based voter mobilization strategy in Texas would have to be undertaken with some caution. In Texas, the share of registered nonvoters is also relatively high, perhaps indicating that previous efforts have registered citizens without mobilizing them to vote.

The state-based snapshots of citizen voting and nonvoting demonstrate several important characteristics of these populations. First, the number of nonvoting citizen adults exceeded the number of voters in five of the nine largest Latino states. With the exception of Florida, the states with more Latino voters than nonvoters were small. Second, the Reluctants present a greater pool of nonvoters than do the Reticents. Seeing them through to voting may require a greater commitment of resources and presents greater organizational requirements. As I indicate in the next section, the Reluctants are also most likely to have the sociodemographic characteristics associated with nonvoting.

Characteristics

The sociodemographic characteristics of citizen nonvoters broadly followed the patterns that would be predicted by previous analysis of the relationship between demographic characteristics—age, education, and income—and the propensity to vote and to participate in other forms of politics. With a unique exception among some Cuban

TABLE 4.3. Demographics of the Reticents (registered nonvoters)

Characteristic	Mexican American	Puerto Rican	Cuban American
Age, mean	37 years	36 years	40 years
Gender			
Male	43.4%	47.2%	41.8%
Female	56.6%	52.8%	58.2%
Race			
White	58.4%	56.6%	96.0%
Black	0.1%	8.1%	0.0%
Latino referent	41.5%	35.3%	4.0%
Education, mean	10 years	10 years	13 years
Household income, mean	$23,421	$20,430	$32,674
Work status			
In labor force	59.9%	46.4%	68.3%
Temporarily unemployed	14.4%	19.0%	12.1%
Not in labor force	25.7%	34.6%	19.5%
Home owner	38.9%	5.0%	37.7%
Self-evaluated language skills			
English stronger	50.4%	22.9%	7.1%
Bilingual	41.3%	42.2%	54.6%
Spanish stronger	8.2%	34.9%	38.4%
Identification			
National origin	60.3%	83.4%	64.9%
Panethnic	31.5%	11.2%	20.9%
American	8.2%	5.5%	14.2%
Religion			
Catholic	64.0%	65.9%	83.4%
Protestant	18.4%	19.7%	12.7%
Other/			
No preference	17.6%	14.3%	3.9%
Immigration generation			
First	8.7%	59.7%	79.9%
Second	15.4%	32.6%	14.0%
Third	26.7%	2.4%	0.0%
Fourth	49.3%	5.3%	6.1%
Age at immigration			
(foreign born), mean	11 years	18 years	19 years
Social milieu			
Mostly Latino	16.3%	34.2%	38.6%
Mixed Latino and Anglo	55.9%	55.8%	59.2%
Mostly Anglo	16.3%	9.9%	2.3%
n	236	131	46

SOURCE: Latino National Political Survey.

Americans, Reticents and, particularly, Reluctants were younger, had similar or less education, and had lower family incomes, as well as other characteristics that distinguished them from the voters.

The Reticents (Registered Nonvoters). On average, Latino voters were in their forties, had 10 to 12 years of education, and had average family incomes ranging from $22,344 for Puerto Ricans to $34,824 for Cuban Americans (see table 3.3). Among the Reticents, the averages for the national-origin groups were as follows: ages ranged from 36 to 40; education levels equaled 10 to 13 years; and incomes ranged from $20,430 for the Puerto Ricans to $32,674 for the Cuban Americans (see table 4.3). For each of the national-origin groups, the Reticents were much less likely to own homes and slightly less likely to be in the workforce. The Reticents were less likely than the voters to be foreign-born (more on this in chapter 5) and, among the foreign-born, likely to have immigrated at a younger age. The differences between voters and Reticents varied between national-origin groups in other important characteristics such as identification, religion, and social milieu. Work status and self-evaluated language skills seemed little influenced by nonvoting.

The Reluctants (Nonregistered U.S. Citizens). The pattern of difference between the Reluctants and the voters was less consistent. Mexican Americans and Puerto Ricans followed the anticipated patterns with average ages and family incomes well below those of the voters and equal or lower levels of education (see table 4.4). The Mexican American and Puerto Rican Reluctants were slightly less likely to be in the workforce and considerably less likely to own homes. Their levels of Catholicism dropped off as well. Among the foreign-born, the Reluctants were slightly older at the time of immigration.[2]

National Origin. One final characteristic deserves note. The Mexican American Reticents and Reluctants differed from the Puerto Ricans and Cuban Americans in terms of immigration generation. The Mexican Americans were more likely to be, at a minimum, the grandchildren of immigrants. This longer-term residence in the United States also appeared in the language variable: the majority were stronger in English. Despite this length of residence and English language use, these Mexican Americans remain outside the electorate.

These multigeneration, U.S. citizen, nonvoters may be one of the legacies of the manipulation and passive exclusion that characterized Mexican American voting prior to the Voting Rights Act. These Reticents and Reluctants were raised in households where they could not be socialized into voting. It is they, in fact, whom the Voting Rights Act was designed to affect.

TABLE 4.4. Demographics of the Reluctants (nonregistered U.S. citizens)

Characteristic	Mexican American	Puerto Rican	Cuban American
Age, mean	30 years	34 years	32 years
Gender			
Male	49.7%	40.8%	48.9%
Female	50.3%	59.2%	51.1%
Race			
White	55.5%	57.9%	90.9%
Black	1.0%	1.4%	0.0%
Latino referent	43.6%	40.8%	9.1%
Education, mean	10 years	10 years	11 years
Household income, mean	$24,708	$15,860	$39,453
Work status			
In labor force	56.0%	44.8%	67.9%
Temporarily unemployed	18.3%	11.5%	13.9%
Not in labor force	25.6%	43.7%	18.2%
Home owner	25.8%	4.3%	28.9%
Self-evaluated language skills			
English stronger	52.2%	20.7%	12.4%
Bilingual	37.3%	43.6%	58.2%
Spanish stronger	10.5%	35.7%	29.4%
Identification			
National origin	66.9%	78.6%	60.2%
Panethnic	25.8%	14.5%	20.9%
American	7.3%	6.9%	18.9%
Religion			
Catholic	70.7%	63.9%	59.2%
Protestant	19.7%	20.6%	14.6%
Other/No preference	9.6%	15.5%	26.2%
Immigration generation			
First	21.0%	59.8%	43.5%
Second	19.4%	28.1%	51.8%
Third	19.1%	7.5%	1.0%
Fourth	40.6%	4.6%	3.7%
Age at immigration (foreign born), mean	14 years	21 years	21 years
Social milieu			
Mostly Latino	24.7%	33.8%	34.9%
Mixed Latino and Anglo	65.5%	55.4%	58.5%
Mostly Anglo	9.8%	10.6%	6.7%
n	201	154	55

SOURCE: Latino National Political Survey.

Differentiating Voters from the Reticents and the Reluctants

Logistic regression models of the citizen nonregistered and the registered nonvoters emphasize the importance of the core demographic variables (see table 4.5). Age, education, and language distinguished the

TABLE 4.5. Determinants of Latino electoral participation, 1988

Independent variables	Reluctants: citizen nonregistered versus voters		Reticents: registered nonvoters versus voters	
	B	(SE)	B	(SE)
Age (18–24)[a]				
25–34	1.0812**	(.20)	.0399	(.20)
35–50	1.9029**	(.21)	.7305**	(.21)
51+	3.1675**	(.27)	1.2967**	(.25)
Family income (less than $13,000)				
$13,000–$19,999	.2761	(.22)	.6400**	(.21)
$20,000–$34,999	.3500	(.20)	.6076**	(.19)
$35,000+	.6901**	(.22)	.7777**	(.20)
Education (high school diploma)				
0–8 years	−.7632**	(.23)	−.0369	(.22)
9–12 years, no diploma	−.8187**	(.19)	−.2856	(.19)
Post–high school diploma	1.1296**	(.28)	.7969**	(.23)
National origin or ancestry (Mexico)				
Puerto Rico	.1885	(.17)	.3814*	(.16)
Cuba	.0910	(.23)	.4541*	(.22)
Usual language (Spanish stronger)				
English stronger	.4143*	(.21)	−.0214	(.21)
Bilingual	.5929**	(.20)	−.1596	(.19)
Self-identification (national origin term)				
Panethnic term	.0928	(.18)	.0925	(.16)
American	.2681	(.26)	.4210	(.24)
Work situation (in labor force)				
Temporarily unemployed	−.0922	(.24)	−.5066*	(.23)
Not in labor force	−.1930	(.19)	−.1709	(.32)
Constant	−1.1180**	(.30)	−.3449	(.29)
Log likelihood	1519.0772		1523.7123	
Total cases	1,246		1,261	
Predicted correctly	76.67%		71.69%	

SOURCE: Latino National Political Survey.
[a]Category in parentheses is the comparison category against which the other categories are compared.
*$p < 0.05$; **$p < 0.01$.

nonregistered citizens from the voters. With the exception of usual language of the respondent, all of the independent variables had impacts in the anticipated directions: voters were older, with higher incomes, and had more formal education. With language, bilingual respondents were more likely to be voters than the English dominant.

Income levels, age, and to a lesser degree, education distinguished Reticents from voters. In addition to these core demographic variables, national origin distinguished these groups. Also, the temporarily unemployed were less likely than those in the labor force to vote. Among the registered, when one controls for all these variables, both Puerto Ricans and Cubans were more likely than Mexicans to vote.

These results reinforce the continuing importance of age, education, and income in differentiating voters from nonvoters for both the Reticents and the Reluctants. While I believe that it is necessary to maintain an analytical distinction between these two categories of nonvoters (Merriam and Gosnell 1924; Kelley, Ayres, and Bowen 1967), these two new electorates can be combined briefly for analytical purposes. A model contrasting *all* citizen nonvoters with the voters offers less overall predictive capability than either of the models discussed here. It indicates that age, higher family incomes, and increased education are related to a greater voting likelihood. In this combined model, Puerto Ricans were also more likely to vote than Mexicans (at the .05 level), when one controls for all these factors.

This finding needs to be emphasized. Mobilization of these citizens as voters will require either an increase in the education and income levels of nonvoting Latinos as well as their steady aging, or some sort of incentive to participate that overcomes their sociodemographic limitations.

Voter Registration Resources and the Latino Communities

Because a significant portion of the Latino communities' efforts to mobilize new electorates 2 and 3 has been invested in voter registration efforts, it is worthwhile to examine in some detail the impact of these efforts. Their impact, I should note at the outset, is generally positive, but insufficient to overcome the sociodemographic limits on Latino participation.

Despite extensive investment in voter registration, the efforts have reached only a minority (37.7 percent) of Latino citizen adults. Although registration efforts have reached all residential density strata, contact is slightly more likely among Latinos who resided in high-density Latino areas.

Once contacted, the result appears to be positive. More than four in five (84.0 percent) of those contacted have registered, and three in four (77.5 percent) were currently registered. Of those currently registered, three in four (78.8 percent) went to the polls in 1988, generating a voter turnout rate of 61 percent. This turnout rate was significantly higher than the rate for respondents who have never been contacted (44.8 percent). As these findings would predict, the voters were much more likely to have been contacted than were the Reticents or the Reluctants.

Equally importantly, those who reported that they had been contacted and that they had registered had a higher rate of continuing registration than those who had registered in the past but had not been contacted. Of those who had not been contacted but had registered in the past, 15.6 percent were not currently registered compared to 8.5 percent of those who had been contacted and had registered in the past.

When I add voter registration contact to the model presented in table 4.5, contact proved a significant positive predictor of voting, for both the difference between the Reluctants and voters and that between the Reticents and voters. As would be anticipated, the impact of this variable is stronger in differentiating the Reluctants from the voters since contact so often leads to registration. Despite the addition of this variable, however, age, income, and education remain significant predictors of nonvoting. Thus, this model indicates that while contact with someone who encouraged voter registration did advance Latino voting, it alone did not overcome the impediments of age, education, and income.

These data do not allow me to determine cause and effect. Voter registration efforts may be more likely to come into contact with people likely to vote anyway. Thus, there could be a self-selection process in being contacted among those who were likely to register and vote. Cause and effect was also unclear in this question of current registration. People who expose themselves to voter registration efforts may be more likely to stay registered than those who do not.

Despite these concerns, contact appears to be associated with higher turnout, and the contacted were slightly more likely than the currently registered to remain registered. This allows the development of the first estimate of a potential new electorate. If all of those who had not been contacted could be, and if they responded with the same voting behaviors as those who had already been contacted, then the 1992 national

Latino electorate would have increased by 1,300,000. Of these, approximately 325,000 would be in Texas and 250,000 would be in California. Turnout would drop slightly in New York, where the contacted turned out less than the noncontacted.

That said, I believe this to be an unrealistically high estimate for several reasons. Not everyone can be contacted. The ongoing voter registration efforts seek potential registrants in public places, such as supermarkets and shopping malls. While some strategies do rely on door-to-door contact, this strategy is expensive. Thus, even if voter registration efforts were to be expanded, they could not reach and successfully register all nonregistered U.S. citizens. Further, even if they could be, the currently unregistered may well be less likely to respond to voter mobilization efforts than have the previously contacted. Their lack of interest in registration may reflect, in part, a lack of interest in voting or a lack of knowledge about the electoral process sufficient to feel confident in exercising the vote. Nevertheless, this estimate offers a possible indicator of the impact of previously unseen levels of Latino voter registration.

The LNPS indicates that voter registration efforts have penetrated states differently. In only one state (California) had the majority (51.9 percent) of Latino citizen adults been contacted. In other states with large numbers of Latino citizen respondents, the rates were lower: New Mexico, 43.1 percent; Illinois, 38.1 percent; New York, 37.7 percent; Texas, 35.9 percent; and New Jersey, 17.5 percent.

Despite this high level of contact in California, it is worth remembering that in the 1992 election, California had the second highest share of Reluctants and among the highest shares of Reticents (see table 4.2). Thus, if California is a model, relatively widespread contact by voter registration drives alone does not overcome other barriers in transforming nonvoters into voters.

Interestingly, the state with the highest levels of Latino participation had the lowest levels of contacts to register to vote. In Florida, just 16.7 percent of citizen adults had been contacted to register. These data probably reflect the pervasiveness of electoral politics among Cuban Americans in South Florida. Voter mobilization efforts are continual and have not been reduced in respondents' minds to inquiries about a single act—registering to vote.

The Miami case also offers a model that parallels the African American community (Stowers 1990; Grenier et al. 1994). Mobilization to participate in politics is so high that all sectors of the Cuban American community participate, not just the richer, better educated, and older.

In sum, then, voter registration alone is not going to resolve low Latino voter turnout rates. The data indicate that it can have a positive
influence, but that other strategies will be needed to overcome the traditional class and education barriers to voting in the United States. Despite extensive investments in voter registration by Latino and community organizations, less than half the adult citizens report that they have
been contacted to register. For those who were contacted and registered
as a result, the contact proved to lead to a higher voter turnout; almost
three quarters voted in 1988. When I added this contact to the basic
voting model, it proved a positive predictor, but not a sufficiently strong
influence to overcome the impacts of age, education, and income. While
these factors indicate a positive overall impact of voter registration outreach, several considerations limit its utility. The state with the highest
rates of Latino participation is the one with the lowest levels of voter
registration contact and the state with the highest contact rate has the
second lowest turnout among all citizen adults. In the former case, voters did not require this contact; they had something that was more important to get Latinos to the polls: mobilization. This mobilization, I
will suggest, is the key to Latino empowerment.

New Electorates 2 and 3:
Political Stance and Possible Impact

The discussion so far in this chapter has analyzed some of the difficulties in making voters out of the Reticents and Reluctants. The evidence presented indicates that although voter registration can be an
effective strategy, it has not bested the impact of youth, low formal education, and low incomes among Latinos and has yet to reach a majority
of Latino citizens. In this section, I shift focus and examine the possible
impacts that these potential voters could have and where this impact
might be felt. For reasons that should be clear from the foregoing discussion, I suggest caution in overly optimistic expectations of making
voters out of the Reticents and Reluctants. Based on previous electoral,
registration, and organizational behavior and knowledge of U.S. politics, I indicate some attainable goals for these populations.

Partisanship, Ideology, and Policy Preferences

Were the Reluctants to begin to vote in greater numbers, they would
add to the overall Latino turnout and, with minor exceptions, intensify
its current ideological and policy preferences while also adding to the
Republican Latino vote. With two exceptions, the Reticents would in-

tensify current partisan as well as ideological and policy preferences. The exceptions appear in the partisan preferences of the Mexican American Reluctants, who are slightly more likely than the current voters to be Republican, and in the partisan and policy preferences of the Cuban American Reluctants. They display an uncharacteristic support for the Democratic Party and take positions on several public policy issues that are more traditionally centrist than are common among Cuban American voters.

Among Latino Reluctants, between 17 and 27 percent reported that they were independent, a rate much higher than Anglo Reluctants and voters, regardless of national origin. Among those with partisan preferences, Republican adherence was much more common among the Reluctants than among the voters. This pattern was most evident among the Mexican Americans. Almost 28 percent of Mexican American Reluctants reported that they were Republicans, compared to 17 percent of Mexican American voters. The combined impact of increased Republican and independent adherence was a reduced attraction to the Democratic Party. This finding is surprising when one considers the class position of these Reluctants. Further, it belies the suggestion that increased Mexican American and Puerto Rican voter turnout would necessarily help the Democrats, if one assumes this voter turnout were to come from today's nonregistered U.S. citizens.

The candidate preferences of the Reluctants indicated an even stronger Republican leaning (as I indicated at the beginning of the chapter, these results should be interpreted cautiously since the LNPS gathered these data between eight and 18 months after the election). Of the Mexican American and Puerto Rican Reluctants with a preference for Bush or Dukakis, more than half reported that they would have supported Bush. More than eight in 10 Cuban Americans with a candidate preference also said they supported Bush. Again, the Mexican American and Puerto Rican support for Bush countered expectations based on the class position of these nonvoters.

Like their coethnics who voted, Latino Reluctants reported more conservative than liberal leanings. Conflicting with popular stereotypes, Puerto Ricans reported themselves to be more conservative than Cuban Americans. Of the three Latino national-origin groups, Mexican Americans were the only ones to place themselves more often in the middle than on the left or the right. Particularly among Puerto Ricans and Cuban Americans who include many foreign-born among their U.S. citizen populations, these various ideological stances and their somewhat surprising positioning on the right side of the scale may reflect notions of conservatism and liberalism carried from Cuba and Puerto Rico.

On a range of public policy questions, the Reluctants took positions not widely different from those of their coethnics who voted (see table 4.6). Particularly in terms of language policy, these positions distinguished Latinos from Anglos. On several issues, however, differences did appear between coethnic Reluctants and voters. Mexican American

TABLE 4.6. Public policy perspectives of nonregistered U.S. citizen adults (by national origin)

Policy area	Mexican American (%)	Puerto Rican (%)	Cuban American (%)	Anglo (%)
Language policy				
English should be the official language	43.0[a]	49.2	36.3	82.4
Public services should be provided in Spanish	86.7	93.1	94.3	57.1
Immigration policy				
Preference should be given to Latin American immigrants	37.1	31.2	26.0	NA[b]
There are too many immigrants	70.5	82.3	57.8	70.0
U.S. citizens should be hired over noncitizens	42.2	59.0	41.2	45.2
Foreign policy				
More concerned with U.S. politics	88.0	56.4	67.1	NA
The United States should establish relations with Cuba	46.6	40.1	41.6	49.6
Puerto Rico should remain a commonwealth	57.8	72.0	51.6	62.5
The cause of Mexico's problems is internal corruption	82.6	84.4	93.1	75.2
The United States should be more involved in Central America	46.9	55.8	69.6	NA
The cause of Central America's problems is poverty and lack of human rights	70.2	51.6	48.5	NA
Other issues				
Support for government quotas for jobs and college admission	34.6	33.0	13.2	2.6
Support for capital punishment for murderers	68.4	46.3	68.0	NA
Abortion should never be permitted	20.4	27.0	6.0	NA

SOURCE: The Latino National Political Survey.
[a] Percentage who agree or strongly agree; [b] NA, not asked.

Reluctants were much less likely than voters to believe that U.S. citizens should be hired over noncitizens (42 percent versus 61 percent). While this might indicate a greater closeness to noncitizens, it should be remembered that Mexican American Reluctants have a high share of second- and third-generation U.S. citizens. Though still a minority, Cuban American Reluctants were somewhat more likely than Cuban American voters to believe that the United States should establish diplomatic relations with Cuba (42 percent versus 29 percent). The Cuban American Reluctants also took a more traditionally liberal position on the cause of unrest in Central America. More, although again still a minority, believed that the cause was poverty and lack of human rights (49 percent for the Reluctants versus 34 percent for the voters). All in all, however, the policy positions and intensity of feeling of the Reluctants closely mirrored those of their coethnics who voted. When one considers the differences of opinion on partisanship, this finding indicates that ethnicity—in this case national-origin-based ethnicity—drove the public policy world of the Reluctants more closely than it did their partisan political world.

Regardless of the specifics, these findings on the Reluctants' candidate preferences, ideologies, and public policy preferences are very important. They demonstrate that Reluctants were not apolitical. They took ideological positions such that they did not cluster around the middle. Fewer respondents failed to answer this question of ideology than the questions of partisanship or candidate preference. Thus, while they may be marginalized from electoral politics, basic questions of U.S. politics were not remote to them.

In sum, the partisanship and candidate preferences of the Reticents also diverged from those of voters, although in a different direction from the Reluctants. Among the Reticents, each of the national-origin groups had a higher share of the nonpartisans than did the voters. These rates of partisan independence were at nowhere near the levels found among the Reluctants. Among those Reticents with partisan preferences, the majority of Mexican Americans and Puerto Ricans were Democrats. Although the Mexican Americans were slightly more likely to be Republican and the Puerto Ricans even more strongly Democrat than their coethnics who voted, these findings for Reticents generally follow the patterns for the voters. Unexpectedly, among Cuban Americans, loyalty was virtually evenly split, with the Democrats holding a slight lead.

Despite this pattern of self-reported Democratic leanings among Latino Reticents regardless of national origin, more of each national-origin group reported that they would have voted for George Bush in the 1988 presidential race than would have voted for Michael Dukakis. Bush would have won an outright majority among these self-reported Cuban American Democrats and a plurality among the strongly Democratic Puerto Ricans. Among Mexican Americans, Bush beat Dukakis narrowly in the two-person results.

Ideologically, the Reticents were slightly more likely to report liberal leanings than the voters and considerably more likely than the Reluctants. Right of center, however, remained the most common ideological position. In this, Latino Reticents differed considerably from Anglo Reticents, two thirds of whom reported either that they were moderate or left of center.

As with the Reluctants, the Reticents generally followed the directions and intensities of the voters' policy choices. The most common differences appeared between the Cuban American Reticents and voters. On several foreign policy issues, the Cuban American Reticents were more likely to take what could be characterized as left-leaning positions (see table 4.7). Slightly less than a majority said that the United States should establish diplomatic relations with Cuba, and more than two thirds said that the cause of Central America's problems was poverty and lack of human rights. Compared to the voters, fewer (though, in both cases, majorities) said that the cause of Mexico's problems was internal corruption and that the United States should be more involved in Central America. Cuban Reticents also differed from Cuban voters in one area of language policy. The majority of the Reticents (compared to one third of the voters) believed that English should be the official language. Puerto Rican Reticents showed variation from voters on two issues: diplomatic relations with Cuba and quotas for college admissions and jobs. Mexican Americans differed from their coethnics who voted when it came to Puerto Rico's status. Anglo Reticents were much more likely than Anglo voters to say that public services should be provided in Spanish.

In sum, the Reticents and Reluctants diverged from the voters on partisanship, but followed patterns similar to their coethnics who voted on ideology and policy preferences. While these findings confuse the question of what their impact would be on specific elections were they to start voting, they offer two useful insights. First, the nonvoters are not apolitical; they had opinions on political and public policy questions facing the country. Were they to begin to vote, they could do so with a policy awareness similar to today's voters. Second, despite their differences with the voters over partisanship, they shared the voters' views on

TABLE 4.7. Public policy perspectives of registered nonvoters
(by national origin)

Policy area	Mexican American (%)	Puerto Rican (%)	Cuban American (%)	Anglo (%)
Language policy				
English should be the official language	50.0[a]	45.3	56.3	76.8
Public services should be provided in Spanish	93.5	96.3	96.5	84.3
Immigration policy				
Preference should be given to Latin American immigrants	40.5	39.1	34.1	NA[b]
There are too many immigrants	72.2	80.5	74.3	78.3
U.S. citizens should be hired over noncitizens	53.3	47.0	38.7	57.6
Foreign policy				
More concerned with U.S. politics	90.0	51.4	79.3	NA
The United States should establish relations with Cuba	46.3	47.6	47.4	59.6
Puerto Rico should remain a commonwealth	62.9	69.6	63.6	49.0
The cause of Mexico's problems is internal corruption	88.8	87.8	78.7	89.9
The United States should be more involved in Central America	37.1	56.1	59.9	NA
The cause of Central America's problems is poverty and lack of human rights	64.3	61.5	67.3	NA
Other issues				
Support for government quotas for jobs and college admission	30.5	42.7	15.8	10.3
Support for capital punishment for murderers	66.4	50.6	75.3	NA
Abortion should never be permitted	20.1	23.2	12.6	NA

SOURCE: The Latino National Political Survey.
[a]Percentage who agree or strongly agree; [b]NA, not asked.

policy issues and the seeming contradiction between ideology (and in some cases partisanship) and attitudes toward policy issues. As a result, were they to begin voting, they might give more votes to the Republicans (or, perhaps, to Republican presidential candidates) than the present Latino electorate or, at a minimum, would appear to be open to the right Republican presidential candidate. They would advocate a public policy agenda that opposes new immigration, but is sensitive to the needs of current immigrants, recognizes the symbolic value of Spanish, opposes admission or hiring quotas, supports capital punishment, and generally supports the direction of U.S. foreign policy (with the possible exception of Central America policy).

Estimating the Sizes of New Electorates 2 and 3

As demonstrated in table 4.5, the primary factors differentiating voters from nonvoters were sociodemographic. Short of a community-wide mobilization of a scale not yet achieved among Latinos, it is unrealistic to expect that large numbers of new electorates 2 and 3 will vote. Yet some, if not many, will eventually become regular voters. To the extent, however, that this is a process of accretion, as today's nonvoters come to share the sociodemographic characteristics associated with voting, this pattern does not fit the definition that I have established for a *new electorate*—a relatively rapid mobilization or conversion of a cohesive bloc of voters.

Realistically, then, absent a massive community-wide mobilization effort and given the demographic characteristics of the Latino communities, the upper limit for these efforts can be seen as the turnout levels for the electorate as a whole in each of the states. The rates vary based on local political environments and reflect the opportunities available to Latinos and other citizens joining the electorate.

This upper boundary based on current state registration levels is lower than my estimate for the impact of a universal Latino voter registration drive. The gap between this estimate and the "realistic maximum" levels for each of the states that I am about to present further indicates that there is some self-selection process toward voting among those who reported voter registration contacts.

The estimate based on statewide turnout levels indicates that in several states, the turnout among Latino citizens is near the rate for the citizen population as a whole. Increases of 9 percent in Florida, 10 percent in New Mexico, or 13 percent in Colorado would bring Latinos and the general population to parity. Thus, absent a broad-based mobilization that makes Latinos more likely than the population as a whole to vote, few votes can be gained from among the Reluctants and Reticents in these states (in Florida, these numbers may reflect the mobilization that has occurred there). In each of the other six states, on the other hand, raising the Latino turnout rate to that of the states' populations as a whole would increase Latino turnout by between 32 and 50 percent, adding 500,000 Latino votes in California and 300,000 in Texas.

Within both the Reluctants and the Reticents, subgroups have shown behavioral or attitudinal signs that they could be in the process of becoming voters. I identify three overlapping groups that would make potentially fruitful targets for mobilization. I should note that this sort of targeted effort differs from current voter registration that tends to be more scattershot in approach. Nevertheless, the exercise of examining the impact that groups of these magnitudes could have is useful, even if voter registration efforts do not follow this agenda.

The Politically Knowledgeable. Among the nonregistered citizens, approximately 20 percent demonstrated a broad knowledge of American politics. On a scale constructed of six items (identifying the offices held by Dan Quayle and William Rehnquist; the party controlling the most seats in the U.S. House of Representatives; the ideological positions of Ronald Reagan and Jesse Jackson; and reporting that they follow current events some or most of the time), these politically informed Reluctants answered at least four with the factually correct answer or, in the case of following current events, with the answer that they followed the news some or all of the time. For comparison, 31 percent of registered nonvoters and 48 percent of voters answered at least four of the six items (and few, of any group, answered all six correctly). If these politically informed nonvoters were to begin to vote, they would add slightly more than 500,000 to the 1992 Latino vote total. While this number may seem small, these new voters would represent more than one in eight Latino voters.

The raw number of these politically informed nonvoter respondents in the sample is small. As a result, I do not analyze their state-level impact, except to say that they were not concentrated in any state. Although I am hesitant to collapse the national-origin groups into a single Latino category, it is necessary in order to say that these politically informed nonvoters leaned to the Democrats, though not as strongly as do Latino voters (when collapsed). These politically informed Reluctants reported that they would have voted Republican by a margin of almost three to one in 1988, though this again may reflect the fact that the LNPS collected this information long after the election.

In that there is a larger sample of politically informed Reticents, I can develop two state-level estimates for this group's potential impact. As I indicated, they made up approximately 31 percent of the Reticents. Were they to have voted, they would have added 276,000 Latino votes in 1992. Slightly more than one quarter of these would have come in California, adding 8 percent to the California Latino vote totals and an almost negligible share of the statewide vote of 11.8 million. Another 16 percent were Texas Latinos. Again, their impact would be small; had the politically informed Reticents joined the electorate, they would have added 50,000 new Texas Latino votes (out of 6.8 million votes cast).

While the Politically Knowledgeable offer a rich lode of potential new voters, they are a difficult population for voter mobilization strategies to reach. Their knowledge has not translated into electoral political behaviors. As a result, I would argue that their move into electoral politics will be self-generated. Candidates and campaigns seeking their votes can target messages to them. As they are informed, they will hear these messages.

The Community Active. A second behavioral indicator of possible interest in voting is membership in community-based organizations. Regardless of voting status, membership was far from universal among Latino citizens. Almost two thirds of Puerto Ricans were not members of any community-based organizations. Bare majorities of Mexican Americans and Cuban Americans were members of at least one organization (de la Garza et al. 1992, table 8.2). Voters were much more likely to be active in community organizations than were nonvoters. Hence, those nonvoters who were active are another group that could be targeted for mobilization. Approximately 23 percent of the Reluctants and 26 percent of the Reticents were members of at least one organization.

Should these organizationally active Reluctants be mobilized, they would add 600,000 new Latino voters to the 4.2 million who voted in 1992. Of these, 150,000 would be California Latinos and 100,000 would be Texans. Nationally, the organizationally active Reluctants reported that a slight majority of their votes would have gone to the Republicans and that they would have supported George Bush over Michael Dukakis by a margin of three to two.

The mobilization of the organizationally active Reticents would create 225,000 new voters with 75,000 in California. They were as solidly Democratic as the voters and included few independents. Nevertheless, they reported a four to three margin of support for Dukakis in 1988.

The Community Active offer an easier target for voter mobilization than do the politically informed. To reach these potential voters, candidates and campaigns must ensure that they reach out to community organizations. Although this is already a part of most competitive campaigns, many elections in Latino communities (and the nation as a whole) are noncompetitive. These noncompetitive campaigns prevent the development of a connection between organizational activity and electoral politics and may, in part, explain the high rates of citizens who are active in community politics, but not in electoral politics.

The Former Voters. One final group of Reticents could be mobilized relatively easily. Approximately 38 percent voted in either the 1986 Congressional race or the 1984 presidential race. Were these 1988 non-voters to be included in the regular electorate, they would add 341,000 new Latino voters including 76,000 in California and 50,000 in Texas. Nationally, they reported Democratic adherence at rates comparable to the voters. Despite their high levels of Democratic partisanship, they reported that their 1988 votes would have been divided almost evenly between Bush and Dukakis, with Bush carrying a slight majority. The gap between partisanship and candidate preference may partially explain the decision not to vote in 1988.

As I have suggested, the 1988 election was a low point for voter turnout in the electorate as a whole. This high number of former voters reflects the absence of targeted Latino mobilization. In the general elections, neither George Bush nor Michael Dukakis undertook these efforts. Neither the candidates nor their surrogates spoke to issues of concern to Latinos.[3]

The Former Voters are at once the easiest and most difficult potential electorate to reach. They are likely mobilized by candidates and issues. When these factors are present, their votes are more likely. When they are absent, they are hard to reach. They offer a lesson, however, that has not been lost on electoral institutions. In close elections, candidates and issues that directly connect with Former Voters will expand the electorate. Often campaigns and institutions do not seek an expanded electorate, as new voters can be unpredictable.

The Strategic Value of New Electorates 2 and 3

Having explored the potential impact of these electorates, I want to move into a more subjective area—that of strategy, particularly to explore who can benefit from the mobilization of these new electorates. I look at who will benefit for two reasons. First, I want to know what organizations might take the lead in moving these nonvoters into voting. Second, I want to indicate the possible future directions of Latino politics. This discussion will lead into a broader and more in-depth discussion of why new electorates 2 and 3 do not offer a larger pool of potential voters.

Each of the pools of potential new voters I have identified offers possibilities for Latino leaders, community organizations, and political parties concerned with Latino electoral participation. If Latino leaders seek new voters, the easiest to mobilize are the Reticents. They are registered, and almost four in 10 had voted in one of the last two national elections.

Conscious outreach may not even be necessary. Mobilization of these registered nonvoters could well occur naturally in a tight national race (which 1988 was not). The 1992 presidential race offers a counter-example where Latinos were more actively mobilized in several small Southwestern states. In this close national race, Latino electorates in as many as six states played important roles in selecting the state's winning candidate (de la Garza and DeSipio 1996). Overall nonparticipation among U.S.-citizen Latinos declined from 54.1 percent in 1988 to 51.7 percent in 1992 (Census 1989; 1993a).

If these Reticents were to begin to vote regularly, then as many as 76,000 new Latinos would vote in California and 50,000 would vote in Texas (see table 4.8). As I argued in chapter 3, small additions of this volume can, in the exceptional election, make a difference in the outcome.

The Reluctants, whether the politically informed or the organizationally active, offer a deeper pool of potential voters: between 500,000 and 600,000. For reasons that I have discussed, mobilizing Reluctants, even those who are politically aware or organizationally active, is a difficult task even among those who have begun in a concrete manner to participate in politics.

The partisan impact of incorporating the broader pool of Reticents and Reluctants is unclear. The Reluctants reported relatively high levels of Republican adherence and supported Bush. The Reticents, particularly the organizationally active and the former voters, followed more traditional patterns of Democratic support, but with surprisingly high levels of reported support for Bush over Dukakis. These seemingly contradictory findings offer opportunities for either of the parties to engage segments of the Latino communities in voter mobilization efforts. The Democrats have a tailor-made target for mobilization in the Reticents. They could also gamble that the Reluctants' reported Republican leanings would not remain if they became voters based on their policy preferences and the behaviors of their coethnic voters.

For similar reasons, a Republican strategy based on the Reluctants would be risky but potentially rewarding. Their numbers are far greater, and Reluctants reported Republican adherence. Yet their demographics and the voting behavior of their coethnics who voted raise the possibility that this reported Republican adherence would not materialize if the Reluctants were to go to the polls. For any of these scenarios to unfold, however, a concerted voter mobilization effort, whether from within the community or without, will be necessary.

For the most part, however, these two potential new electorates do

TABLE 4.8. Estimates of potential new voters among various target groups (nationally and in selected states)

Strategy 1: Voter registration contacts to all Latino adults

Strategy:	Voter registration contacts to all Latino adults. These newly contacted adults follow the same participation patterns as the previously contacted.
Source of voters:	Reticents and Reluctants (mostly Reluctants)
Size of population:	1,300,000
State impact:[a]	
California	275,000
Texas	325,000

*Strategy 2: Latino voter registration and turnout
at rates comparable to the population as a whole*

Strategy:	Mobilization to ensure that Latinos turn out at rates comparable to populations in their native states. This mobilization must overcome class and education limits of Latinos relative to statewide populations.
Source of voters:	Reticents and Reluctants (mostly Reluctants)
Size of population:	1,131,000
State impact:	
Arizona	69,000
California	511,000
Colorado	18,000
Florida	38,000
Illinois	86,000
New Jersey	54,000
New Mexico	18,000
New York	138,000
Texas	310,000

Strategy 3: The Politically Knowledgeable

Strategy:	Mobilization and outreach to nonvoters who have a knowledge of U.S. politics.
Source of voters:	Reticents and Reluctants (mostly Reluctants)
Size of population:	
Reluctants	500,000
Reticents	276,000
State impact:	
California Reticents	75,000
Texas Reticents	50,000

Strategy 4: The Community Active

Strategy:	Mobilization and outreach to nonvoters who are members of community organizations.
Source of votes:	Reticents and Reluctants (mostly Reluctants)
Size of population:	
Reluctants	600,000
Reticents	225,000
State impact:	
California	
Reluctants	225,000
Reticents	75,000
Texas	
Reluctants	100,000

TABLE 4.8. (*continued*)

	Strategy 5: The Former Voters
Strategy:	Mobilization and outreach to 1988 nonvoters who voted in 1986 or 1984.
Source of voters:	Reticents
Size of population:	341,000
State impact:	
California	76,000
Texas	50,000

SOURCES: Latino National Political Survey; U.S. Bureau of the Census 1993c.
[a]I derive the state-level estimates for the various target groups by examining the portion of respondents sharing the behavioral characteristic in question from each of the states. Because of the small subsample sizes, I cannot report on state impacts for states other than California and Texas.

not currently offer a strong likelihood of contributing large numbers of new voters. In none of the scenarios that I have developed does a majority show some characteristics associated with voting.

Certainly, this could change: mobilization efforts targeted at the informed or the active, or some other component of these nonvoters that I have not identified, could spill over to capture others who are less politically informed or not organizationally active. In the next section, I explore why I believe voter mobilization has been less successful at overcoming the sociodemographic limits on voting among Latinos than among African Americans.

Voter Registration and Latino Communities: The Potential for Broad-Based Mobilization

These findings offer little likelihood of making voters of many of the Reticents and the Reluctants. Throughout the discussion, however, I hint that a mobilization of a scale that has not previously been seen among Latinos could overcome some of the structural barriers and make more voters out of nonvoters than I predict here. A model for an effort of this sort is the Civil Rights movement. As I suggest, Latino leaders may have modeled their voter registration efforts on similar drives in the black community. The black efforts had an advantage. They grew from the mass awareness and mobilization of the Civil Rights movement. The Latino efforts never had the community-wide popular appeal that the black efforts did. I argue that this can be seen in their relative outcomes, which I discuss in some detail. Through this comparison, I show that simply offering the voter registration materials and providing rides to the polls is not enough (though they must be there as well). Voter registration must include mobilization—a reason to vote. This is what has not been done so well.

Beginning in the 1970s, Latino leaders began to promote voter registration as central to Latino electoral empowerment (Southwest Voter Registration and Education Project 1983). Although the origins for community-level Latino voter registration can be traced to small efforts by Mexican Americans as early as the 1920s, the impetus for large-scale voter registration among Latinos was the success in registering large numbers of African Americans in the 1960s and 1970s after the passage of the Voting Rights Act. Despite a great financial and organizational investment in this type of voter mobilization, the results of these efforts have been mixed for the Latino communities.

The Voting Rights Act, Voter Registration, and African Americans

Voter registration rates of African Americans increased rapidly in the 1960s after the passage of the Voting Rights Act. Prior to 1965, black voter registration rates tended to be low, particularly in the core southern states, and they varied widely from state to state and within states. The earliest national estimate finds that 3 percent of blacks were registered in 1940 (Lawson 1991, 85). In the late 1940s, Key noted that "so few have been Negro voters in the South that to estimate their number seems futile" (1984 [1949], 517). Key found that indeed few blacks voted in the core southern states of Mississippi, Louisiana, South Carolina, and Alabama. In the states on the fringe of the South (Tennessee, Florida, Virginia, and Texas), some, mostly urban, blacks voted. By 1960, Garrow reported that 29.1 percent of blacks were registered nationwide. State registration levels varied from 5.2 percent in Mississippi to 58.9 percent in Tennessee (1978, 7–19).

The patterns documented by Key and Garrow continued into the early 1960s. The North and border southern states saw increasing opportunities for black voting while the core southern states resisted any effort to register black voters (Branch 1988). By 1964, a majority of voting-age blacks in Tennessee, Texas, and Florida were registered (Lawson 1991, 85). In the Deep South, however, rates remained very low: 31.6 percent in Louisiana, 27.4 percent in Georgia, 19.3 percent in Alabama, and 6.7 percent in Mississippi (Parker 1990, 23). These rates of voter registration in both the high- and low-rate states were accomplished through concerted local black-led efforts to register voters and were assisted by Justice Department efforts after 1962 to file voting rights suits (Parker 1990; Davidson and Grofman 1994).

The passage of the Voting Rights Act removed many of the structural barriers that had kept blacks from registering and voting, particularly in the core southern states that had the lowest black voter registration rates. In order to take advantage of these new opportunities, African American organizations quickly converted their mobilization strategy from the passage of the Voting Rights Act to voter registration. The impact of these efforts was dramatic. Black voter registration rates increased to within 10 percent of white registration rates by 1968; in 1988, this white-black registration gap had narrowed to less than 4 percent (Census 1989, table B). The increase in black voter registration in the 1960s occurred in the states with both low and high black voter registration prior to 1965. Considering the age structure and the class and educational status of blacks, this accomplishment is all the more notable. This lesson was not lost on Latino leaders and organizations.

The Voting Rights Act, Voter Registration, and Latinos

Although it was promoted with similar strategies and with similar access to philanthropic support, voter registration has not proved as effective at increasing Latino registration and turnout as it was among African Americans. Although they note that there are few studies of pre-1970s Latino voting, de la Garza and DeSipio (1993) document that the Voting Rights Act (VRA) has not been as successful in increasing the number of Latinos going to the polls as it was for blacks. They cite four pre-VRA studies—three from the 1960s and one from 1972. The three studies of voter registration and turnout rates from the 1960s indicate that by that decade Latinos were not excluded from the Texas or Los Angeles electorates, and in some specific cases, their registration and turnout levels exceeded those of Anglos (McCleskey and Nimmo 1968; Grebler, Moore, and Guzman 1970, 564; McCleskey and Merrill 1973). Undoubtedly, the period before the 1960s saw outright exclusion. Throughout Mexican American and Latino political history, however, the more common pattern was one of voter manipulation. Thus, some of the voter participation levels documented in the 1960s may represent a manipulated vote, or voters who were originally mobilized to participate in corrupt local elections (de la Garza and DeSipio 1993).

The findings of these three studies of the 1960s were confirmed by the first Census Bureau analysis of Latino voting patterns. In the 1972 presidential election, 44 percent of the "Spanish surnamed population" registered and 37 percent voted (Census 1973, table one). These census data included non–Mexican Americans. Perhaps more importantly, they included noncitizens among the nonvoters, so they underestimate registration and voting rates among Latino U.S. citizens.

For comparison, Latino U.S.-citizen registration in 1992 was 58.7 percent and turnout was 48.4 percent (Census 1993a). While these rates appear, and may actually be, higher than the rates for 1972, the inclusion of noncitizens in the 1972 data makes them broadly comparable. Further, the 1992 data indicate lower participation rates than those found in some of the studies from the 1960s (specifically Los Angeles in Grebler, Moore, and Guzman; and Texas "Mexican American counties" in McCleskey and Merrill). Thus, even if registration and turnout rates are the same as those found prior to 1975, the Voting Rights Act and the wave of Latino-led voter registration efforts that surrounded it have not had much impact on the aggregate share of Latinos registered to vote and actually voting.

Black and Latino Experiences with Voter Registration

What then differentiated the black and Latino experiences with voter registration after the passage of the Voting Rights Act? Voter registration efforts targeting blacks went hand-in-hand with a community-wide mobilization for civil rights. This effort took many years and involved leadership, institutions, and individuals. By the 1960s, the demands of the Civil Rights movement transcended the African American community to involve whites and, eventually, the federal government. Once it became an achievable goal, voter registration and voting were the natural end-products of this mobilization. The evidence for this appears in the Wolfinger and Rosenstone (1980) finding that blacks vote at levels much higher than would be predicted by their class, education, and age.

If this is the case, then, one might anticipate a decline in black voter mobilization as the fervor of the movement declined. This pattern appears in several forms. Based on the National Survey of Black Americans, Brown finds that (controlling for education and poverty) post–Civil Rights movement age groups (18-to 26-year-olds) are less likely to vote than the civil rights generation (27- to 41-year-olds), who are themselves less likely than older blacks to vote (1991, 261–62). Although Brown recognizes that increasing age usually predicts higher voting rates, he also indicates that older blacks are more likely to recognize the intrinsic importance of the vote because of the Civil Rights movement.

A less quantitative example of the decline in salience of voter mobilization in the black community was the closing of the Atlanta-based Voter Education Project (VEP) in early 1992. The VEP had worked to register blacks since 1962. Its demise came as part of a larger move by the philanthropic community away from funding voter participation (in both the black and Latino communities). After contributing several million dollars to nonpartisan voter registration in 1984 without seeing much impact, the funders began to question the effectiveness of these expenditures and to reduce grants in this area (Barnes 1992). Broadly, then, this pattern indicates that funding to support registration and the opportunity to vote are not enough to ensure steadily increasing levels of voter registration and turnout. Instead, voter mobilization must be tied to a broader effort at using the vote to accomplish a desired social end as it was during the height of the Civil Rights movement.

It is interesting to note that in the same period that the philanthropic community became dissatisfied with the results of its efforts, the religious right was registering several million new voters to support Ronald Reagan and a moralist conservative agenda. Here, again, the voter mobilization was tied to a social end desired by the new registrants.

If, as this argument suggests, voter mobilization that overcomes class, education, and age barriers must come as part of a broader social movement, the lack of success of Latino voter registration is better understood. Although the goal of electoral empowerment is meaningful and important to community leaders, it is less than a rousing call for individuals. This point was not lost on one of the first leaders of the Latino voter registration efforts. Willie Velásquez, the founder of the Southwest Voter Registration and Education Project, often observed that issues of extreme local importance (paving the streets to avoid floods after storms, in his example) were the ones that aroused community interest (Velásquez 1983). Yet it was difficult in many circumstances to link filling out a voter registration card at a supermarket or community fair to getting the streets paved. Thus, on the whole, for poorer, younger, or less educated African Americans, at least during the 1960s and 1970s, the relevance of the vote was manifestly evident; for Latinos, the negligible increase in the share of citizen adults registered and voting would seem to indicate that the relevance was not so clear.

Velásquez's efforts grew from the same popular discontent that spawned the Raza Unida Party (RUP), the centerpiece of the Chicano movement organizations (García 1989). More interestingly, he was a college friend of RUP leaders and shared in its formative experiences. His and Southwest's efforts, then, which emerged as the RUP was in decline, were a variation on the demand for social change of the Chicano movement, though with a much more mainstream and, Velásquez would argue, a much more genuine strategy.

The efforts of Southwest Voter and other community-based organizations notwithstanding, an increasing body of literature indicates that Latino leaders are not being particularly effective at demonstrating the relevance of the vote to the mass of the U.S. citizen population (Skerry 1993; de la Garza, Menchaca, and DeSipio 1994). There is no systematic study of these questions. Instead, these studies are specific to narrow geographic areas (Los Angeles, Houston, San Antonio, Chicago, Miami, and New York), but the pattern of disconnection between Latino leaders and Latino communities is consistent across cities, with just one exception—Miami.

I do not mean to present this discussion as a dismissal of voter registration–based empowerment strategies for Latinos. The empirical evidence from the LNPS presented here is testimony to the strengths of past voter registration efforts nationwide. Equally important, there is no way to estimate what Latino registration and voting rates would have been in the 1980s without these efforts. Instead, my goal has been to indicate that to ensure a broader pool of newly registered voters, the new voter must view voting as relevant to solving community problems, particularly local ones. A lesson here can be learned from the experience of the African American community. The initial wave of voter registration and electoral participation grew from the demand for social inclusion of the Civil Rights movement. As the legacy of this movement began to decline, local variation appeared. The areas with the highest levels of black participation were those where electoral participation had a direct connection to solving community problems and addressing local needs.

This pattern has occurred successfully on some occasions in Latino communities. Raymond Telles won El Paso's mayoralty in 1957 through the deft combination of registering (and paying poll taxes for) Mexican Americans and running as a nonethnic populist to attract the votes of some poor whites (García 1989, chapter 3). Federico Peña's first election as Denver's mayor required extensive new voter mobilization and high Latino turnout (Hero 1987; 1992). Cuban Americans in Miami have based their rapid rise in local politics on a high sense of community needs and commensurate high registration and turnout rates (Portes and Mozo 1985; Grenier et al. 1994). In each of these cases, the sense of community need and the widely shared perception that individual voters could affect outcomes ensured that poorer, younger, and less educated Latino voters mobilized. In each of these examples, Latino voters were not only active members of the electoral coalitions but also key players in the victor's margin of victory.

Over the past several years, organizations conducting Latino voter registration have had to shift their focus. Partially in response to reduced financial support, their efforts have increasingly targeted communities where Latino candidates have lost electoral races to non-Latino candidates by narrow margins. These strategies have the benefit of offering the newly registered voter a concrete reward for participation; if successful, new voters can see an immediate benefit (the election of a coethnic) in voting. The downside of this new strategy is that it targets relatively few nonregistered voters.

The mobilization of new electorates 2 and 3, then, requires more than just investment in voter registration and get-out-the-vote efforts. Campaigns, candidates, and electoral institutions must woo these new voters so that they have the linkages to the electoral process that are necessary to vote regularly. As I indicated in the discussion of Latino electoral participation in chapter 2, these linkages are frequently absent.

Conclusions

The second and third new electorates offer opportunities for the expansion of the Latino vote. Had all the Reluctants and Reticents voted in 1992, the Latino vote would have doubled overnight; had they just voted at rates comparable to the population as a whole, the Latino vote would have increased by one third. Despite this potential, I find that realistic levels of new voting from these electorates are much lower.

The reasons should not be oversimplified, but age, income, and education are strong predictors of voting. This finding is not new and confirms much previous analysis of nonvoting. What is new from these data, however, relates to the questions of national origin and the value of voter registration. Mexican Americans, the largest of the Latino national-origin groups, are significantly less likely to vote than Cuban Americans and Puerto Ricans, when one controls for all the other sociodemographic factors. As a result, analysis of Latinos that does not disaggregate by national origin fails to account for the differential voting patterns of Mexican Americans and all other Latinos. The second new finding is the positive value of voter registration, at least among the minority that it reaches. While causality is unclear, those who reported contacts to register were more likely to have voted and to stay registered. An extrapolation from these figures indicates that if all Latinos received voter registration contacts, Latino voting would increase by one third. Even if this could be done, however, I suspect that the effect would be more muted because these nonregistrants have the sociodemographic characteristics of nonvoters. Thus, many need not only a voter registration contact but also a more direct sense of connection to candidates, campaigns, or electoral institutions.

I have identified components among the Reticents and Reluctants who offer a potentially greater reward for voter registration and get-out-the-vote efforts. Some Reluctants and Reticents have high levels of political knowledge. Others are active in community organizations. Some Reticents have voted in recent elections. Each of these segments of new electorates 2 and 3 offer inviting targets for mobilization efforts. Although relatively small in number (either absolute or as a share of statewide or national votes), these potential voters offer an inroad into Latino nonvoting. As I explore further in chapter 5, the ability to mobilize increasing numbers of new voters may itself generate more new voters. In other words, the cost to mobilize the earlier votes is higher than the cost to mobilize later votes.

The ultimate success or failure in moving these Reticents and Reluctants as a group into the electorate, however, will come from a broader mobilization. In the next chapters, I discuss naturalization as a tool to make voters of noncitizens. If naturalization were to accomplish this as a short-term goal, I argue that it could have a longer-term impact of creating a mobilized environment in which the Reticents and the Reluctants will come to participate as well. In chapter 5, I ask whether naturalization promotion is an empowerment stimulus that could have an impact comparable to the Civil Rights movement on black voting.

CHAPTER 5

Naturalization and New Voters

NUMERICALLY, THE GREATEST pool of Latino nonvoters is the noncitizen population—the Recruits. As indicated in chapter 3, more than half of Latinos who did not vote in the 1992 elections could not do so because they were not citizens. Formally, these Latinos are furthest from the voting booth. Before they can vote, they must naturalize and register. Their practical distance from the polls, however, varies. Based on recentness of immigration or immigrant status, some are ineligible to naturalize; others are eligible, but unwilling; others are eligible and anxious to naturalize.

Those who are interested face several steps to naturalize prior to registration and voting. These include psychological ones—transferring their primary political loyalties from their countries of origin to the United States. They must also prepare for the naturalization process that requires both specific knowledge—English language proficiency and knowledge of U.S. civics and history—and the ability to meet a series of confusing bureaucratic requirements. Only after developing the psychological attachment to the United States, developing the requisite knowledge, and meeting the bureaucratic requirements imposed by the U.S. Immigration and Naturalization Service (INS) can these Latino immigrants consider the possibility of voting in most jurisdictions.

Despite these steps, many Latino immigrants with the statutory minimum residence for naturalization of five years of legal residence (three if married to a U.S. citizen), have made the psychological bond with the United States. Further, many of those who have passed the psychological step have initiated the naturalization process on their own despite the absence of a community-wide ethic to promote this activity.

This chapter, then, examines these indicators of attachment within the Latino noncitizen population. I then analyze factors that distinguish the naturalized from the nonnaturalized and conclude by developing several estimates of possible new electorates that can be found among the Recruits.

The following chapter continues to focus on the noncitizen new electorate. My concern, however, shifts from analyzing its characteristics and size to assessing its potential impact. These questions of strategy generate a discussion of the potential importance of Latino naturalization, not just for making citizens out of immigrants, but as importantly, for overcoming some of the limits on citizen electoral participation.

Latino Non-U.S. Citizen Attachment to the United States

Naturalization is a voluntary process. Once admitted to permanent residence, an immigrant may remain a denizen of the United States until death. Although it may be changing slightly, the historic policy of the U.S. Government has been not to promote naturalization among its denizens, instead leaving the decision to the individual (Duarte 1985). Since the first decades of this century when the federal government centralized administration of naturalization, state and local governments have taken only sporadic interest in promoting citizenship. Urban political machines drove much of this local promotion.

The Constitution and judicial interpretation of the equal protection clauses of the fifth and fourteenth amendments also limit immigrant incentives to naturalize. Equal protection guarantees ensure that noncitizens receive all of the constitutional protections of U.S. citizens and, until recently, most of the programmatic benefits (Fuchs 1990, 477–82). Further, the grant of birth-right citizenship in the fourteenth amendment ensures that the immigrant's decision to remain a denizen will have no impact on his or her U.S.-born children or grandchildren.

The voluntary nature of this decision and the absence of state encouragement to naturalize, coupled with assumptions about the enduring loyalty between the immigrant and the country of origin, may explain much about the low naturalization rates of some immigrant groups (Pachon 1991; DeSipio and Pachon 1992). This contention of enduring loyalty to the country of origin can be seen as a variant of the Latino sojourner thesis discussed in chapter 2. According to its noncitizen variant, those who do not act on the opportunity to naturalize must not be attached to the United States. The results of both the National Latino Immigrant Survey (NLIS) and the Latino National Political Survey (LNPS) indicate otherwise, particularly among immigrants with the five or more years of residence requisite for naturalization. Just as Latino immigrants defy the conventional wisdom by not being sojourners, they defy it again by the intensity of their interest in U.S. citizenship despite low naturalization rates.

Evidence of Emerging Attachment to the United States

The great majority of Latino immigrants reported that they intended to make the United States their permanent home. Regardless of national origin, more than 95 percent of NLIS respondents reported that they "presently plan to make the United States their permanent home." The LNPS shows equally strong though not as universal intent to stay in the United States. Among respondents with five or more years of residence, 79.3 percent of Mexican and 87.5 percent of Cuban immigrants reported that they planned to remain in the United States. Just 7.2 and 4.9 percent of Mexican and Cuban immigrants reported an intent to return to Mexico and Cuba, respectively. One explanation for the discrepancy between these findings is the possibility that the LNPS contains undocumented immigrants.

This reported intention to reside here permanently was reinforced by a series of positive attitudes toward life in the United States. Overwhelmingly, immigrants reported that life is better here and that they expect their children's lives to be better than their own. This attachment and expectation for a better life was true of each of the national-origin groups. Latinos from Central and South America were the least likely to express a perception of a life in the United States as being better. Yet more than two thirds of the noncitizen Latinos from Central and South America reported that life in the United States was better, and again, 95 percent planned to make the United States their permanent home.

The LNPS offers a final indication of this attachment. Nearly 80 percent of the Cuban immigrants and almost two thirds of the Mexican immigrants with five or more years of residence reported either an extremely strong or very strong love for the United States. At the other extreme, just 11 percent of Mexicans and 4 percent of Cuban citizen-eligible immigrants reported "not very strong" love of the U.S.

Emerging Political Attachment to the United States

The intention to live in the United States and attachment to it were tempered, however, by the political reality of noncitizenship. Among the noncitizens, the dominant political allegiance remained to the country of origin (Pachon and DeSipio 1994, table 6.3). Despite their non-citizenship, more than one third of each of the national-origin groups and nearly half of the Dominican immigrants already were more connected to the United States.

As this discussion should imply, Latino immigrants seek to make their attachment to the United States more formal. Among NLIS respondents, between 82 and 95 percent of each national-origin group had applied for or planned to apply for U.S. citizenship. Among respondents who had not yet naturalized, 78 percent of Cuban immigrants, 79 percent of Mexican immigrants, 93 percent of Dominican immigrants, and 81 percent of other Latino immigrants intended to apply for citizenship in the future.

Among noncitizens in the NLIS, approximately 60 percent of each of the national-origin groups reported that naturalizing was "very important." At the other extreme, between 3 percent of Mexican immigrants and 6 percent of Cuban immigrants felt the converse, that naturalizing was "not at all" important.

The LNPS echoed these high rates of intent to apply for naturalization. For Mexican immigrant respondents, 73.3 percent were either currently applying or planned to apply. Among Cuban-origin respondents to the LNPS, 67.5 percent were applying or would in the future. Although somewhat lower than the NLIS, particularly among the Cuban immigrants, these data demonstrated the strong interest in naturalization among Latino immigrants.

With their high levels of intent to remain permanently in the United States, their strong love for the United States, and their considerable interest in naturalization, one might expect that Latinos are quick to naturalize once they achieve statutory eligibility. The reality is quite different. Among the immigrant groups making up a major share of the immigrant pool, Latinos are consistently among the slowest to naturalize (U.S. INS 1992, 114–21).[1] Until the mid-1980s, Cuban immigrants proved the exception to this rule. Today, however, they are among the slowest to naturalize. In the next chapter, I develop a hypothesis to explain this discrepancy between interest in and successful naturalization.

This gap between interest in naturalization and U.S. citizenship rates is somewhat more complicated than this discussion suggests. Many Latinos initiate the naturalization process but fail to become U.S. citizens. According to the NLIS, 38 percent of Mexican immigrants, 51 percent of Cuban immigrants, 41 percent of Dominican immigrants, and 48 percent of other Latino immigrants had begun to naturalize in some concrete manner, but had not yet completed the process (Pachon and DeSipio 1994, table 7.1).

Because the NLIS was designed in part to track the INS's administration of naturalization, it offers precise measures of each step in the naturalization process. In the analysis that follows based on the NLIS, I define immigrants who had initiated naturalization as those who had either (a) obtained the application for naturalization from the INS or (b) took classes in English or civics with the intention of preparing for the citizenship exam.[2]

The LNPS does not offer similarly precise measures of the behavioral initiation of naturalization. Its findings, however, offer useful insights into the question of the share of immigrants in the process of becoming U.S. citizens. Instead of defining a starting point for naturalization, the LNPS asked noncitizen respondents if they were currently applying or intended to in the future. Just 21.1 percent of Mexican and 9.6 percent of Cuban immigrants reported that they were in the process of applying at the time of the interview.

This margin between self-reported applying status and the broader category of having initiated the process provides an indicator of the size of the pool of discouraged applicants. For Mexican immigrants, 38.2 percent had at some time begun the process in a concrete way. Yet barely half still saw their applications as moving forward. Among Cuban immigrants, the pool of discouraged applicants made up an even larger share of the eligible immigrants, with 51.4 percent beginning the process and just 9.6 percent still pursuing their applications. Admittedly, some may have voluntarily decided to halt their move toward U.S. citizenship after initiating the process and, thus, were not discouraged, but merely back in the pool of the disinterested. As I indicate in the next chapter, however, the bureaucratic complexity of the process discourages many people so that they give up, not because of lack of interest, but because of confusion.

These results are really quite startling. They indicate that over one third of Mexican and one half of Cuban immigrants desire U.S. citizenship, but are not actively pursuing it. The presence of these populations (and similar Dominican and other Latino immigrant populations) begins to indicate the size of this potential new electorate. For analysts, however, these citizenship-inactive populations also indicate the need to examine the naturalization process to see what impedes these interested immigrants from achieving their goals and what discourages those who have taken the behavioral step of initiating naturalization.

Distinguishing Naturalized U.S. Citizens from the Discouraged and the Disinterested

The National Latino Immigrant Survey offers a portrait of the process of becoming a U.S. citizen. It distinguishes between nonnaturalized and naturalized citizens on a series of behavioral and attitudinal dimensions. In this discussion, I focus primarily on the behavioral dimension of U.S. citizenship acquisition. Specifically, I examine what characteristics distinguished those who had not behaviorally initiated naturalization, and those who have begun but not completed the process from those who had naturalized.

I exclude from this discussion naturalized citizens who obtained citizenship as children through the naturalization of their parents (whom the INS calls "derivative citizens") because they themselves did not have to make any decisions about whether to apply, and did not personally experience any of the difficulties associated with the INS's administration of naturalization. As a reminder, I define the behavioral initiation of naturalization as either obtaining the naturalization application from the INS or taking classes in English or civics in order to prepare for the citizenship exam.

The Disinterested

Approximately 37 percent of Latino immigrants eligible for naturalization had taken neither of these actions. The first question is, Did these apparently disinterested immigrants want to stay in the United States and become citizens? Overwhelmingly, the answer to this question is yes. Among the disinterested, more than 97 percent planned to make the United States their permanent homes and over 80 percent believed that becoming a citizen is either very or somewhat important. The comparable rates for naturalized citizens were 99 percent and 95 percent, respectively. Thus, in terms of residential plans and beliefs about naturalization, the noninitiators and the naturalized were similar in that both planned to remain in the United States and both saw the importance of naturalization.

What, then, distinguishes these disinterested immigrants from the naturalized? The answer, in part, will sound like a familiar refrain: age, education, and income again played a significant role (see table 5.1). These traditional demographic factors for distinguishing voters from nonvoters were joined by age at immigration, self-evaluated English language ability, associations with U.S. citizens, national origin, and, in one case, reason for immigration.

Older and more educated immigrants were significantly more likely to be naturalized. Higher incomes also appeared to predict naturalization, though the pattern is not monotonic. English competence was also linked to naturalization, though not as strongly as were age and education. Immigrants who arrived in the United States at older ages were less likely to naturalize than those who came to the United States when they

TABLE 5.1. Predictors of naturalization

Independent variables	Have not begun process versus naturalized		Have begun process versus naturalized	
	B	(SE)	B	(SE)
Age (18–34)[a]				
35–50	1.0684**	.24	.6916**	.25
51+	1.9358**	.31	1.4916**	.31
Education (0–8 years)				
9–12 years	.8697**	.24	.1383	.24
Post–high school	1.4891**	.28	.1865	.26
Yearly family income ($12,000 or less)				
$12,001–$21,000	.6426*	.23	.5337*	.22
$21,001+	.3079	.25	.7436**	.24
Workforce status (in workforce)				
Not in workforce	−.0001	.20	−.2159	.20
Reason for immigration (family)				
Political	−.1244	.38	−.0091	.35
Economic	.5612*	.24	.2265	.24
Other	.1799	.28	−.2934	.28
Citizenship milieu (mixed U.S. citizens and noncitizens)				
Mostly noncitizens	−1.1272*	.47	−1.6281**	.49
Mostly U.S. citizens	−.2234	.19	−.1534	.18
Gender (male)				
Female	.1767	.19	.4849*	.18
Home ownership (yes)				
No	−.3617	.19	−.3265	.19
Self-evaluated English ability (speaks English not well)				
Mixed language ability	.7503**	.25	.7933**	.26
Speaks well	.7923*	.37	1.1994**	.35
Social milieu (all Latino)				
Mixed Latino and non-Latino	−.3696	.20	−.1647	.20
Age at immigration (1–12)				
13–18	−.6444*	.32	−.8178**	.30
19–29	−.9853**	.33	−.4802	.29
30+	−1.5084**	.36	−1.3877**	.34
National origin (Mexico)				
Cuba	1.3090**	.34	1.1595**	.32
Dominican Republic	.9630**	.35	.6665	.37
Other Latin America	.1875	.25	.3172	.24
Constant	−2.2887**	.63	−1.6088*	.64
Log likelihood	−1133.12		−996.02	
Total cases	835		719	
Predicted correctly	78.20%		74.46%	

SOURCE: National Latino Immigrant Survey.
[a]Category in parentheses is the comparison category against which the other categories are compared.
*p < 0.05 **p < 0.01.

were 12 years or younger. This relationship is not linear: immigrants who arrived at older ages were increasingly less likely to naturalize.

The citizenship milieu of the immigrants appeared to influence the likelihood of naturalization. Association with noncitizens proved a significant negative predictor compared to association with a combination of citizens and noncitizens. The opposite situation, association mostly with U.S. citizens, however, did not prove to be a significant predictor of naturalization. Finally, if one controls for these factors and the others in the model presented in table 5.1, Cuban and Dominican[3] immigrants were consistently more likely than Mexican immigrants to naturalize.

The Discouraged

Latino immigrants who had initiated but not completed naturalization were even closer to the residential and attitudinal positions of the naturalized. Ninety-eight percent planned to reside in the United States permanently, and 91 percent believed that becoming a U.S. citizen was either very or somewhat important.

The mix of the relative importance of the independent variables shifted slightly in differentiating those who had begun the naturalization process but were not able to naturalize, from those who had naturalized. Age was a strong positive predictor differentiating the groups, though the impact of age was not as great as with the first model. Higher incomes also predicted successful naturalization, this time in a more monotonic pattern. Interestingly, education proved not to be a significant differentiating factor between immigrants who had begun to naturalize but had not succeeded, from those who had naturalized.

In this model, age and income were joined by gender, language ability, age at immigration, citizenship milieu, and national origin. Once they had initiated the process, women were more likely than men to naturalize. Those who felt they spoke English well were more likely to naturalize than those who reported that their Spanish was better. Immigrants with mixed language abilities also did better than did the Spanish dominant. Immigrants who arrived in the United States in their teens and in their thirties and beyond were less likely than those who had arrived as children to naturalize. Finally, Cuban immigrants were more likely than Mexicans to naturalize.

Noncitizens versus Citizens

When I combine these two models to distinguish all noncitizens from the naturalized, age, education, income, self-evaluated English ability, age at immigration, and national origin all proved to be significant positive predictors of the likelihood to naturalize. Each followed the patterns discussed above, with largely linear effects on the demographic variables. In the combined model, association mostly with non-U.S. citizens had a negative impact on naturalization compared to immigrants who associated with both citizens and noncitizens. Overall, the strongest positive predictors of naturalization were age, particularly those over 50 years, income over $21,000 per year, strong abilities in English, and lastly, origins in Cuba.

As I have suggested, the NLIS offers more precise indicators of the steps from immigrant to citizen. As a control, however, I applied a similar logistic regression model to the intending, the currently applying, and the naturalized in the LNPS (the LNPS data do not allow for the exclusion of derivative citizens). These are attitudinal as opposed to behavioral indicators. Similar patterns appear to distinguish between its more narrow "currently applying" category and naturalized citizens. Age proved the most influential positive predictor of naturalization. Other significant positive predictors were higher levels of education, home ownership, and age at immigration. Among LNPS respondents, the impact of age at immigration was monotonic, with the immigrants who arrived at the youngest ages being the most likely to naturalize.

The LNPS offered an insight into immigrants with five years of residence who were uninterested in citizenship that can be better developed from its attitudinal measures than from the NLIS's behavioral indicators. I should acknowledge that some of these disinterested immigrants in the LNPS are undocumented. Age and age at immigration remain reliable predictors of naturalization (see table 5.2). The disinterested were either young or immigrated in their twenties or thirties and beyond. They lived in a mostly Spanish-language world and were more likely to be out of the workforce. Mexican immigrants were more likely to be disinterested than Cuban immigrants. Important to notice also, however, are several characteristics that did not statistically distinguish the disinterested from the naturalized citizen. Higher education levels and income, for example, have no independent significant effect.

Though they vary slightly, these models indicate that those who had naturalized differed from those who had not across a series of variables relating to aspects of socioeconomic status and acculturation: immigration at a young age, increasing age, English language ability, home ownership, and current workforce participation. Immigration at a young age allows Latino immigrants the opportunity of education in the United States. Older immigrants, in many cases, have been here longer and, in any case, are at ages when they are more likely to settle down.

TABLE 5.2. Predictors of naturalization, distinguishing those who express no interest in naturalization

Independent variables	Not interested in U.S. citizenship versus naturalized	
	B	(SE)
Age (18–24)[a]		
25–34	.5985	.65
35–50	2.0140**	.69
51+	3.5106**	.74
Education (high school diploma)		
0–8 years	−1.1155**	.34
9–12 years, no diploma	−.6107	.50
Post–high school	.8631	.48
Yearly family income ($13,000 or less)		
$13,001–$19,999	−.3701	.40
$20,000–$34,999	−.1691	.39
$35,000+	−.2746	.46
Workforce status (in workforce)		
Temporary labor force	.2127	.57
Not in workforce	−.9332**	.35
Gender (female)		
Male	.4439	.28
Home ownership (no)		
Yes	.7573*	.29
Language used (all or mostly Spanish)		
Mixed	1.6319*	.75
All or mostly English	.9794*	.43
Social milieu (mostly Latino)		
Mostly Anglo	−.5529	.82
Mixed Latino and Anglo	.0687	.29
Age at immigration (1–12)		
13–18	−.9333	.53
19–29	−2.1890**	.52
30+	−3.8195**	.63
National origin (Mexico)		
Cuba	.8795**	.19
Self-identification (national-origin term)		
Panethnic term	.2971	.41
American	7.5708	14.98
Constant	−1.4756*	.76
Log likelihood	−620.95	
Total cases	489	
Predicted correctly	82.57%	

SOURCE: Latino National Political Survey.

[a]Category in parentheses is the comparison category against which the other categories are compared.

*p < 0.05; **p < 0.01.

English language ability is certainly a primary indicator of acculturation. The finding in one of the models that bilinguals were more likely than the predominant English user to naturalize does not undermine this. In fact, bilingualism provides an ability to move in both the immigrant and the citizen worlds. Finally, homeownership and workforce participation are also indicators of permanence in the United States and longer-term community ties.

The characteristics that do *not* distinguish the noncitizens from the citizens reinforce the notion that a loosely defined acculturation explains why some immigrants naturalize and some do not. Education and income are inconsistent in their importance. Low education appears as a negative predictor intermittently, perhaps reflecting the skill-based nature of the naturalization exam. High incomes appear as positive indicators in some models. This may be a function of limitations on some economic opportunities to U.S. citizens and also that the more affluent immigrants are more culturally and experientially distant from the majority of immigrants. Associational characteristics have mixed influence. Association only with noncitizens diminishes the likelihood of naturalization, but ethnic associations seem to have no influence. Despite being identified as a positive predictor of naturalization in a previous study, homeownership had no impact in the behavioral (NLIS) models (Portes and Curtis 1987). Immigration-related experiences have little predictive ability; reason for immigration has only sporadic influence.

National origin makes a difference. Controlling for a wide range of characteristics, Mexicans are consistently less likely to naturalize than Cuban immigrants (in the LNPS) and than Cuban and Dominican immigrants (in the NLIS). In part, this must reflect the added opportunities to naturalize among Cuban immigrants and the greater affluence and education of many Cuban immigrants.

The model, however, indicates that if one controls for all of the demographic factors, Dominican immigrants also have a higher likelihood of naturalizing than do Mexican immigrants. These differences may reflect more than simply cultural differences. Dominicans began large-scale migration in the 1960s. The first immigrants brought higher class and education status than did most Mexican immigrants, and consequently, they naturalized rapidly. These early Dominican immigrants set a pattern for subsequent waves of immigrants. Thus, as the Dominican immigrant pool comes to reflect the patterns of the later, relatively lower status immigrants and the heritage of these early naturalizations is lost, Dominican immigrants may not differ from Mexican immigrants, unless there is some targeted effort at naturalization mobilization.

One additional factor must be considered in explaining low rates of naturalization for Mexican immigrants. The closeness of Mexico to the United States may act as a dampening influence on Mexican naturalization. As evidence for this proposition, I offer the low rates of naturalization among Canadian immigrants to the United States. Although many Canadian immigrants bring the high sociodemographic traits normally associated with naturalization as well as, in most cases, English language skills, they are among the slowest to naturalize. In the case of a cohort of 1977 immigrants studied by the INS, they naturalize at lower rates than do Mexican immigrants (U.S. INS 1992, table K). Thus, the shared border with the United States and the resulting easy access to the country of origin may limit the impetus to naturalize among many Mexican and Canadian immigrants. Although this finding of low naturalization rates among Canadians and Mexicans has long been a part of the naturalization literature, there has been no systematic examination of why. My best conjecture would be that the proximity allows Mexican and Canadian immigrants more than immigrants from other parts of the world to remain an ongoing part of life in the sending country. As a result, although the cultural and political attachment to the United States steadily grows, it takes longer for them to make the attachment formal through naturalization than for other immigrants because many Canadians and Mexicans are able to maintain involvement in the life and politics of their home countries.

Finally, these models offer an important point to an ongoing debate in the Latino and immigrant advocacy communities. Many advocates have argued that noncitizens should be given the vote, at least in local elections. In defense of this position, these advocates raise a historical argument: this was the norm in parts of the country in the nineteenth and early twentieth centuries, with no particular harm to the polity (Rosberg 1977). They also raise a justice-based argument, that the noncitizens pay taxes and receive government services, so they should have a say in electing officials. While both of these arguments have merit, these advocates of noncitizen voting neglect an important point: most Latino noncitizens have the demographic characteristics associated with nonvoting and are not likely to vote even if granted the right, without some sort of accompanying voter mobilization. An example is in the election of New York school board members in which noncitizens have been able to vote since 1968. Despite the large numbers of noncitizens in New York, few vote in these elections.

With one exception, then, the energies being used to advocate non-citizen voting could be better channeled into promoting naturalization and its concomitant socialization in American politics, than into ensuring a right that would be largely unused. The exception is a proposal that Rodolfo de la Garza and I make that a limited five-year noncitizen voting privilege be granted to new immigrants. If during this five-year period, the immigrant regularly exercises the vote, he or she will have been deemed to have demonstrated the behavior of a good citizen and will have the naturalization examination requirements waived (de la Garza and DeSipio 1993, 1521–23). We propose, then, to add a second route to naturalization to the present, knowledge-based route. In this new alternative, the measure of commitment to the values and principles of the United States is behavioral. While implementation of such a plan might well stir a backlash among those who believe that a knowledge-based system is the only adequate test for the award of naturalization, we argue that those immigrants who demonstrate commitment to the United States in a concrete manner should be offered naturalization as U.S. citizens.

Latino Non-U.S. Citizens and New Electorates: Who Are the Likely Recruits?

The Latino non-U.S. citizen population contains diverse populations (Pachon 1991, 72–75). Among these are long-term legal permanent residents, recently arrived legal permanent residents, beneficiaries of the legalization provisions of the Immigration Reform and Control Act of 1986, the undocumented, and temporary visitors. For several reasons, immigration analysts have not been able to develop reliable estimates of any of these populations. Two factors consistently prevent the development of estimates across each of these populations. First, there is neither data nor consensus on how many permanent residents emigrate. Second, no record exists of the mortality of these immigrants. Since it is not possible to develop an estimate based on a count of legal immigrants, subtracting those who have naturalized, emigrated, or died, I count backward from the census count of noncitizen Latinos. This too presents problems because this figure includes populations ineligible to naturalize.

In appendix 2, I develop an estimate of 2.5 to 3 million currently eligible noncitizens. This calculation begins with the 5.9 million Latino noncitizens present in 1992 according to the Current Population Survey (CPS) and excludes three populations not eligible for U.S. citizenship:

the undocumented; recent-arrival legal permanent residents; and the beneficiaries of the legalization and Special Agricultural Worker (SAW) provisions of the Immigration Reform and Control Act (IRCA) of 1986. My estimate also seeks to adjust the CPS estimate upward to account for persistent undercounts of Latinos in the census. This "current" estimate of 2.5 to 3 million currently eligible noncitizens excludes the approximately 2.6 million Latino beneficiaries of the legalization and SAW programs who are beginning to become eligible for citizenship at this writing.

Were these naturalization-eligible noncitizens to naturalize and vote (neither of which should be assumed), they could increase the Latino vote nationally by between 50 and 75 percent. This is the maximum possible new electorate and assumes that a steadily broadening interest among immigrants in naturalization has what Alejandro Portes has characterized as a "cumulative causation" effect across the Latino immigrant community.

Portes (in NALEO 1994, 67–69) raises this notion in terms of Latino naturalization. He defines cumulative causation as "the more there is of something, the more there is going to be." Hence, he contends that as naturalization increases in a specific immigrant community, the rate becomes faster among those not yet naturalized. The initial pool of naturalizing immigrants accomplishes this for subsequent applicants by reducing the costs of naturalization, increasing its salience, establishing social networks for those not yet naturalized, increasing the political reward for naturalization by raising local and state political influence, and generally familiarizing the community with the benefits of naturalization and strategies for overcoming the bureaucratic hurdles. According to Portes, then, the difficulties lie in initiating the process. Once it is started, it is reasonable to anticipate "accelerating rates of citizenship acquisition once it has become part of the 'culture' of an immigrant group" (69). Were this cumulative causation to include the legalization applicants, it could more than double the Latino vote.

The pattern of cumulative causation is not unique to naturalization. The model of the Civil Rights movement presented in the previous chapter offers a parallel (Kluger 1976). The new electorate created by the New Deal offers a second (Allswang 1971). In each of these cases, a racial or ethnic elite developed a community-wide expectation, in the case of the Civil Rights movement for equal participation and in the case of the New Deal realignment, for a shift in governmental priorities. Alone these elites could not accomplish their objectives through democratic means. By creating a mass movement around their objectives, however, the elites were able not only to make a claim on the society but also to succeed in implementing this claim.

In the case of naturalization, immigrant or ethnic leaders could galvanize a movement by claiming that immigrants have a stake in the U.S. political order and that the only way they can ensure that their voices will be heard is through naturalization. The initial naturalizees will not necessarily achieve their goals, as their number will be small. With increasing numbers, however, naturalized citizens will be able to influence political outcomes, which will serve to create an incentive for more to naturalize.

In the next chapter, I examine a contemporary example of this cumulative causation phenomenon based on a claim of political exclusion—that is, the Cuban community's efforts to naturalize in South Florida in the early 1980s. It is important to note now that Miami Cubans were able to achieve significant local and statewide political influence by the early 1990s, not through universal or immediate naturalization, but instead through widespread naturalization of 125,000 to 150,000 new citizens over an eight-year period.

Potential New Electorates among Latino Non-U.S. Citizens

Naturalization of all eligible Latino immigrants and their exercise of the franchise at rates comparable to the current pool of naturalized citizens would add between 50 and 75 percent to the national Latino electorate. Regardless of how realistic the cumulative causation model, I believe that this is an unattainable goal. To develop more realistic estimates of the potential impact of this electorate, I limit my discussion in several ways. First, I look at the Latino immigrants who behaviorally or psychologically have begun the process of becoming American. These are the "Frustrated." Second, I investigate noncitizen Latinos who have a history of political participation either in their countries of origin or in the United States, whether or not they have initiated naturalization. I call these the "(Previously) Electorally Active." Third, I examine eligible noncitizens who participate in community organizations and in their children's schools in the United States; these are the "Community Active." Each of these populations has demonstrated a behavior or attitude that is associated with engaging the polity, a characteristic that may indicate they are well along in the process of becoming U.S. citizens.

I intentionally use the word *process* to describe the passage from immigrant to citizen because a series of recent studies indicates that

TABLE 5.3. Estimates of the potential newly naturalized Latino population using various target groups (nationally and in selected states)

Target Group 1: The Frustrated	
Strategy 1.1:	Outreach to those who have initiated naturalization
Size of population:	1,100,000 to 1,300,000
State impact:[a]	
California	260,000
Florida	210,000
New York	210,000
Texas	288,000
Strategy 1.2:	Outreach to those who report they are "currently applying" to see that they see the process through to naturalization
Size of population:	525,000 to 630,000
State impact:[b, c]	
California	250,000
Target Group 2: The (Previously) Electorally Active	
Strategy 2.1:	Mobilization of immigrants who participated in politics or followed politics in their country of origin
Size of population:	1,100,000 to 1,400,000
State impact:	
California	225,000
New York	275,000
Texas	275,000
Strategy 2.2:	Mobilization of immigrants who have participated in politics or followed politics in the United States
Size of population:	1,400,000 to 1,700,000
State impact:	
California	300,000
Florida	225,000
New York	280,000
Texas	390,000
Strategy 2.3	Mobilization of immigrants who participated in politics in their country of origin
Size of population:	900,000 to 1,000,000
State impact:	
New York	250,000
Strategy 2.4:	Mobilization of immigrants who have participated in politics in the United States
Size of population:	387,500 to 450,000
Target Group 3: The Community Active	
Strategy 3.1:	Mobilization of eligible immigrants who have been active in politically oriented community organizations
Size of population:	850,000 to 1,000,000
State impact:	
California	230,000
Florida	125,000
New York	200,000
Texas	200,000

TABLE 5.3. (*continued*)

	Target Group 3: The Community Active
Strategy 3.2:	Mobilization of eligible immigrants who have been active in community organizations or schools
Size of population:	1,500,000 to 1,800,000
State impact:[c]	
California	750,000
Texas	150,000

SOURCES: National Latino Immigrant Survey and Latino National Political Survey.
[a] I derive the state-level estimates for the various target groups by examining the share of respondents performing the behavioral act in question from each of the states to the low estimate of the national population with those characteristics. Because of the small subsample sizes, I cannot report on state impacts of each strategy for all states. [b] For some of the smaller estimates of noncitizen populations that could potentially be mobilized, it is not possible to develop state-level impact estimates because of small sample sizes. [c] Estimate derived from the Latino National Political Survey. LNPS estimates do not capture the influence of non–Mexican American, non–Puerto Rican, and non–Cuban American Latino noncitizens in New York State. Further, in state-level analysis, they reflect the relative proportions of the three major Latino national-origin groups.

naturalization is not just a single behavioral act, but rather the cumulative result of shifting allegiances and the preparation for a confusing, and sometimes threatening, series of bureaucratic encounters (Alvarez 1987; García 1987; Portes and Curtis 1987; Pachon, DeSipio, and Sullivan 1991). In my discussion, I fix each of these identifiable subgroups in this process.

In each case, I use these populations—the Frustrated, the (Previously) Electorally Active, and the Community Active—as estimators for realistic levels of new Latino voters that can be anticipated from the Recruits, the fourth new electorate. Needless to say, these populations overlap. I conclude by examining immigrants who share the characteristics or behaviors of all three categories of potential U.S. citizens.

Over the next several pages, I present many estimates that often appear similar. I present a summary of the various estimates in table 5.3.

The Frustrated

According to the NLIS, 43 percent of eligible immigrants who had not yet naturalized had begun to naturalize in some concrete way. Were these Latino immigrants to naturalize and vote—a more realistic goal than seeking to naturalize all eligible non-U.S. citizens—the national Latino electorate would increase by between 1.1 and 1.3 million. Using 1992 election figures, an increase of this magnitude would add more than one quarter to the total Latino vote nationally.

Even relying on the lower of the lower-end estimate of naturalization-eligible noncitizens (2.5 million),[4] increases of this magnitude could add one quarter to the state Latino votes in the two largest Latino states. Slightly more than one quarter of the Frustrated immigrants, or 288,000, reside in Texas, and slightly less than one quarter, or 260,000, reside in California. Other states that could potentially gain significantly from outreach to the Frustrated are New York and Florida. Each would gain approximately 210,000 new Latino voters. As the current Latino votes in these latter two states are smaller than in either California or Texas, increases of this magnitude would increase the 1992 vote by half.

The LNPS does not offer a behavioral indicator of the initiation of the naturalization process. Instead, it relies on self-reporting of interest in citizenship. Its "currently applying" category is narrower since it excludes discouraged applicants. Slightly more than one fifth (21.1 percent) of the non-U.S. citizens report that they are in this status. If just the currently active could be mobilized, the national Latino vote would increase by between 525,000 and 630,000. Over half of the currently applying reside in California, potentially adding 250,000 voters.[5]

Were the Frustrated to become the focus of a naturalization effort, they could be relatively easily identified. The INS would be able to identify immigrants who have formally applied but not pursued their applications or who failed their exams. Public schools offering citizenship classes have student records that could be used to identify former students, some of whom would be Frustrated immigrants. Finally, community-based organizations offering citizenship assistance have extensive data on immigrants who have sought citizenship assistance. At present, they do not have sufficient resources to assist these applicants, but as part of a mass naturalization effort they could broaden their outreach. In each of these points of access, contact must be linked with the availability of education, form assistance, and preparation for the citizenship exam so that these potential citizens do not return to the Frustrated category.

The (Previously) Electorally Active

Among adult noncitizens who immigrated to the United States, almost 60 percent participated in some form of political activity before they left their countries of origin. Of course, many immigrated as children and did not have the opportunity to participate in home country political activities. As a result, the total share of noncitizen adults with these characteristics declines to 45 percent. These activities included the passive—following politics in the news—or the active—marching and voting in elections. While denied the vote in most cases, almost two thirds of the noncitizens had participated in U.S. politics in some form. Again, a passive activity such as following politics in the news was the most frequent, but others included writing a letter to an elected official, distributing leaflets, marching, or attending fundraisers.

These electoral behaviors define another target for U.S. citizenship mobilization. Were those who were politically active abroad able to be channeled into naturalization and then voting in the United States, the new voters could number between 1.1 and 1.4 million, with 275,000 in New York and Texas and 225,000 in California. These politically active individuals would offer a particularly inviting target in New York, which has a high share of the non-U.S. citizen population that was active politically abroad. These 275,000 potential new Latino voters would add over 70 percent to the 1992 Latino vote totals.

An organizational strategy built around naturalizing Latino immigrants who had been active in U.S. electoral activity could add between 1.4 and 1.7 million citizens. The most sizable state gain that could be derived from this strategy would be seen in Texas where as many as 390,000 noncitizens have taken part in some political activity. California, New York, and Florida would gain 300,000, 280,000, and 225,000 votes, respectively.

Each of these measures of political activity included the passive activity of following politics in the news, which may mean little more than watching the television news. In order to develop a measure of immigrants who participated in more active political behaviors, I develop estimates of those immigrants who participated in group political activities. The rate for participation in U.S. political activities drops considerably to 16 percent, reducing the potential new electorate to between 387,500 and 450,000. The share who engage in active political behaviors in their countries of origin does not decrease as greatly, leaving 35 percent of the noncitizen population. Again, these noncitizens who participated in active political behaviors before emigrating could add 900,000 to 1,000,000 new voters. New York has a particularly high share of these home country political actives. It could add 250,000 new potential voters, and Texas could add almost as many.

The (Previously) Electorally Active are the most difficult of the Recruits to reach. Their activity in electoral politics may be only sporadic (or only in the country of origin). Instead of seeking to identify immigrants who have been active in past political activities, this new electorate can most effectively be reached by beginning to identify noncitizens in local political activities and ensuring that they have sufficient information and resources to pursue naturalization if they are interested. The short time-frame of campaigns makes it unlikely that candidates or campaigns will lead this informational effort. Instead, the mobilization of the (Previously) Electorally Active must be the focus of an independent, nonpartisan agency within immigrant communities.

The Community Active

As mentioned in chapter 4, a bare majority of Mexican American and Cuban American U.S. citizens were active in community organizations. Among the noncitizens, levels of community organizational activity were even lower, with just 23 percent of Mexican immigrants and 17 percent of Cuban immigrants with five or more years of residence active. The NLIS found slightly higher levels of community organizational activity, with approximately 34 percent of the noncitizens participating in community organizational activities. This difference emerges most probably from differences in questionnaire design. The NLIS probed on a broader range of specific types of organizations than did the LNPS. A new electorate based solely on those noncitizens who have been active in politically oriented community organizations would add between 850,000 and 1,000,000 to the national electorate, with 230,000 in California and 200,000 in New York and Texas. Florida could see as many as 125,000 of these new voters.

Parenthetically, if membership in churches, national-origin-based organizations, and sports clubs were to be added, the rates of membership in a community activity would rise to two thirds among the noncitizens. I treat churches, sports clubs, and national-origin-based organizations as potentially nonpolitical and exclude their members who were not also members of more political community organizations from these estimates. It is quite possible that some members of these less overtly political organizations receive political socialization through these group activities, and these types of organizations certainly offer a second-level strategy for citizenship mobilization among organizational members.

This estimate of 850,000 to 1,000,000 Community Active immigrants who could be targeted for naturalization may, however, present too narrow a view of Community Active non-U.S. citizens. Many participated in another form of community involvement. These were parents who participated in school-based activities. Again, the intensity of these school-based activities varied from the passive, and not necessarily voluntary, meeting with a teacher to more active tasks, such as meeting with the principal and attending school board meetings. I hesitate to examine the potential impact of this category alone as it excludes non-parents. As a result, I combine those who have been active in potentially political community organizations with those active in the schools to create a composite community activity measure.

If naturalization efforts were to target Latino immigrants who have been active in their communities or have been active in their children's schools, they could reach 61 percent of the eligible noncitizen population. These new citizens would number between 1.5 and 1.8 million, potentially adding nearly half to the current national Latino electorate. As these estimates are based on the LNPS, the state estimates are of potential new Mexican ancestry and Cuban ancestry voters. California could see 750,000 new voters from the Community Active and Texas could see 150,000.

Targeting the Community Active is most likely a longer-term strategy than either of the other two mentioned here. The experiences with community- or school-based activity are not necessarily ongoing. Instead, they may have come in response to a specific policy issue or personal concern. Thus, to target the Community Active, U.S. citizenship proponents will have to develop ongoing relationships with community-based organizations and the schools to identify politically active noncitizens so that they can be funneled into the citizenship assistance networks that will be necessary to ensure naturalization of the scale proposed here.

The Most Likely Recruits

These three components of the Latino immigrant community are possible beneficiaries of mass naturalization efforts. Their behaviors and attitudes place them on the road to participation in American politics, if not U.S. citizenship. Clearly these categories are not mutually exclusive. Many of the Electorally Active are also active in their communities and many of these active immigrants are also found among the Frustrated applicants. Although the estimate is somewhat limited by the use of two separate data sets to generate the individual estimates of each of the pools of potential citizens, approximately 13 percent shared all three of these characteristics: having begun the application process with a behavioral act, participating in politics either in the country of origin or in the United States, and joining organizational or school-based activities. Almost one third of these immigrants who share all of these traits reside in Texas.

These components of the Latino immigrant community should be treated as discrete, however, because, each offers a distinct avenue for naturalization mobilization. Returning to Alejandro Portes's notion of cumulative causation, an effort to target any of these groups, matched by resources and organization to meet their needs, would serve to bring in the other noncitizens who are on the road to participation in the U.S. political system. Their example would serve as a guide. Their experience would overcome confusion among many immigrants about how to naturalize, and their political activities would demonstrate a tangible benefit to naturalization. Thus, the immigrants receiving the outreach would offer a model for those not receiving outreach. As Portes notes, what has been lacking is the incentive to stimulate naturalization among most Latinos. Although Cuban immigrants had this incentive and are reaping the cumulative benefits of a large and energized electorate, Cuban naturalization has recently diminished. Thus, a concentrated, well-organized, and ongoing effort to target any of these groups, whether eligible noncitizen parents active in the schools or noncitizens who have attended meetings or marched over a specific community issue, would raise the salience of U.S. citizenship among Latinos in general and reduce their costs in pursuing naturalization.

The benefit of mass naturalization should be clear from the estimates presented here. Depending on the effort, a targeted outreach to Frustrated applicants or to Political or Community Actives could add between 387,500 and 1,800,000 new Latino citizens and, arguably, nearly as many voters. California could see between 225,000 and 750,000 new Latino citizens and Texas between 150,000 and 390,000 (see table 5.3). Again, these are estimates based on initial efforts, not accounting for any possible cumulative causation impact. Further, they do not include the numbers of potential citizens and voters from the pool of legalization beneficiaries who began to become eligible in 1993.

Conclusions

Despite the low levels of U.S. citizenship among Latino immigrants, many have developed a psychological attachment to the United States and have made behavioral steps toward naturalization. These preliminary efforts to become U.S. citizens, however, end in frustration for many. Despite this frustration, many noncitizens have demonstrated an engagement with government and would make for good citizens.

Were this frustration to be overcome, Latino legal permanent residents offer a huge pool of new citizens and new voters. With three target populations identified, sufficient numbers could naturalize to have influence in the next close election. Their impact would add to the incentive structure for other interested immigrants who have the desire to stay in the United States, who believe U.S. citizenship is very important, and who desire to make their attachment more formal through naturalization.

The new electorate that could be created from this pool of citizenship-eligible noncitizens offers an unmeasurable quality that increases the likelihood of their electoral participation. This is a quality that is less likely to be present among many of the Reticents and Reluctants. Once socialized into politics, they would bring an optimism and vibrancy to the electoral process that can be felt only among voluntary citizens who consciously had to seek membership in the polity. As I have indicated, many Recruits share the sociodemographic characteristics associated with nonvoting. Yet arguably, some of the dampening effect of these traits on voting would be counterbalanced by the energy and vibrancy of their new, voluntary commitment to the United States. Thus, in addition to their slightly greater numbers, the Recruits offer a more promising new electorate than the Reticents and the Reluctants for a second reason. They have a tie to the United States and its political system that cannot be duplicated among the native-born.

CHAPTER 6

Including the Excluded

Strategies for Making Voters of Latino
Non-U.S. Citizens

IN THE PREVIOUS chapter, I examined various aspects of attachment to the United States among Latino immigrants with five years of legal residence. Having found evidence of attachment, including the desire for citizenship, I discussed the sociodemographic factors that distinguished the naturalized from the nonnaturalized. Finally, I looked within the citizenship-eligible population to see if some noncitizens had experiences or behaviors that might be associated with a greater likelihood of naturalization. Among the noncitizens, I found three populations that manifested this higher likelihood: the Frustrated, the (Previously) Electorally Active, and the Community Active. The Frustrated have tried to naturalize. The (Previously) Electorally Active have been involved in politics whether in their home country or in the United States. Finally, the Community Active are members of community-based organizations and a subset are involved in community activities with a political focus. I see these three populations as the potential targets for a mass naturalization effort because they could be relatively easily identified, and once identified, they would be more responsive to naturalization promotion efforts. Overwhelming majorities of each of these populations intend to reside permanently in the United States and believe that becoming a U.S. citizen is very important. Many, though not a majority, feel that they are politically more a part of the United States than they are a part of their home countries.

These populations currently offer between 387,500 and 1,800,000 potential new citizens. I concluded chapter 5 by suggesting that were these noncitizens to naturalize, the process of formal inclusion would make them more likely to vote than would comparably situated native-born U.S. citizens.

This discussion begged two very important questions. First, considering the high interest in U.S. citizenship and the large number of applicants who have taken a behavioral step to achieve this goal, why have so few naturalized? Second, what would be the impact of their votes were they to naturalize? I explore this first question of impediments to naturalization in two ways. I examine the structure of the naturalization bureaucracy to suggest that despite increasing but minimal formal standards, it is not designed to meet the needs of applicants with the education and experiences that most have. Second, I look within the Latino community to see what sort of resources are available to immigrants seeking naturalization. As to the second strategic question—the potential impact of the citizenship-eligible—I examine the voting behaviors of the previously naturalized and then return to the questions of partisanship, ideology, and policy preferences.

Immigrants and the Naturalization Process

Naturalization is an individual choice. Two institutions, however, can contribute to or impede this process. These are, first, the government (until the turn of the century, national, state, and local, but today, in practical terms, the Immigration Service); and second, the immigrant support networks (these have shifted over time, but today potentially include ethnic and community organizations and a few local governments, political parties, and elected officials). Traditionally, the state's role has been formally neutral and informally encouraging. Increasingly, however, as it has centralized its administration, it has created bureaucratic impediments that frustrate applicants. Historically, immigrant support networks have developed that played an active and encouraging role in naturalization. Today, with one major exception, few are active, leaving the Latino immigrant at a loss for assistance. I look in turn at each of these institutions in order to examine possible explanations for the gaps between interest in naturalization and U.S. citizenship.

U.S. Naturalization Policy and Administration

Until recently, it was not possible to measure the disparity between interest in naturalization and successful achievement of U.S. citizenship. Some aspects of the administration of naturalization, however, are evident throughout its history. The first is a slowly increasing set of standards that, though bewildering for many applicants, can be met by most denizens with a reasonable amount of preparation. The second is a continuing pattern of decentralization of administration that has made the application process increasingly adverse and confusing for the applicant and the potential applicant (DeSipio and Pachon 1992).

Until the first decade of this century, state and local governments administered naturalization. In areas with high concentrations of immigrants, local political machines ensured that some nationalities naturalized even, in some cases, if the interest was absent or the immigrant had not quite arrived in the United States (Erie 1988, 51). Where machines were reticent to help, national-origin-specific immigrant assistance societies emerged to assist with naturalization. During the first several decades of federal administration of naturalization, the role of the machine declined, but preexisting immigrant assistance societies ensured that knowledge about and assistance with naturalization remained available to the European immigrants of the era. After the hiatus in immigration caused by the immigration restrictions enacted in the 1920s, however, the post-1965[1] immigrants had little or no assistance in naturalizing.

Formal Naturalization Requirements. The formal requirements for naturalization have increased slowly in the past 205 years (Franklin 1906; Gettys 1934; Kettner 1978; U.S. Senate 1980; U.S. INS 1992, appendix one). For almost the entire period, the law required five years of legal residence and the ill-defined, and sometimes misused, "good moral character." In 1795, Congress added a requirement that remains today to forswear any allegiance to foreign nobility or hereditary titles. In 1798, Congress required immigrants to file a Declaration of Intention prior to applying for naturalization. This new requirement appeared in legislation associated with the Alien and Sedition Acts that extended the statutory period of residence to 14 years. By 1802, the period of residence was returned to five years (where it has remained since), but the Declaration of Intention remained.

After this change in 1802, the naturalization law remained largely untouched in the nineteenth century. The fourteenth amendment resolved the status of the freed slaves, but also formalized what had been the informal practice in some states of granting birth-right citizenship (*United States v. Wong Kim Ark*, 169 U.S. Rep. 649 [1898]; Schuck and Smith 1985, chapter 2). The only major statutory change in naturalization in the nineteenth century was the Chinese Exclusion Act of 1882 which provided, among other things, that "no state court or court of the United States shall admit Chinese to citizenship" (Chan 1991; Sandmeyer 1991 [1939]).

The twentieth century saw more Congressional attention to naturalization than did the nineteenth. In 1906, Congress added a requirement that applicants speak English. Congress also amended the oath to include a promise of permanent residence in the United States.

In 1907, Congress centralized the administration of naturalization in the federal government and created a Bureau of Naturalization. Prior to 1907, states and cities administered naturalization with only minor federal oversight. State and local administration allowed disparate practices to flourish, including fraudulent naturalization by urban political machines and illegal exclusion of some nationalities in some regions. Although centralization added only slightly to the formal requirements (by requiring federal agents to do background checks of applicants), it substantively changed the context of naturalization administration.

The next major change in naturalization requirements occurred in 1950. Congress made membership in a communist or totalitarian organization grounds for denying naturalization. It also required that applicants be able to read and write English (adding to the earlier speaking requirement) and "demonstrate a knowledge and understanding of the fundamentals of the history, and the principles and form of government, of the United States." The Immigration and Nationality Act of 1952 (the McCarran-Walter Act) eliminated the racial barriers to naturalization and the requirement to file a Declaration of Intention prior to naturalization.

In 1990, Congress again altered the administration of naturalization. In an attempt to speed the processing of naturalization applications, Congress transferred exclusive jurisdiction over naturalization from the federal and state courts to the Justice Department (in practice, the INS).

This discussion should indicate that while the formal naturalization requirements have steadily increased, Congress has focused most of its attention on the administration of naturalization. It is in this area of administration that impediments to naturalization can be found.

Naturalization Administration. While the formal requirements for naturalization have remained largely untouched (and limited relative to other countries [Brubaker 1989b]), the administration has varied considerably over time. Through each of these phases of administration, however, one characteristic has endured: decentralization and concerns about its impact on naturalization.

The first century of U.S. naturalization processing featured state- and local-level administration. Although noted as early as 1845 (Ueda 1980), decentralization in this period resulted from state-level authority to administer naturalization such that municipal judges and justices of the peace naturalized immigrants. While formally responsible, clerks of the state courts had no resources to ensure that these local officials followed standard guidelines or even ensured that applicants met the five-year statutory residence requirement. Further, there was no standard certificate of naturalization, and many officials provided no proof of naturalization. Local officials kept a high share of the application fee and had a financial stake in keeping the number of applicants high.

The effect of this decentralization became a subject of concern around the turn of the century. Corruption was a particular problem in the cities under the control of political machines. Tammany Hall, for example, used naturalization as a tool for increasing the number of voters. In his study of Irish political machines in the United States, Erie (1988) offers the example of when Tammany Hall printed 105,000 blank naturalization applications and 69,000 certificates of naturalization before a particularly crucial election. "Immigrants fresh off the boat," he finds, "were given red tickets, allowing them to get their citizenship papers free. Tammany paid the required court fees and provided false witnesses to testify that the immigrants had been in the country for the necessary five years" (1988, 51).

President Theodore Roosevelt appointed an interagency commission in 1905 to examine these concerns; it formulated the broad outline for the administration of our current federal naturalization system. It created a federal agency, the Bureau of Naturalization, to oversee and establish guidelines for naturalization. The new bureau promised uniformity in administration. Courts continued to have final power to award naturalization, but Congress required judicial clerks to file standardized forms with a newly formed bureau.

These reforms eliminated one form of decentralization—local variation in administration—but created another. Individual judges established different standards.[2] Congress addressed this discrepancy by giving the Immigration and Naturalization Service (formed in 1933) the authority to review all applicants before judicial processing (U.S. Senate 1980, 41–42). Although the courts retained the final authority to award naturalization, the INS recommendations for award or denial became the final word for most applicants.

Problems associated with decentralization were not necessarily eliminated with this reform. The problem, however, disappeared from public and legislative attention for a while. With the implementation of the national-origin immigration reforms in the 1920s, the flow of immigrants declined. Although the pre-1920 immigrants as well as the few who continued to immigrate did seek naturalization, their numbers remained small and relatively constant (at about 100,000 to 125,000 per year) from year to year with the exception of a surge during World War II. As a result of the smaller pool and the generally reduced salience of immigration as an issue, the general public, policy analysts, and Congress stopped paying much attention to naturalization.

When immigration again entered the public's consciousness in the mid-1970s, coincidentally, naturalization also began to rise (U.S. INS 1992, table 41). Interestingly, and predictably, the pattern of decentralization that had been established in this earlier history reappeared.

Despite the reemergence of concern about naturalization in the 1980s, it has received much less attention than other INS functions. Of greater concern have been border control, legal immigration (appropriate levels and composition), and implementation of the Immigration Reform and Control Act of 1986, including legalization, the Special Agricultural Worker, and employer-sanction programs. The ability of the INS to focus on naturalization has been further reduced by ongoing management problems within the INS (National Academy of Public Administration 1991; U.S. General Accounting Office 1991, and internal Department of Justice memoranda). Despite the competing policy concerns and distraction among top INS managers, two recent studies have examined the contemporary management of naturalization. They demonstrate that the problems of decentralization that have traditionally plagued the program remain. Further, they demonstrate why potential applicants, particularly potential Latino applicants, have become frustrated in their efforts to naturalize.

In *The Long Grey Welcome*, North (1985) paints a picture of a decentralized INS that processes most citizenship applicants with fairness, but that lacks effective administrative controls to ensure equal treatment. The study also finds that many immigrants interested in U.S. citizenship who apply for naturalization disappear in the INS administrative process and fail to obtain U.S. citizenship. Prior to North's research, this "administrative" denial was unknown outside of the INS. He found that on its own authority, the INS dismissed or encouraged applicants to withdraw as many as one quarter of the applications before the judiciary had the opportunity to review them. Hence, formal denial rates (usually in the 2 to 4 percent range) vastly underestimated the true level of frustrated applicants.

The Long Grey Welcome documented what had been a mystery in the naturalization process. Naturalization advocates had long reported that the requirements were difficult for many immigrants to meet (Pachon and DeSipio 1986). Yet INS naturalization statistics suggested that these claims were invalid. In the 86 years for which naturalization data have been available (1907–93), just 604,346 of the 14,381,613 applications for naturalization filed have resulted in the denial of U.S. citizenship, a denial rate of 4.2 percent that declined to just 2.1 percent between 1981 and 1993 (U.S. INS 1994, table 45).

North's review of INS administrative records explained this discrepancy between advocates' perceptions and INS data. INS personnel (not the courts) effectively rejected 10.4 percent of naturalization applications based on the applicant's failure to complete the materials properly and 13.2 percent of naturalization applicants at the examination level. In other words, rejections at the administrative level equaled 23.6 percent of all naturalization applications (U.S. Senate 1987 and U.S. INS internal reports). By including these administratively denied applications, the nonapproval rate for naturalization applicants soared from 4 percent to 28 percent. If these trends continue, the INS will administratively deny U.S. citizenship to 1 million applicants during the 1990s.

The second set of studies of contemporary INS practices stemmed from Congressional concern with North's findings. Two in-depth studies of INS data on administrative denials (NALEO 1988; 1991) demonstrate that they affect some nationalities more than others and are used at vastly different levels among INS district offices, reinforcing the contemporary evidence of decentralization. Naturalization applicants from Mexico, Central and South America, and Africa were found to be more likely than immigrants from other regions of the world to experience administrative denials. Arguably, these results could reflect differences in the skills applicants from different regions of the world bring to the process. Countering this notion, however, was the finding that administrative denial rates vary dramatically among INS district offices. Just 3.1 percent of applicants in Denver experienced administrative denials. In Miami, on the other hand, 27.2 percent faced the same result. When one considers the mix of applicants in these two cities, and others at the extremes (Atlanta, Newark, San Antonio, and San Jose), it would have been hard to argue that these contradictory results were solely a function of the applicant pool (NALEO 1988).

A follow-up report (NALEO 1991) demonstrated that these were not isolated findings. Applicants from Spanish-speaking Latin American countries continued to face the highest administrative denial rates, followed in this sample by Asian applicants. District offices continued to see different administrative denial rates. Varying from a low of 0.1 percent in Boston to a high of 23.6 percent in San Antonio, the findings confirmed that decentralization remained a problem within the INS.

Latinos, the INS, and Naturalization. Reinforcing these findings, the NLIS demonstrates that the naturalization application process is an impediment for many interested Latino applicants. At an aggregate level, the NLIS demonstrates that more than twice as many applicants begin the process as those who naturalize. This gap, of course, cannot entirely be explained by the INS administration of the program. Confusion about the process does, however, appear both among discouraged applicants and among those who have naturalized.

The application step that deters the most applicants is completing the application. Nearly 15 percent of Latino immigrants eligible for U.S. citizenship had obtained the application forms but had been unable to complete them. While some reported that they had not filed the application because they were preparing for the exam, many were deterred by the complexity of the form, which consists of four pages of small print plus a two-page supplement (as well as requirements to obtain photos and fingerprints). Among other questions, the form asks applicants whether they have ever "bourne any hereditary title or . . . been any order of nobility in a foreign state" or "knowingly committed any crime for which [the applicant] has not been arrested."

The format and the substance of these and the other 34 (some multipart) questions deterred many applicants from filing. Latino immigrants had lower than average levels of formal education. Further, many had little experience at dealing with government bureaucracies. Hence, the first formal step in the application process is not designed to welcome potential applicants.

Among those who are able to file, the application again proved a detriment. Failure to complete the application accurately was the major cause of administrative rejection among Latino naturalization applicants. Among those applicants in the NLIS who experienced administrative rejection (about 8 percent of those who had filed), just one (of 46) had failed to meet the statutory requirements for citizenship. The remaining 45 faced administrative rejection because of clerical errors on the application. Again, an application not targeted to the education and skill levels of the applicant must be seen as an explanation. Thus, not only did the application deter some from filing, it also subjected others who were able to file to administrative denial.

Among those who naturalized, the NLIS documents a diversity of experiences with the naturalization bureaucracy. INS examiners asked the average applicant nine questions. Yet almost half of applicants received five or fewer questions while some examiners asked as many as 50 questions. District office variation also appeared in these results. While 20 percent of NLIS respondents who had taken the citizenship exam resided in Miami, almost half of those who were asked 20 or more questions resided there.

Despite these examples of inconsistency in the administration of naturalization exams, individual applicants overwhelmingly reported that they found the examiner to be helpful (79.8 percent) and the exam to be very easy (48.0 percent) or somewhat easy (27.2 percent). Yet while the individual experience may well have been positive, these diverse experiences suggest why there may be confusion about the process among the nonnaturalized.

Conclusions. Despite the minimal formal requirements for naturalization, the decentralization of INS management has proved to be an ongoing and vexing problem for Congress and advocates. Congress attempted to remedy these problems in a comprehensive manner twice, but they remain today. Thus, despite a positive perception of the INS among many applicants, their experiences demonstrate inconsistent administration by the current naturalization bureaucracy. Further, the first formal step, the application, discourages many who have demonstrated an interest from pursuing U.S. citizenship.

Clearly, these impediments can be overcome. The solutions can come from one of several sources. The INS can move toward greater consistency in examination and retool the application to be sensitive to applicants with low levels of formal education and bureaucratic coping skills. It has begun this effort. Beginning in 1989, applicants have been able to meet the English reading and writing, civics, and history requirements through an exam designed by the Educational Testing Service and administered by community organizations. While this offers some guarantee of consistency, applicants must still complete the application and be examined on spoken English by an examiner who has the power to deny the application.

Educators and community leaders can also help overcome impediments in the application process by preparing applicants to meet the knowledge-based requirements of the exam (English, history, and civics) and reducing the overall fear applicants face in engaging the INS. With sufficient resources, these skills can be taught at such a level that inconsistency in evaluation becomes a rare problem.

The answer, of course, lies in both of these institutions. For now, however, the wide gap between immigrants who desire citizenship and those who have naturalized lies partly in the perception that the application and the examination are difficult and partly in the actual experiences applicants have faced with the INS.

Immigrant Communities and the Promotion of Naturalization

One strategy for overcoming the confusing nature of naturalization and preparing applicants for its requirements is community-based preparation. The model for this sort of effort is the resources that were available to many turn-of-the-century immigrants. Despite the potential importance of widespread naturalization, little mobilization has traditionally existed around this issue in Latino communities.

As I indicated, in the nineteenth century urban political machines played an important role in encouraging naturalization. Studies of this role have documented two phases. During the first, when the pool of immigrants was less diverse, and national, state, and local elections were highly competitive, the machines served as mass naturalization factories (Werner 1932, 134–38; Myers 1968 [1917], 128–30, 209–10, 217–18). Beginning in the 1890s as southern and eastern Europeans began to dominate the immigrant stream and elections became less competitive, however, the machines began to use their resources more selectively, so that some nationalities were excluded from mass naturalization promotion. Erie reports that the New York machine naturalized "Irish en masse and the Southern and Eastern Europeans en individuel" (1988, 95). In other cities, one-party or one-group rule caused differential naturalization assistance levels among various nationalities.

Even after these machine resources disappeared, nationality-based organizations provided assistance that many immigrants needed. Each nationality faced different opportunities and was able to marshal different resources (Peel 1935, chapter 23). These differential experiences among immigrants in this period led to the first great academic debate over naturalization (U.S. Immigration Commission 1911; Gavit 1922; Carpenter 1927) regarding the relative Americanization potential of newer immigrants compared to older immigrants.

The lessons of this debate are important for understanding contemporary naturalization. Once the machine raised the salience of naturalization, some nationalities were able to develop an elite of naturalized citizens and an institutional resource of the skills necessary to prepare for naturalization. Nevertheless, after the machine declined as a force promoting naturalization, the raw numbers tailed off considerably. Exceptions, however, occurred under two circumstances. First, some nationalities (or religious groups) experienced high pressure or leadership from within to naturalize rapidly. Most prominent among these were Jewish, Armenian, and Northern Italian immigrants (Gavit 1922, table 10). Second, national political issues sparked a generalized interest in naturalization among long-term immigrants. The most notable of these periods was World War II. Long-term legal residents, most of whom held citizenship in European countries against which the United States was at war, naturalized in great numbers. Although partly because of processing delays, the year with the single highest number of naturalizees (441,979) was 1944 (U.S. INS 1966, table 37). The numbers naturalizing in the late 1920s and early 1930s were also quite high. This period saw the roots of the mobilization of the new voters discussed in chapter 1. Thus, historically, high rates of naturalization have needed an outside trigger—community-wide encouragement in the case of the early machines or nationality-group leadership in the case of the Jewish immigrants—or periods of national political activity that cause immigrants to call into question their attachment to the United States, such as the period between 1928 and 1936 or World War II.

Latino Community Efforts to Promote Naturalization. With few exceptions, these sorts of motivations have been absent in the Latino communities. The two exceptions are efforts in the Miami Cuban community to naturalize large numbers in the late 1970s and 1980s (Portes and Mozo 1985) and the recent efforts by the National Association of Latino Elected Officials to coordinate a national U.S. citizenship education and promotion campaign (NALEO 1985; Pachon 1987, 1991).

Traditionally, naturalization has not been a national, ongoing priority for Mexican American organizations. LULAC offers an example. Although it encouraged "Americanization," its membership excluded non-U.S. citizens, and its outreach to immigrants varied from local chapter to local chapter. Several factors explain this neglect. First, it saw a need to stop immigration to ensure the integration of Mexican immigrants already in the United States. Thus, while it advocated naturalization, it organized only among U.S. citizens and left to individual chapters the responsibility for offering naturalization services. Second, the class position of many of its members distanced LULAC from many Mexican immigrants. LULAC's desire for political accommodation with the Anglo power structures in Texas and the Southwest encouraged them to maintain distance from immigrants. Third, they advocated a self-help mentality that discouraged unsolicited naturalization promotion and assistance. Finally, the majority of Mexican immigrants in this period were agricultural and, as a result, hard to reach, let alone mobilize (Orozco 1992; Márquez 1993; Gutiérrez 1995).

As immigration from Mexico and the rest of Latin America increased after 1965, Mexican American and Latino organizations were in a stronger position to help immigrants naturalize. Two factors militated against this. First, the ideology of the Chicano movement prevented support for naturalization. Instead, to the extent that nationality was discussed, it focused on the mythical nation of Aztlán. As a result, the Chicano movement sought to create a separate identity, a cultural nationalism that transcended U.S. or Mexican nationality. Second, many of the post–Chicano movement organizations fought for civil rights for those of Mexican (or Latino) ancestry, regardless of citizenship or legal status. Thus, instead of helping immigrants naturalize, they reduced the incentives for U.S. citizenship (Fuchs 1990).

Three patterns characterize the relationship between the native-born and the foreign-born in both the historical and contemporary periods. First and foremost, the native-born have consistently sought to distinguish themselves from the foreign-born. Second, many perceived that naturalization was the natural final step in immigration and did not need encouragement. Third, the native-born focused on their own political needs and tended to neglect the foreign-born. As a result, there was no community-wide mobilization to promote Latino naturalization (Browning and de la Garza 1986; Gutiérrez 1995).

There have been two major exceptions to this pattern (as well as many local one-time efforts directed by community-based organizations). The first occurred within the Miami Cuban community. As its focus shifted and its self-perception changed from that of an exile to an immigrant community in the mid-1970s (Boswell and Curtis 1984, 168–69), Cuban American leaders in Miami promoted naturalization. They presented U.S. citizenship as a tool to accomplish political ends as well as to sever political ties with the Cuban Government. They also recognized that many of the exiles would not return to Cuba, even if Castro fell. Naturalization served the Cuban American leadership's national political ends by giving it increased leverage to promote the overthrow of Castro and Cuban communism in Washington as well as its local ends, to garner local political power in Miami and Dade County. This political power was increasingly important to ensure the continued growth of Cuban economic power in the region.

This community-wide effort to promote naturalization was not solely driven by the Cuban community. The national and local Republican Parties offered key political support for this endeavor. The apogee of this alliance was a mass naturalization ceremony held at the Orange Bowl in which more than 5,000 Cubans and other new citizens from the

Miami area naturalized, conveniently just before the deadline for registering to vote for the 1984 presidential elections. Seeing a political opportunity in an election year, Ronald Reagan attended. Although a success in terms of numbers, it should be noted that the INS does not like to hold ceremonies of this size; people naturalized at a single ceremony usually number from 25 to several hundred. The Cuban community leadership was, however, able to conduct this sort of attention-grabbing and politically efficient ceremony.

This Cuban American–driven naturalization promotion had the desired impact. Naturalization rates among early Cuban immigrants are among the highest of any immigrant group (Portes and Mozo 1985). This high rate of naturalization has translated into local and national political influence (Moreno and Warren 1992; Portes and Stepik 1993). The path of this effort—early naturalization among elites leading to widespread mass naturalization—follows the cumulative causation model proposed by Portes (in NALEO 1994, 67–69).

To some extent, community-wide mobilization toward naturalization has declined in recent years. This probably reflects the combined impacts of declining immigration in the 1970s (reducing the pool), a change in composition of the Cuban immigrant and refugee pool (with the Mariel boatlift), and the ability to increase the electorate through the mobilization of U.S.-born Cuban Americans.

The other exception to the pattern of limited Latino interest in encouraging and assisting naturalization is, to date, more diffuse than the efforts in the Cuban community, but in the end much more ambitious. Beginning in 1985, the National Association of Latino Elected Officials[3] initiated a research and demonstration project on the causes of low naturalization rates in the Latino communities. In addition to research, the project advocated before Congress and the executive branch to raise the salience of naturalization, promoted its importance nationally and before Latino leaders, and established a national toll-free telephone number to provide citizenship information to applicants. By 1987, this project research (including preparation for the NLIS) led to the development of a prototype citizenship service center in East Los Angeles. The U.S. citizenship center tested several models for the delivery of direct citizenship services while promoting U.S. citizenship to immigrants in California and nationwide. The most efficient and effective model— mass citizenship workshops followed by individual assistance in completing the application, supplemented, if necessary, by civics and history classes—is now being implemented on an ongoing basis by coalitions including NALEO and local community service organizations in California, Texas, Illinois, and New York and on an irregular basis in Arizona and Florida. To date, the NALEO hotline has received over 250,000 calls from potential citizenship applicants. The NALEO workshops have individually assisted at least 20,000 immigrants who have since naturalized. NALEO is developing a national U.S. citizenship coalition to ensure that the workshop model is available and implemented nationally in areas with high concentrations of immigrants. This coalition includes organizations that serve non-Latino immigrants as well.

NALEO's success has caused other national and local Latino organizations to recognize the importance of naturalization and the need for administrative reform and direct citizenship assistance (National Council of La Raza 1991). NALEO's initiatives have also spurred community groups to conduct ongoing citizenship promotion and assistance activities. One of these operates with active support from the Chicago Democratic Party.

Yet the efforts of one organization, however impressive, cannot overcome the traditionally low salience of naturalization among Latino leaders and organizations. As a result, the gap remains between high levels of interest in naturalization among individual immigrants and the lack of community resources to help them meet their citizenship goals. The result is that the Latino communities as a whole continue to suffer from the impact of low rates of citizenship acquisition—a reduced vote. In the next section, I suggest an alternative by indicating that naturalization not only makes citizens but can also, under the right circumstances, make new voters.

The Naturalized and the Vote

The discussion of new electorate 2—the Reticents, the registered nonvoters—and new electorate 3—the Recruits, the nonregistered citizens—spoke of the need for mobilization as a tool to overcome the demographic limits that reduce the Latino vote. This chapter has discussed the need for community-wide mobilization to overcome the barriers that keep interested Latinos from naturalization. In both cases, the impetus for these recommended mobilizations must come from leaders and organizations, not from the individual. While individuals undoubtedly will continue to register and vote (and naturalize), individually directed mobilization of this sort tends to exclude the poor, less educated and young, who are majorities of the Latino populations. For there to be a large-scale mobilization of the new Latino electorates, people with just these characteristics must be included. In this section, I present the results of what has been, for Mexican Americans, a largely individual mobilization and for Cuban Americans, a more community-wide experience. Differences in the electoral outcomes of these naturalizations can rest, in part, on these divergent mobilization strategies.

The results of both the NLIS and the LNPS indicate high voter registration rates for naturalized Cuban Americans (88 percent and 85 percent, respectively). The NLIS demonstrates similarly high registration rates for naturalized Dominican Americans and other Latinos (86 percent and 82 percent, respectively). For each of these nationality groups, self-reported registration rates exceeded 80 percent, considerably surpassing the Census Bureau's registration estimate for both Latino U.S. citizens (57 percent) and white U.S. citizens (74 percent) (the Census Bureau does not report registration or turnout data for Latino national-origin groups). Although they exceeded the national Latino rate, naturalized Mexican Americans had somewhat lower voter registration rates than these other Latino nationalities, with between 59.4 percent (LNPS) and 69.3 percent (NLIS) reporting that they were registered.

The LNPS offers a comparison between the naturalized and the non-naturalized for both registration and voting. The Cuban American naturalized registered at rates 25 percent higher than the native-born. Mexican American naturalized citizens, on the other hand, registered at a rate approximately 7 percent lower than that of the Mexican American native-born. These patterns reverse themselves when it comes to voting. The Mexican American naturalized voted at rates exceeding the native-born, and the Cuban American naturalized voted at rates marginally lower than their coethnics who were born in the United States. Combining registration and voting rates, naturalization made a slight, but positive, difference in Mexican American turnout. Out of every 1,000 citizen adults, 424 of the native-born and 427 of the naturalized went to the polls. For Cuban Americans, however, naturalization made a large and positive difference. For every 1,000 native-born Cuban adults, 510 went to the polls. Among the naturalized, 1,000 adults generated 692 voters, a rate that exceeded that of the white population.

The NLIS offers some further indicators of the voting patterns of the naturalized. Because the survey was in the field in the months prior to the 1988 election, it does not have data directly comparable to the LNPS on the 1988 presidential election. It did, however, ask respondents who were naturalized in or before 1984 whether or not they had voted in the presidential election that year. Although these data may reflect some blurring of respondents' memories, the naturalized reported turnout rates of between 77 percent for Mexican Americans and 92 percent for Cuban Americans (Pachon and DeSipio 1994, table 5.12). All Dominicans reported that they voted, but the sample was too small to lend much significance to these findings. In the most recent state election, naturalized citizens reported turnout rates of between 45 percent for the Dominican-origin naturalized and 63 percent for naturalized Cuban Americans and Mexican Americans.

These findings indicate that naturalization has a mixed but generally positive impact on registration and voting, a finding, however, that must remain tentative. The addition of naturalization status to the model for voting presented in table 4.5 indicates that naturalization has a negative impact. In regressions for all Latino U.S. citizens, the naturalized proved less likely to register and to vote than did native-born Latinos. As is predicted by the above discussion of the different naturalization experiences of Mexican and Cuban immigrants, this negative impact proved stronger in a regression just of Mexican Americans and did not appear in a regression just of Cuban American respondents. Thus, among Cuban Americans, source of U.S. citizenship does not prove to be a significant predictor of either registration or of voting (DeSipio 1995c).

The aggregate sociodemographic characteristics of the naturalized voters confirm this continuing importance of age, income, and education (see table 6.1). The naturalized voters were older, significantly more affluent, and much better educated, and had immigrated at a younger age than the nonnaturalized. The Cuban American pool of naturalized voters had sociodemographic characteristics closer to those of the noncitizens than do the Mexican American naturalized voters. Although not borne out by the regression equation, these sociodemographic characteristics of Cuban American naturalized voters indicate that the community mobilization that induced many Cuban Americans to naturalize reached deeper into the mass of Cuban immigrants than it has among Mexican Americans.

These aggregate findings demonstrate several important characteristics of the role of naturalization in developing the Latino vote. As suggested, Cuban American naturalization emerged from a different environment than did the Mexican American. Cuban American naturalization has been organized and assisted while the Mexican American has been largely left to the individual. I would hypothesize that the community-wide interest in naturalization may partially explain these different outcomes. In Miami, naturalization was not perceived simply as an end in itself but rather as a tool to achieve the vote. These data would indicate that the naturalized took advantage of this opportunity. These findings suggest a second important point. The naturalized

TABLE 6.1. Demographics of naturalized U.S. citizen voters

Characteristic	Mexican ancestry	Cuban ancestry
Age, mean	47 years	53 years
Gender		
Male	59.6%	39.0%
Female	40.4%	61.0%
Race		
White	55.2%	97.5%
Black	0.0%	1.3%
Latino referent	44.8%	1.1%
Education, mean	10 years	12 years
Income, mean	$34,207	$32,298
Work status		
In labor force	64.5%	65.0%
Temporarily unemployed	3.7%	3.1%
Not in labor force	31.8%	31.9%
Home owner	76.6%	60.7%
Self-evaluated language skills		
English stronger	28.9%	4.8%
Bilingual	45.0%	27.7%
Spanish stronger	26.1%	67.5%
Identification		
National origin	78.1%	75.8%
Panethnic	20.5%	17.0%
American	1.4%	7.2%
Religion		
Catholic	83.9%	79.6%
Protestant	6.5%	15.9%
Other/No preference	9.5%	4.5%
Age at immigration (foreign born), mean	11 years	27 years
Social milieu		
Mostly Latino	30.6%	40.9%
Mixed Latino and Anglo	64.0%	56.8%
Mostly Anglo	5.4%	2.3%

SOURCE: Latino National Political Survey.

Cuban American drives the community's vote in two ways: First, it constitutes a majority of the voting age population. Second, it registers at much higher rates, and the registered turn out at comparable rates to the native-born. As the first of these conditions will soon change, the community's leadership should be concerned about the relatively low levels of voter turnout among the native-born.

Despite this positive impact on voting rates, particularly for Cuban Americans, naturalization has not significantly reduced the class bias in voting. The several impediments to contemporary naturalization and the general absence of community-level support networks outlined in this chapter offer an explanation. The system as it stands now rewards education and bureaucratic competence and not an underlying attachment to the United States. These rewarded skills serve to select a relatively elite group among the immigrants for naturalization. It is these immigrants, then, who share the demographic characteristics of those most likely to vote.

Recruits and the Latino Vote

In chapter 5, I developed estimates of several elements of the citizenship-eligible population who have shown behaviors or attitudes that bring them closer to U.S. citizenship. The specific impact of any of these groups is difficult to calculate and tedious to review because there is much overlap between groups and the variations in partisanship, ideology, and policy preferences between them are narrow. Also, many of the estimates are generated from the NLIS, which does not include questions on ideology and policy preferences. As a result, I limit my discussion of the political impact of these potential new voters to the more limited categories determined by their attitudinal or behavioral stage in the naturalization application process. I look at what would happen if the "Frustrated" or the "Currently Applying" were to become citizens (the most likely scenario) and then what would happen if the interested, but not yet applying, were to naturalize. In a sense, this pattern follows the cumulative causation model. The currently active pave the way for the currently interested, but inactive. Finally, perhaps, they make today's disinterested interested and, eventually, into U.S. citizens.

As I have indicated, the partisanship of the noncitizen, particularly the Mexican American and Cuban American, was largely unformed (see table 6.2). Those who had begun the process were more likely to have a partisan identification. Nonetheless, among those who had begun to naturalize, the majority of Mexican Americans and Dominican Americans were unaffiliated. Almost two thirds of Cuban Americans identified as Republicans. Other Latinos were slightly more likely to have a partisan identification than not to have it. Their nascent partisanship was divided quite evenly between the Democrats and the Republicans. Among those who had not begun, the majority of each national-origin group was unaffiliated.

TABLE 6.2. Partisanship among non-U.S. citizens (by stage in application process and national origin)

Partisanship	Mexican ancestry (%)	Cuban ancestry (%)	Dominican ancestry (%)	Other Latino (%)
Stage 1: Have not applied				
Democrat	14.0	4.0	16.9	22.8
Independent	6.6	2.1	4.0	8.8
Republican	5.1	34.0	6.0	11.9
Other party	0.7	0.4	3.2	0.0
Unaffiliated	73.6	59.4	69.9	56.5
n	236	94	42	119
Stage 2: Initiated naturalization process, not naturalized				
Democrat	17.7	10.0	20.9	23.1
Independent	7.0	1.2	0.0	10.8
Republican	8.5	65.0	10.1	19.7
Other party	0.6	0.0	9.2	0.0
Unaffiliated	66.2	23.8	59.8	46.5
n	197	101	34	111

SOURCE: National Latino Immigrant Survey.

I would hypothesize that the most likely course would be for these unaffiliated noncitizens to follow the partisanship patterns of their coethnics who are citizens. One indicator of this is the noncitizens who reported a partisanship. Nevertheless, the high rate of unaffiliation offers opportunities for both parties, should either take the initiative. Note also that I have said that they will follow the patterns of their coethnic citizens, not their coethnics who vote. Coethnic citizens are much less likely than voters to have the very high rates of Democratic adherence.

Ideologically, those who were applying and planning to apply arrayed around the center much more than the voters did, with bare pluralities of Cuban Americans and Mexican Americans selecting one of the conservative positions. Although these reported conservative ideologies followed the general patterns of the citizens and the citizens who voted, the noncitizen Cuban immigrants were more likely to report liberal positions. These results should be interpreted cautiously, however, because the bunching around the center may reflect an ignorance of American politics or an unfamiliarity with the meanings of "liberal" and "conservative" in the American political order.

Even if these noncitizens were ignorant of American politics, they had views regarding a series of public policy issues. In many of these cases, they had the option of taking a middle, or neutral, position, and in all cases, they had the option of not answering questions. Although the rates of both of these types of (non)response were higher among the noncitizens, the vast majority had opinions on these issues.[4] On several issues, the Mexican immigrants who were applying for U.S. citizenship took positions not associated with immigrants (see table 6.3). More than two thirds agreed that English should be the official language, and more than half felt that U.S. citizens should be hired over noncitizens. As a comparison, Mexican American voters took a similar position on

TABLE 6.3. Public policy perspectives of "currently applying" citizens (by national origin)

Policy area	Mexican ancestry (%)	Cuban ancestry[a] (%)
Language policy		
English should be the official language	67.5[b]	17.9
Public services should be provided in Spanish	94.2	93.1
Immigration policy		
Preference should be given to Latin American immigrants	69.4	47.1
There are too many immigrants	79.0	78.2
U.S. citizens should be hired over noncitizens	52.8	64.7
Foreign policy		
More concerned with U.S. politics	44.1	47.9
The United States should establish relations with Cuba	51.0	43.8
Puerto Rico should remain a commonwealth	68.8	47.1
The cause of Mexico's problems is internal corruption	85.8	96.1
The United States should be more involved in Central America	54.2	66.0
The cause of Central America's problems is poverty and lack of human rights	75.1	29.4
Other issues		
Support for government quotas for jobs and college admission	28.0	19.8
Support for capital punishment for murderers	43.4	50.8
Abortion should never be permitted	25.8	5.7

SOURCE: The Latino National Political Survey.
[a]There are few Cuban Americans in the "currently applying" status (n = 36). As a result, these findings should be interpreted with some caution. [b]Percentage who agree or strongly agree.

hiring, but gave only minority support for the question of English as the official language (see table 3.4). The currently applying Mexican Americans also differed with their coethnics who voted on several foreign policy issues. The applying citizens were more likely to say that the United States should establish diplomatic relations with Cuba, that Puerto Rico should remain a commonwealth, and that the United States should be more involved in Central America. Finally, they were approximately one third less likely to support capital punishment for murderers. These differences did not follow a consistent ideological pattern. Instead, it can be said that the Mexican Americans who were applying for citizenship were equally aware of these policies as the citizens who voted and shared many positions, but differed on some, particularly in foreign policy.

The Mexican Americans who were planing to apply for U.S. citizenship agreed more often with the voters than not (see table 6.4). Their differences appeared in immigration policy and foreign policy. Immigrants planning to apply showed almost twice as much support as the voters for the proposition that Latin American immigrants should be given preference in the immigration system. They were less than half as likely to say that citizens should be hired over noncitizens. These differences can be easily explained by the immigrant status of these respondents.

The differences in foreign policy offered no obvious explanations. The Mexican-origin noncitizens planning to apply were more likely to assert that the United States should establish diplomatic relations with Cuba and that Puerto Rico should remain a commonwealth than were the voters. Finally, they were much less likely to support capital punishment for murderers and half-again more likely to believe that abortion should never be permitted.

Interestingly, the Cuban immigrants planning to apply differed from their coethnics who voted on several of the same issues and in the same direction as the Mexican immigrants planning to apply. The overall percentages, however, often differed more between the national-origin groups than between the voters and the intending citizens. The Cuban immigrants who were planning to apply were more likely than the voters to believe that preference should be given to Latin American immigrants. They were also more supportive of Puerto Rico's remaining a commonwealth. They differed with their coethnics on the role of the United States in Central America and the cause of the region's problems. More of the noncitizens than the voters believed that the United States should be more involved; they were less likely than the voters to believe

TABLE 6.4. Public policy perspectives among noncitizens planning to apply for naturalization (by national origin)

Policy area	Mexican ancestry (%)	Cuban ancestry (%)
Language policy		
English should be the official language	36.2[a]	39.6
Public services should be provided in Spanish	96.6	94.4
Immigration policy		
Preference should be given to Latin American immigrants	76.9	42.4
There are too many immigrants	83.3	72.4
U.S. citizens should be hired over noncitizens	24.2	37.9
Foreign policy		
More concerned with U.S. politics	40.8	56.0
The United States should establish relations with Cuba	56.8	37.4
Puerto Rico should remain a commonwealth	65.5	73.9
The cause of Mexico's problems is internal corruption	86.2	94.0
The United States should be more involved in Central America	38.4	85.3
The cause of Central America's problems is poverty and lack of human rights	64.2	23.6
Other issues		
Support for government quotas for jobs and college admission	35.4	21.7
Support for capital punishment for murderers	41.9	71.6
Abortion should never be permitted	30.3	18.1

SOURCE: The Latino National Political Survey.
[a]Percentage who agree or strongly agree.

that the causes of the region's problems were poverty and lack of human rights. These final two positions could be characterized as more conservative than their already conservative coethnics.

Finally, the Cuban immigrants planning to apply were just two thirds as likely to report more concern with U.S. politics than with Cuban politics. The majority of these immigrants were, however, more concerned with U.S. politics than with Cuban politics or evinced some mixture of the two.

In sum, Latino immigrants on the road to U.S. citizenship share their citizen coethnics' views on public policy issues, are somewhat more centrist ideologically, and, with the exception of the Cuban immigrants and other Latinos, are not yet firmly rooted in either of the dominant political parties. Should they naturalize and vote, their policy positions indicated that they would reinforce and intensify the current Latino positions to the extent that these positions are distinct from those of the national population as a whole. Most importantly among these, perhaps, is that they could have the numbers to influence what increasingly appears to be becoming a topic of national debate again: immigration. They shared a concern about the numbers of immigrants. Yet they sought to protect the rights, particularly the language rights, of immigrants.

Even though it appears that were today's noncitizens to vote in large numbers they would not significantly change the policy positions of the Mexican American and Cuban American communities, the lack of party affiliation offers an opportunity, particularly for Republicans who have traditionally been the weaker party among non-Cuban American Latinos. Should the Republicans galvanize and mobilize these Latino noncitizens, who are at least nominally open to such an appeal, the party might be able to ensure a generation of support from this growing potential electorate as the Democrats did during the New Deal. Realistically, considering the existing constituencies in the Republican Party, targeted outreach to Mexican-, Dominican-, or other Latino-ancestry populations and the inclusion of their issues in the Republican agenda may not be possible on a large scale. Yet over the past several elections, the national Republican Party has invested in efforts to target elements of the Latino electorate (de la Garza and DeSipio 1996). Similarly, the Democrats could mobilize these nonvoters. Nonetheless, despite many years of opportunity, and the need to develop increased state-level support, particularly in the Southwest, the party has not shown much inclination to promote naturalization. The impact of this Democratic neglect is evident, among both the noncitizens and the nonvoters. As I have suggested, Democratic adherence among the partisans in these populations is lower than it is among the voters.

Conclusions

Despite high levels of interest in U.S. citizenship, many Latino immigrants have been impeded in accomplishing this goal. I develop two explanations for this failure. First, the bureaucratic administration of naturalization is ill-designed to assist the average Latin American applicant. While the statutory requirements are relatively minimal, the administrative requirements and procedures deter many from applying and others from completing the process. Second, with the exception of the Cuban American community, Latino leaders and organizations as well as nonethnic political and community leaders have largely failed to promote naturalization or to assist immigrants interested in pursuing U.S. citizenship. Again, sensitivity to the skills and experiences of many Latino immigrants, even long-term legal residents, should suggest that this is a population in need of mobilization and assistance to achieve this end.

The results of this neglect of naturalization are evident both in the low rates of naturalization among those Latinos who have expressed interest in or pursued U.S. citizenship and in the sociodemographics of the naturalized who vote. A large-scale Latino community mobilization, even if just targeted at those who have expressed some concrete interest in naturalization, could reverse these trends. Further, it would develop a new electorate of a size greater than can reasonably be anticipated from either the Recruits or the Reluctants.

Similar factors distance the nonnaturalized from naturalization as distance the nonvoter from voting. Two fundamental differences, however, distinguish these types of civic nonparticipation. First, the nonvoters have had many opportunities and encouragements to register. With recent electoral reforms such as the Motor Voter bill, they will have even more. Yet many stay away from the polls, whether through decision, indecision, or ignorance. Few Latino noncitizens, with the exception of Cuban Americans, on the other hand, have had much encouragement or assistance to naturalize. Second, since the mid-1970s and probably before, few nonvoters have experienced personal discouragement in their effort to exercise the franchise. Thus, their decision not to vote is private. Although there are costs associated with registering and voting, today these can be overcome with a minimum of effort. This is not to say that there cannot be more encouragement, particularly in terms of competition for their votes, but the opportunity to register and vote is there. Noncitizens contemplating naturalization, however, face more active discouragement. Dealing with the INS is intimidating. The application form is not sensitive to the education levels of many of its users. Confusion abounds about the risks in failing the exam. Applicants have few places to turn to get assistance when they have questions or concerns. Finally, unlike voter registration or voting, applying for naturalization can take months, even a year or more in some cases. Thus, the reward—naturalization—which many reported they have sought or would like to seek, is often in the long-term future.

My final reason for asserting that a community-wide naturalization promotion strategy is viable for promoting an increased Latino electoral impact is based on the experiences of U.S. citizens who have benefited from this type of mobilization. Those who naturalized in response to community-wide assistance and encouragement participate electorally at high rates. Hence, the process of naturalization, particularly a large-scale community-wide naturalization, offers a tool for community electoral mobilization. The level of activity necessary to naturalize the 2.5 to 3.0 million eligible noncitizens will achieve a mobilization among Latinos that could rival the Civil Rights movement experience of the African American community. If successful, then, this naturalization mobilization could serve to overcome not only non-U.S. citizenship but also some of the class, education, and income limitations on Latino voting.

A complete empowerment strategy needs to incorporate the desires for citizenship among the 2.5 to 3.0 million Latinos currently eligible and the 2.4 to 2.6 million legalization and Special Agricultural Worker applicants who are becoming eligible at this writing. The desire is there among immigrants. The numbers required to have a significant impact, perhaps an impact as great as registration of every nonvoter, are there. What has been lacking, however, are the strategy, commitment, supportive political environment, and the resources to assist these potential new citizens and voters.

CHAPTER 7

Conclusions

Counting on Latino Votes Old and New

By WAY OF conclusion, I return to two themes raised in the first chapter that I have not addressed directly in the intervening analysis. First, I evaluate the likelihood that Latinos will form a new electorate, as women, youth, African Americans, and southern and eastern Europeans did earlier in the century. If they do, I ask where they fit on the continuum of possible electoral outcomes established by these other twentieth-century new electorates. Second, I question the role of ethnicity in future Latino political activity. As I suggested, ethnicity is a very fluid force in politics. Thus it is important to know how Latinos view themselves ethnically and what these feelings portend for their political behaviors. Finally, I conclude with a suggestion about the role of naturalization, not just as a tool to make more citizens, but as a broader stimulus to fuel incorporation among Reticents and Reluctants as well as Recruits.

This discussion raises a question that transcends the experiences of Latinos. It assesses how the original mode of group-based political incorporation is linked to short- and long-term political behaviors and, potentially, political influence. Thus, the models developed here can be applied equally to other populations that either do not participate politically or participate at low levels.

Does the New Electorate Model Apply to Latinos?

In the first chapter, I outlined examples of four populations—women, African Americans, youth, and turn-of-the-century immigrants—who moved from being largely excluded from electoral politics to being formally included. The focus was on what circumstances led to their inclusion and what the short- and long-term outcomes of this inclusion were. Here, I would like to look for some patterns that applied to all of these groups and examine their applicability to today's Latino new electorates. Each offers lessons for Latino political mobilization.

The first pattern worth noting is the basic characteristic that made each a new electorate. They either gained a previously denied right to vote or began to exercise that right on a widespread basis for the first time. This access to the polls takes place as a group, not as an individual, phenomenon. What defines a new electorate, then, is the ability to vote at previously unachievable levels. Some groups had an immediate impact, whereas others did not. Thus, electoral influence is not a necessary condition. Instead, new electorates exist upon the establishment of a reasonable potential for group political influence.

For three of the new electorates—blacks, women, and youth—laws had to be changed to allow participation. For the southern and eastern Europeans and other New Deal–era immigrants and their children, existing laws allowed their participation, but many did not take advantage of these opportunities nor did the political order encourage or reward their participation. They began to vote in large numbers only when the electoral system convulsed sufficiently to need their votes and to solicit their participation.

On the surface these patterns may seem quite different. The de jure exclusion of southern blacks and most women and youth was patronizing and debilitating. In denying them the vote, the nation told these groups that they were not equal citizens. The de facto exclusion of many of the turn-of-the-century immigrants and their children was, on the other hand, a relatively routine part of U.S. immigrant history. By establishing the five-year residence threshold for naturalization, Congress asserted that there *should* be a period between immigration and full political participation. Thus, although these electorates share the property of acquiring participatory rights or a routine pattern of participation over a short period in the twentieth century, the character of their previous exclusion differs dramatically.

Yet in all four cases, the polity formally or informally excluded the majority of each of these groups prior to their becoming a new electorate. If the history of the U.S. political process is one of progressive inclusion of previously excluded groups, then the twentieth-century new electorates share a common experience. They represent examples of this progressive inclusiveness and reflect also the polity's perception of itself as inclusive. All four new electorates challenged the organizing principles of the country. African Americans in particular, but also women and youth, based their claims not on power but, instead, on their more abstract status as citizens who deserved equal treatment. While this formal or informal exclusion may seem to distinguish the experiences of the other twentieth-century new electorates from those of contemporary Latino immigrants, each, including Latinos today, sought equal treatment as well as the entitlement to participation.

Do the southern and eastern European immigrants and their children figure as a category that the political order excluded? The answer, I believe, is yes. Even though the political system decided that it was justified in delaying the enfranchisement of the recent immigrants, it faced a dilemma with these long-term denizens. They were no longer recent immigrants. Many had resided in the United States for twenty years or more. Equally disturbing for a democratic system premised on universal white adult franchise (Bryce 1921; Tocqueville 1981; Fuchs 1990), this new electorate included immigrants' children who, though U.S. citizens, followed their parents' patterns of nonparticipation. Thus, to the extent that the polity premised itself on universal white electoral inclusion, the presence of large numbers of nonparticipating southern and eastern Europeans conflicted with this ideal. The scale of their de facto exclusion offered both an opportunity and a challenge for the polity.

In the late 1920s, local Democratic parties, the national Democratic Party, and the Al Smith presidential campaign seized this challenge and mobilized immigrants and their children into a cohesive voting bloc. Had they not—so that the southern and eastern Europeans had remained outside of the electorate—the failure of progressive electoral inclusion would have conflicted with the polity's view of itself. Over time, the response to this informal exclusion might have led to more assertive demands for inclusion. In this period, then, the polity met the challenge: institutions reached out to immigrants and incorporated them into U.S. electoral politics. As long as large-scale immigration continues, however, incorporating immigrants presents a continuing challenge for the polity.

In the wake of the post-1965 immigration, the system again faced this type of challenge to its organizing principles. Among Latinos, more than one third of adults cannot participate as a result of noncitizenship. Among nonvoting citizen Latinos, many are the children of immigrants who are not socialized into U.S. electoral politics. Although not immigrants, first- and second-generation Puerto Ricans are also, in many cases, not regular participants in U.S. politics. Finally, the Mexican American population includes people who were themselves excluded or are the children of the excluded. Again, political socialization may be lacking in these citizens as it was among turn-of-the-century immigrants and their children. At present, there is no way to predict how the political system will respond to this newest challenge.

The experiences of the earlier new electorates offer possible models of incorporation for Latinos. The New Deal new electorate offers the most direct comparison. Latino immigrants, like their turn-of-the-century predecessors, are a large population, the majority of which is politically unincorporated. They are also geographically concentrated. Perhaps the most important comparison is that both populations include various nationalities that have some common interests and traits, but that also have unique national-origin and regional interests.

The comparison, however, should not be overdrawn. Changes in the competitiveness of U.S. elections and the roles of political parties and electoral institutions in the intervening 60 years have limited the opportunities for contemporary immigrants relative to their predecessors. Further, it is impossible to predict the likelihood of the emergence of a new electoral alignment or of an event that could spark a realignment. Scholars also differ on whether the contemporary party system can coherently realign (Petrocik 1981; Shafer 1991).

Naturalization has become more difficult. New requirements added in the 1950s mandate that immigrants be able to pass a knowledge-based exam in addition to speaking English, the only knowledge requirement for the turn-of-the-century immigrants. Further, the bureaucratic requirements have toughened with increased efforts at centralization.

Finally, contemporary Latino immigration differs significantly from turn-of-the-century European immigration. Latino immigration continues at high rates and promises to continue for the foreseeable future. As a result, policymakers and Latino leaders focus their attention on immigration policy, not settlement policy. By the late 1920s, on the other hand, most European immigration was at least a decade old. Immigration policy had been settled with the national-origin–based immigration quotas of the early 1920s. As a result, Congress and ethnic leaders were able to focus on settlement policy.

Hence, the New Deal model offers a possible scenario, but differences between Latinos and turn-of-the-century immigrants make a comparable outcome far from certain. Regardless of similarities or differences between Latinos and earlier immigrants, however, the systemic challenge to incorporate the excluded remains.

To the extent that Latinos perceive or come to perceive that they face formal exclusion from the political order, the new-electorate models of blacks, women, and youth offer parallels for demand making. The experiences of these three new electorates demonstrate that sustained demands for inclusion result, eventually, in electoral access. As I have indicated, to the extent that these demands challenge the systemic guarantee of political inclusion, they will succeed at gaining the right to vote.

These three new electorates differ, however, when it comes to the question of the impact of this participatory access, once gained. Latinos can learn something from these previous experiences: the scope of the movement making the demands for inclusion is very important to the eventual impact of the new vote. The African American vote had an immediate and continuing impact because the drive to gain this right pervaded all levels of African American society; the organizations and leaders that demanded the vote represented a community-wide consensus and common African American vision for a better society. The right to vote was just one demand of many in this African American vision for society. That the community could come together initially reflects the legacy and pervasiveness of the exclusion. That they could largely stay similar in terms of partisanship and policy preferences 30 years after the Voting Rights Act reflects this legacy, but also the nature of the demand making that led to the VRA.

The demands by women and youth for suffrage were no less legitimate. The scope of the organizations that mobilized to win the vote, however, was not as all-encompassing as was the black struggle. The movements seeking the vote for women, for example, could have demanded what would come to be called a "feminist social agenda," or it could have reached out to other excluded groups, such as black women. Instead, it sought and won a single, very important, right. The narrowness of the mobilization, however, ensured that the franchise would not be used initially in great numbers and would not have an immediate impact, as it did nothing to give the new eligible voters a reason to vote.

Trajectories for the Latino Vote

These examples suggest four possible trajectories for Latinos. First, they could follow the pattern of the southern and eastern Europeans. During a period of national electoral change, Latino votes could be sought by a candidate, party, or other electoral institution. Their votes would join with those of existing voters and become important to one of the new coalitions. This form of inclusion could integrate the Reluctants (nonregistered citizens), Reticents (registered nonvoters), and some Recruits (noncitizens). It could also spark conversion among existing Latino voters. The impetus for this first trajectory is largely outside of the Latino community. Thus, the political institutions that drive the mobilization and conversion could be selective in their outreach to Latinos and not necessarily ensure universal mobilization. Equally, the issues that drive the mobilization and conversion would not necessarily be those of central importance to Latinos. If this were the case, then cleavages along sociodemographic, regional, or national-origin lines could quickly divide these new Latino voters. Thus, the long-term legacy of this mobilization would be increased participation, but not necessarily a common voice. The partisan and policy impact of this model would depend on the institution that reaches out to Latinos during the electoral tumult and cannot be predicted in advance.

The second trajectory captures only the Reluctants and the Reticents and follows the examples of women and youth new electorates. Latinos could organize solely to gain mass voter registration. If successful, a narrow focused effort would bring in new eligible voters in large numbers. These new voters would alter the present national partisan and ideological balance slightly and could well shift party control in some states. The leadership for this effort would come largely from Latino (or Mexican, Puerto Rican, or Cuban) leaders. Their message would be narrow and focus on the call for greater levels of participation to ensure greater responsiveness from government. Because this new electorate mobilization would have no organizing principle beyond the vote, however, it would not bring to the political process a unique set of Latino issues, just as women brought no women's issues into national electoral debates in the 1920s. Although not understood in these terms, this has been the empowerment model followed by many Latino (and other excluded electorate) leaders through voter registration efforts. Unless overwhelmingly successful, this strategy faces the limitations of previous voter registration and mobilization efforts: it would tend to exclude poorer, less educated Latinos, reinforcing the existing class bias in American voting.

This strategy would probably benefit the Democrats in the short term, though the data presented here demonstrate that Republicans should not neglect the seeming openness of many immigrants to the party's program. As Latinos would come to be a larger vote, they could incrementally shift national priorities to areas of their concern. The nature of this trajectory, however, militates against the development of a Latino issue agenda. Since the mobilization would not have a policy focus, it would not cause Latinos to question whether there are indeed Latino issues. Thus, this style of ensuring equal participation is a short-term strategy focused solely on expanding the vote.

The third model, based on the African American experience, ties voter or citizenship mobilization to a broader set of policy objectives. Such an effort could be organized around either of two sets of policies that appear to link the Latino communities. These are a general demand for an increase in governmental services targeted at the needs of a poor population and concern with the rights of immigrants, broadly for a coherent settlement policy. This third trajectory assumes that Latino leaders and Latino communities can agree on a common agenda and use voter or citizenship mobilization as one component of a larger community political agenda. Clearly, this strategy assumes that Latino leaders can both link the various Latino communities and find a set of issues that unites them in such a way as to overcome other cleavages in the society. Later in this chapter, I speculate on a scenario in which this could occur.

If Latinos were to follow this third model in today's political environment, it would likely benefit the Democrats, but would challenge the party to return to its New Deal and Great Society roots. If the strategy relied solely on the notion of settlement policy, it could fit into elements of the Republican agenda, but would conflict with vocal elements of the existing Republican constituency. In either case, large-scale mobilization of new Latino voters would likely lead to a countermobilization, or backlash, among non-Latinos who were dissatisfied with the policy choices or partisanship of these new voters. Thus, while the exact impact goes in a number of discrete directions, following this third trajectory ensures increased participation throughout the electorate and, in the end, greater democracy, but not necessarily a stronger voice for Latinos.

A final trajectory is to continue on the present course. If the 1980s and early 1990s are a lesson, this pattern will see a slow, but steady, increase in Latino electoral participation. Some of this increase is individually driven, whereas some involves intermittent mobilization strategies led by Latino leaders or political parties and candidates. This pattern of incremental mobilization will ensure a continued class gap in Latino voting and will do little to move noncitizens interested in naturalization into citizenship and voting. A parallel for this sort of incremental mobilization appears in both the ethnic communities that mobilized and converted as part of the New Deal and in the African American community. After the first waves of mobilization during the realignment and the Civil Rights movement, those who remained outside joined the electorate incrementally and in the self-selective manner predicted by the socioeconomic model of voting. In other words, once the mass-based incentive disappeared, individuals, not groups, entered or left the electorate.

In sum, I have identified four trajectories for the incorporation of new Latino electorates. The first sees selective but widespread mobilization by electoral institutions during periods of electoral tumult. The second involves mobilization narrowly around the franchise either by ethnic leaders or by electoral institutions, or by both. The third links mobilization to a wide range of public policy objectives. The process of identifying and demanding these policy objectives unites the new electorate not just to vote but also to use those votes to achieve a set of societal objectives. The fourth model supplements the process of individual inclusion with intermittent efforts at mobilization for the vote, or for a specific candidate or issue.

Table 7.1 examines each of these trajectories. It evaluates the same factors as does table 1.1 with two exceptions. It assumes that Latinos and all subsequent new electorates have legal access to the franchise and so does not evaluate the process by which the new electorate gains the franchise. This assumption is inaccurate if a new electorate were to be drawn from a grant of the vote to noncitizens. Second, it does not

TABLE 7.1. Trajectories for new electorates

	One	Two	Three	Four
Conditions of mobilization				
Mobilization generated from within new electorate	no	yes	yes	no
Mobilization from outside new electorate	yes	no	yes	no
Racial/Ethnic dimension to mobilization	no	no	yes	no
Electoral impact				
Immediate impact	yes	maybe	yes	maybe
Long-term impact	maybe	maybe	yes	maybe
Reinforce existing political alignments, initially	unknown	yes	unknown	yes
Creation of negative feelings in general population, initially	maybe	no	unknown	no
Presence of cleavages within new electorate, initially	yes	yes	no	yes

KEY: *One*: selective but widespread mobilization by electoral institutions during periods of electoral tumult; *two*: broad mobilization around the franchise either by ethnic leaders or electoral institutions, or both; *three*: mobilization linked to a wide range of public policy objectives in which the process of identifying and demanding these policy objectives unites the new electorate to achieve a set of societal objectives; *four*: individual inclusion of new voters with intermittent efforts at mobilization for the vote, or for a specific candidate or issue.

attempt to assess the long-term interaction of the newly created electorate with future political institutions or other electorates. These factors could be determined only by knowing the structure of the political system that is created as part of the effort to bring the new electorate into the electoral process. Instead, it assesses whether the new electorate will be likely to have a long-term electoral impact.

If I were to speculate which of these patterns the Latino community would follow, I would guess the first, the second, or, in the long term, the fourth, with the second the most likely. During a period of electoral realignment, the Latino nonvote would be too tempting to neglect. In this discussion, I have indicated populations that could be targeted during a period of electoral mobilization. Similarly, in terms of the second pattern, Latino community efforts to mobilize nonvoters or noncitizens could steadily increase the Latino vote.

The third, African American, pattern is less likely because it requires much more investment and coalition building and the development of a common political agenda. The divergent policy positions and cleavages based on national origin, nativity, and citizenship have limited the ability to develop a common Latino political agenda adopted on a mass as well as elite basis.

The final scenario—maintaining the status quo—seems unlikely in the long term. While numbers do not guarantee influence, they do guarantee attention. At today's relatively low levels of participation, Latinos can influence electoral outcomes, frequently at the local level and between 15 and 25 percent of the time in statewide races. Even at current growth rates (and assuming continued partisan competition), these rates will slowly increase each election cycle. As Latino electoral influence becomes better understood, a form of cumulative causation will increase the likelihood that there will be steadily increasing attention given to Latino voters and potential voters from electoral institutions. This process will not occur as rapidly as Latino leaders would like and will not overcome socioeconomic and citizenship limitations on the Latino vote, but the size of the Latino population in some states will be such that even with huge numbers of nonvoters, Latino votes can determine electoral outcomes in close and, eventually, not-so-close races.

Latinos as an Ethnic Group or Ethnic Groups

The potential for the most rewarding of these electoral mobilizations, the one modeled on the Civil Rights movement, depends on the intersection of ethnicity and policy issues. For Latinos to experience broad mobilization, they must perceive some link that unites their experiences and distinguishes them from the rest of the population. To have an impact on politics, this link must be more than cultural (although culture may reinforce the link across national-origin communities or across political cleavages in American society). The tool for developing this link is a set of issues in which Latinos have a particular interest and a distinct perspective.

Regardless of whether Latinos develop as an ethnic vote, the impact of the Latino new electorates will be shaped by the meaning and salience of ethnicity to them. As demonstrated in chapter 1, the political impact of ethnicity in the United States operates on a continuum between the virtual disappearance and the threat, though never the manifestation, of ethnic political separateness. Between these extremes, ethnicity is a political resource to mobilize for a specific political end or a tool to increase participation beyond the levels ensured by class, age, and education. Measuring ethnicity's meaning for Latinos has the added complexity of the possible irrelevance of the panethnic identity to the national-origin groups that make up the panethnic whole.

National-Origin–Focused Ethnicity

Throughout this analysis, I have had to treat the issue of Latino ethnicity or ethnicities very cautiously. This caution operated at two levels. First, the use of the panethnic identity term "Latino" masks national-origin identities that are more salient to these populations. Thus, were these attachments to continue, any new electorate would reflect the smaller national-origin groups and not some broader collectivity.

In the LNPS, Latinos did not view themselves as having common political concerns. Among U.S. citizens of each of the three largest national-origin groups, respondents were more likely to report that their national-origin group was not very similar to either of the other groups than they were to report they were very similar (de la Garza et al. 1992, tables 9.20–9.22). No more than 14 percent of any group reported that any pairing was very similar, and this was Mexican Americans reporting on common political concerns of Puerto Ricans and Cuban Americans, whom they had little knowledge about. Noncitizens were even less likely to report political similarities between any pair of national-origin groups (de la Garza et al. 1992, tables 10.84–10.86). Citizens and noncitizens alike reported that Latinos shared a "somewhat" similar culture. This view was held by the majority of those of Mexican or Puerto Rican ancestry, regardless of citizenship status, and by the majority of Cuban ancestry noncitizens (de la Garza et al. 1992, tables 9.19 and 10.83). Thus, to the extent that I use Latinos' perceptions to guide my efforts, it is important to recognize that Latinos themselves did not see common political or cultural bonds.

The absence of these bonds emerges in part from the low level of contact among the Latino national-origin groups. Vast majorities of Mexican Americans, Puerto Ricans, and Cuban Americans did not interact with Latinos other than those of their own national-origin group. Fifteen percent or less of each group reported "a lot" of contact with people of either of the other national origins (de la Garza et al. 1992, tables 4.13–4.15). When one considers the geographic concentration of the Latino populations, this finding should not be surprising.

Further, the intragroup affinities were lower than with other racial or ethnic groups in U.S. society. Mexican American citizens, for example, reported that they were personally closer to Anglos and African Americans than they were to either Puerto Ricans or those of Cuban ancestry. Puerto Ricans were closer to Anglos than to those of Mexican or Cuban ancestry. They ranked African Americans equally to those of Mexican ancestry in terms of closeness. Cuban American citizens reported that they were closer to Puerto Ricans than any of the other pairings between Latino national-origin groups. Nevertheless, they reported that they were even closer to Anglos (de la Garza et al. 1992, table 4.16). None of the Latino national-origin groups reported negative perceptions about other Latinos. Instead, a neutral response was the most common. This neutrality, I would argue, reflects the lack of awareness of other Latinos. Nevertheless, this lack of affinity results from a lack of contact and leads to a lack of perception of a common political or cultural agenda, thereby reducing the likelihood of a mass-based Latino identity, at least in the near future.

The Roots of a Panethnic Latino Identity

Ethnicity is a fluid concept whose political salience can grow or wane. Several indicators suggest that a collective Latino identity may slowly be increasing in salience (Padilla 1985). None of these indicators, however, suggests that the increasing acceptance of the term "Latino" as an indicator of a common identity carries an overtly political manifestation. In terms of primary ethnic identification, between 12 and 28 percent of those of Mexican, Puerto Rican, and Cuban ancestries used a panethnic identification term (Hispanic, Latino, Hispano, Spanish, or Spanish American). Citizens, regardless of national origin, were more likely to use a panethnic term than were noncitizens, and those of

Mexican ancestry were more likely to use it than those of Puerto Rican or Cuban ancestry (de la Garza et al. 1992, table 2.27). Because the citizens will drive the community's politics, their greater likelihood of adopting a panethnic term is important. Further, in terms of the variety of ethnic identifications used, the majority of Mexican American and Puerto Rican U.S. citizens (56.0 and 58.4 percent, respectively) used one of these panethnic terms as one of their self-identifications. Forty-six percent of Cuban American citizens also used one of these pan-ethnic terms. The rates for Mexican and Cuban ancestry noncitizens were somewhat lower, but still significant at 39.4 and 38.1 percent, respectively.

The use of one of these terms does not necessarily reflect a panethnic meaning. Majorities of each national-origin group had no opinion as to the meaning of "Latino" and "Hispanic." Among those who did, however, the overwhelming majority reported that they referred to some form of commonness among peoples of Latin American origin in the United States (de la Garza et al. 1992, table 4.7). These findings suggested an acceptance, at least among those using one of these pan-ethnic terms as an ethnic identifier, that something is shared beyond the national-origin ties (Oboler 1995).

These findings may appear to be mutually contradictory. They may, however, indicate that while there is currently no politically salient basis for Latino ethnicity, the roots are there among a sufficient share of the population. Given the right circumstances, Latinos, regardless of ancestry, can shape a common political space. Once established, this nascent Latino politics could generate an ethnically driven political participation and mobilization.

As I discussed in the first chapter, the tension with ethnicity in the United States is not just its ebb and flow, but the possibility that it may disappear. The pattern for most previous immigrant groups was to pass through a period of political behavior based on ethnicity, but then to lose these bonds and act on other interests. Despite changed opportunity structures and the continuing inflow of new Latino immigrants, however, this historical pattern may continue.

As the discussion in chapters 5 and 6 suggests, however, the recent immigrants (at least those with five years of residence) seem to be moving quickly toward attachment to the United States. They plan to reside here and see U.S. citizenship as a goal, and more than half have applied in some concrete manner. Most surprisingly, perhaps, between 33 and 35 percent of the noncitizens already viewed their political allegiance more with the United States than with their countries of origin. These

Latino immigrants, then, appear to be well on the road to joining the polity in full.

The roots of an ethnic movement, however, do not have to appear among the foreign-born. The native-born are in many ways a more likely origin of such a movement. With the increasing size of the Latino immigrant population, however, for any such movement to have a genuine appeal throughout the communities, it would have to attract support from immigrants, even if led by the native-born.

Like the foreign-born, citizen Latinos do not show an ethnically driven dissatisfaction with the U.S. political system. In terms of attachment to the United States, between 68 and 88 percent of citizens reported extremely strong or very strong affection for the United States. Levels of pride in the United States were equally high (de la Garza et al. 1992, tables 6.1 and 6.2). At the individual level, approximately 18 percent of Cuban Americans, 30 percent of Puerto Ricans, and 39 percent of Mexican Americans reported having personally experienced discrimination based on national origin. In their reported treatment by public officials, more than 90 percent, regardless of national origin, reported that they were treated as well as anybody else. These low rates of reported discrimination were not matched by perceptions of the absence of discrimination against Latino national-origin groups. The majority of each national-origin group perceived that the Mexican- and Puerto Rican-ancestry populations faced discrimination. Mexican Americans and Puerto Ricans also believed that the Cuban-ancestry population faced discrimination (de la Garza et al. 1992, tables 7.5, 7.6, 7.10–7.12).

In sum, immigrants are moving toward American political life at a rapid clip. The native-born report overall satisfaction with life in the United States, and only a minority report personal exclusion based on their national origin, although the majority perceived that it occurs against their coethnics and other Latinos. This is not fertile ground for an ethnic political movement. Ethnicity offers a resource that Latino leaders and organizations could tap to move Latinos closer to the African American new-electorate model and further from the women and youth models. Continuing immigration ensures that national-origin–based ethnicity will not decline below current levels.

Further, there is always the possibility that de facto or de jure exclusion from political opportunities might encourage the development of a separatist or exclusive ethnic politics that could disrupt the political system. This is one scenario in which Latinos could unite to increase their electoral participation and impact. The spark could come from a variety of areas: an increase in nativism among non-Latino populations, a candidate attractive to Latinos, efforts to reduce policy programs of particular importance to Latinos such as bilingual education, or a general increase in the salience of ethnicity and ethnic-specific policies throughout the society. The data presented here do not indicate that this is a likely cause of mobilization of Latinos as a new electorate. In the next section, I present a more likely cause of Latino mobilization: community-wide response to concerns about the weak political voice of the community due to low rates of citizenship.

Ethnicity and Electoral Mobilization

In the discussion of nonvoters and noncitizens, I developed estimates of possible new electorates based on patterns present in the Latino populations. Among the citizen nonvoters, I developed a high estimate of 1,300,000 potential new voters and what I believed to be more realistic estimates of between 225,000 and 600,000 potential new voters. The noncitizens offered richer pools of potential naturalized citizens who could then move on to voting, ranging between 525,000 and 1,800,000. To achieve voter registration or naturalizations at this level, however, the Latino community would have to experience a previously unprecedented level of mobilization. Among the noncitizens, this mobilization would not only have to guarantee naturalization (a bureaucratically complex and time-consuming process) but also would have to see these new citizens through to voting. A quick review of the demographic characteristics of the noncitizens demonstrates that this final step to political inclusion should not be taken for granted. Should the estimated numbers naturalize, many will share those sociodemographic characteristics that are more common among citizen nonvoters.

One important factor about these estimates deserves note. The majority of the noncitizens fall into a behavioral or attitudinal category—such as frustrated naturalization applicants or members of community-based organizations—that could be targeted in a mass naturalization effort. Among citizen nonvoters, however, barely one third have behavioral traits that might predict future voting—such as membership in politically oriented community organizations or previous electoral activity. While the pool of citizenship-eligible noncitizens is currently smaller than the citizen nonvoters, it will soon be of equal or slightly greater size, when the Immigration Reform and Control Act legalization and Special Agricultural Worker (SAW) program beneficiaries reach their threshold for citizenship eligibility.

The differences between the noncitizen and citizen nonvoting populations are not just quantitative, but also qualitative. The lower levels of possible voters reflect higher numbers of discouraged or disinterested individuals who will not mobilize at any cost. Fewer permanent resident immigrants are discouraged and this is reflected in the relatively high share who have done something to naturalize or have participated in some activity that indicates that they might be interested in seeking U.S. citizenship.

No mobilization of this magnitude has occurred among Latinos. The single major effort—voter registration—has led to mixed results. Where, then, does this unprecedented impetus come from? I would argue that it can be found in the link between new electorates and ethnicity. To the extent that Latinos, initially through Latino leaders, come to perceive that the high levels of noncitizens eligible for naturalization are limiting Latino electoral power and, more importantly, denying Latinos equal access to political participation, they can organize around naturalization as an issue of community-wide concern. Here, ethnicity can be used as a resource in U.S. politics. In this scenario, high rates of nonparticipation may lead to a sense of political exclusion that could cause individual Latinos to perceive that the broader society is denying them the same level of access that other groups have. They would organize to make demands for some form of redress, specifically federal support for and encouragement of naturalization. Broadly, this is a civil rights strategy focused on naturalization.

Were an effort such as this successful, it would create a new electorate along the lines of the four from earlier in the century. If this effort were to include programmatic demands, Latinos could unite broadly in two areas of public policy. Regardless of national origin, Latinos reported the need for increased government services. Most important among these was the need for added educational resources. The second area of broad public policy agreement across the communities involved the need to protect the rights of immigrants. I call this the demand for a settlement policy.

This scenario clearly has difficulties. The current conditions have been present for at least a decade. Yet the community response has not been extensive. Further, naturalization is at best an effort with neutral consequences for Puerto Ricans, since they are U.S. citizens by birth. In a more Machiavellian analysis, large-scale Latino naturalization hurts Puerto Ricans in state and local politics in areas where they are concentrated. Because Puerto Ricans live in the same areas as noncitizen Latinos, the naturalization of the noncitizens reduces their relative influence. Finally, this scenario of community-wide emphasis on naturalization might shift organizational activity away from the citizen new electorates to the noncitizens. Ongoing voter registration efforts, then, might suffer.

The answer to each of these concerns, is the idea of cumulative causation—the idea that the more of something there is, the more there will be. The something is more voters. What has to be identified, then, is where to target efforts so as to make voters out of some traditional nonvoters, who will then show still others the positive impact of greater voting, creating a cycle of inclusion.

The 1994 elections offered an example of what could be the beginning of this process in one state. California voters passed Proposition 187, which limited state services to undocumented immigrants and by extension to some permanent resident- and citizen-children of undocumented immigrants (Tomás Rivera Center 1995). Overwhelmingly, Latino voters opposed Proposition 187, and they expressed this opposition through the ballot box. More California Latino voters went to the polls in 1994 than had in any previous election. Though the Latino voice was muted by high levels of non-Latino voting, the 1994 California elections offer an indication that Latino voters can be mobilized in unprecedented numbers (particularly for an off-year election). The challenge to leaders is to keep this interest high in subsequent elections. The preliminary evidence indicates that the debate around Proposition 187 spurred more than just voting on election day. Naturalization applications in California and nationwide have surged (DeSipio 1995b). Anecdotal evidence indicates that one of the reasons these new applicants give is to be able to vote to protect the rights of immigrants.

The tentative efforts at large-scale Latino naturalization have demonstrated that Latino immigrants are interested in citizenship and have showed the impediments they face in their pursuit of this goal. These efforts have designed strategies to assist potential applicants in the areas where they most need assistance, particularly with meeting the bureaucratic requirements of the process.

Indirectly, cumulative causation also addresses the concerns of Puerto Ricans and others who advocate continued focus on voter registration. Increasing numbers of naturalized citizen voters would raise the general salience of electoral politics in the Latino communities, leading to greater numbers, both citizen and noncitizen, seeking to participate. Increased voting would reverse the cumulative negative effect of high rates of noncitizenship overlapping with low rates of voter registration that I have identified in the states with larger Latino populations. Thus, by tapping into what will soon be the largest pool of nonvoters and targeting those among the noncitizens who have behaviorally or attitudinally positioned themselves on the path to citizenship, the leaders of this mass naturalization effort will be able to initiate more of something that will lead in the end to more voters.

Realistically, this scenario may not unfold for some time. The low level of concern for naturalization promotion that has characterized Mexican American and Latino organizations may well continue. Yet the longer the delay, the greater the potential dilemma for the society as a whole. The Latino population is increasing at a much more rapid rate than either the non-Hispanic white or black populations. By approximately 2020, the Latino population will outnumber the black population. Yet if present trends continue, two thirds of what will be the largest minority population either will not be able to vote because of noncitizenship, or will not vote despite having the right. For a society that prides itself on inclusion, this passive exclusion can only create a more serious challenge to the political system. To the extent, then, that Latinos do not take the lead in naturalization and voter mobilization, political institutions must take responsibility to move Latinos interested in U.S. citizenship from denizenship and, among the citizen population, must seek out their votes.

Appendixes
Notes
Bibliography
Index

Data Sources

The foundation of this research consists of two national studies of Latino political values, attitudes, and behaviors: the National Latino Immigrant Survey and the Latino National Political Survey. Although these studies were conducted by different researchers with different, though comparable, research questions, they together offer a previously unavailable resource for assessing actual and potential Latino political behavior. In this appendix, I discuss the goals and methods of each survey, the common issues raised, and the ways in which I use their data to examine Latino political incorporation.

The National Latino Immigrant Survey

The NALEO Educational Fund, with support from the Ford Foundation, conducted the National Latino Immigrant Survey (NLIS) in 1988. The NLIS is a national probability sample of 1,636 Latino immigrant adults who have naturalized or who are statutorily eligible for naturalization (see table A.1). Respondents had to meet the following conditions: They had to (1) be legally resident in the United States for five years, unless married to a United States citizen in which case the period of legal residence was three years; (2) have emigrated from a Spanish-speaking country in Latin America or the Caribbean; and (3) be 18 years of age or older. The sampling frame for the survey consists of 47 counties in eight states where 80 percent of the Latino foreign-born with five years of United States residence lived in 1980.

The sample consists of 1,636 respondents who were interviewed by telephone. These respondents were selected through random digit dialing in the 47 counties in the sample. The average interview lasted 35 minutes. All interviewers were fully bilingual; 87 percent of the respondents chose to take the survey in Spanish.

Of the 1,636 respondents, 709 (43 percent) were born in Mexico, 429 (26 percent) in Cuba, 110 (7 percent) in the Dominican Republic, and the remainder in 15 other countries in Central and South America and the Caribbean. The average respondent was 40 years of age and had lived in the United States for 15 years. Approximately one third were U.S. citizens. Although just one third had naturalized, 98 percent of respondents stated an intention to make the U.S. their permanent home.

Besides collecting basic sociodemographic data about the Latino immigrant population, NALEO designed the survey with twin purposes. First, it investigated attitudes toward U.S. citizenship and life in the United States. This line of questioning allowed an analysis of different measures of acculturation that precede the immigrant's decision to naturalize. Second, the survey sought to assess the bureau-

TABLE A.I. Sample design of the National Latino Immigrant Survey (NLIS)[a]

Number of interviews	1,636
Type of interview	Telephone
Countries of origin	
Mexico	43.6%
Cuba	25.9%
Central America and the Caribbean	17.2%
South America	13.3%
Period of interviews	August–November 1988
Survey length and content	35 minutes; 110 items focusing on demographics, economic and labor force characteristics, language, associations, attitudes, knowledge of and participation in the naturalization process, and attitudes toward U.S. citizenship.
Sample	Two-stage stratified probability sample of foreign-born Latino immigrants living in the 47 counties that account for 80 percent of all foreign-born Latinos living in the United States at that time. The NLIS defines Latino immigrants as people who emigrated from one of the Spanish-speaking countries in Latin America or the Caribbean.
Respondent selection	Random digit dialing
Limitations	Studies only Latino legal immigrants eligible for U.S. citizenship. As a result, the NLIS excludes most legal immigrants with less than five years of legal residence and all undocumented immigrants.

[a]For more information, see Pachon and DeSipio (1994) and NALEO (1989).

cratic experiences of Latino immigrants, particularly relating to naturalization. To this end, the survey included numerous questions about each stage, formal and informal, of the naturalization application process to assess at what point immigrants interested in citizenship became discouraged in their pursuit of the goal.

Although the focus of the survey was the determinants and structural/bureaucratic limitations on naturalization, the NLIS offers considerable data to assess the potential role of Latinos in the electorate. It included standard measures of community participation such as membership in various types of organizations. The survey, however, added a distinctive component. Questions distinguish between membership in predominantly Latino and predominantly non-Latino organizations.

The NLIS also evaluated the degree to which immigrants participated in political activity, both in the country of origin and in the United States. This question is relevant not just to the U.S. citizen respondents. In some jurisdictions, non-U.S. citizens can vote in school board elections. The NLIS captures this phenomenon. Perhaps more importantly, though, since the majority of respondents were *not* U.S. citizens, the NLIS measured political behaviors such as campaigning and attending political events. The NLIS assessed the partisan preferences and voter registration levels of respondents who were U.S. citizens.

Potentially, the most important contribution of the NLIS to my research here is its focus on the act of "becoming American." An extensive literature is emerging that highlights the voluntary nature of U.S. citizenship (Levinson 1988; Fuchs 1990; DeSipio and de la Garza 1992a; Harles 1993). Thus, one of the most important political acts—joining the polity by choice, that is, through naturalization—is only formally open to immigrants. The NLIS offers an extensive battery of questions for understanding why immigrants become citizens. The survey also asked why immigrants had not sought U.S. citizenship.

Thus, the NLIS offered two dimensions for examining political participation of first-generation Latino immigrants. It assessed political participation—broadly defined—to include activities in which both the naturalized and the nonnaturalized may participate. It also evaluated the politics of why people do not become citizens and the levels of attachment both to the country of origin and to the United States.

The Latino National Political Survey

The Latino National Political Survey (LNPS) used a national probability sample of Mexican-, Cuban-, and Puerto Rican-ancestry (in the continental United States) populations as well as a control sample of non-Latino whites who resided in areas with moderate and high concentrations of the sampled Latino populations to examine two questions about the Latino community (see table A.2). First, the LNPS evaluated whether there was a distinct Latino political community in the United States and whether Latino politics is better understood through the study of the distinct Mexican-, Puerto Rican-, and Cuban-ancestry political communities. Second, to the extent that there is a distinctive Latino political community (or communities), the LNPS gauged the differences and similarities among their political attitudes, values, and behaviors.

The LNPS excludes Latinos who are *not* of Mexican, Puerto Rican, or Cuban ancestry from the sampling frame; these excluded populations are approximately 20 percent of the national Latino population. The rationale for this exclusion appears in García et al. (1989) and de la Garza et al. (1992).

The LNPS was conducted in person in 38 cities and two rural counties in 15 states. These communities represented areas in which at least 90 percent of the Mexican, Cuban, and Puerto Rican populations in the United States (excluding Puerto Rico) reside. Within these areas, the sampling design selected four density strata—from high-density Latino to very low-density Latino—to ensure that Latinos who resided in non-Latino areas would be included. Just as Latinos who resided in non-Latino areas were captured in this sample design, individuals of one national-origin group who reside in an area of another's concentration—for example, a person of Mexican ancestry in Miami or a Puerto Rican in Albuquerque—were included.

Temple Survey Research collected these data between July 1989 and April 1990. The average survey took 91 minutes to complete (59 minutes to survey Anglos, who were asked fewer questions). The respondents were: 1,546 of Mexican ancestry, 589 of Puerto Rican ancestry living in the continental United States, 682 of Cuban ancestry, and 438 non-Latino whites. Slightly more than half of

TABLE A.2. Sample design of the Latino National Political Survey (LNPS)[a]

Number of interviews	3,415
Type of interview	In-Person
Countries of origin or ancestry	
Mexico	47.3%
Cuba	20.8%
Puerto Rico	18.0%
Anglos	13.9%
Period of interviews	July 1989–April 1990
Survey length and content	90 minutes / 184 items focusing on demographics, psychological, cultural, linguistic and associational characteristics, information environment, political values, public policy perspectives, organizational and electoral behavior, and ethnic attitudes.
Sample	Stratified probability sample of Mexican-, Puerto Rican-, and Cuban-origin residents of 38 cities and two rural counties. The 40 areas were selected so as to be representative of 90 percent of each of these populations residing in the United States. Latinos were selected from high-, medium-, and low-density areas of Latino population concentration. The sample of Anglos was drawn from areas in which Latinos reside.
Limitations	Does not study Latinos who are not of Mexican, Puerto Rican, or Cuban origin or ancestry. Includes some undocumented residents who cannot be identified. The Anglo sample is not representative of Anglos nationwide. The sociodemographics of the Anglos in the sample are higher than those of Anglos nationwide because national Anglo samples include more older Anglos and more Anglos from rural areas.

[a]For more information, see de la Garza et al. (1992).

the LNPS respondents were born abroad (including the Puerto Ricans born in Puerto Rico). Of those born in Cuba and Mexico, approximately 25 percent had naturalized.

As with the NLIS, the LNPS offers a rich lode of material to assess the future ways in which Latinos will incorporate politically into the United States. The LNPS matched the NLIS in assessing the levels and the types of formal and informal political participation and organizational membership. Since the size of the U.S. citizen respondent pool is larger than in the NLIS, the LNPS can better evaluate registration, voting, and partisan preferences. The LNPS also has the advantage of having been conducted after the 1988 election; it therefore asked questions on how respondents participated in the elections (as well as previous national elections).

Unlike the NLIS, the LNPS featured a series of questions about the political values of immigrants. Traditional measures were used to assess the level of expectations for state or individual solutions to problems. The LNPS measured the salience of national, local, and community issues to respondents and examined respondents' expectations for being able to solve problems they identified as important. The respondents' expectations about the likelihood of solving these problems and the likely source of that solution relate directly to current and future expectations about the political system.

The LNPS also evaluated the respondents' ideologies. The survey supplemented self-evaluation by asking people to evaluate the ideologies of public figures (Jesse Jackson and Ronald Reagan). The survey also asked questions about specific public policy issues such as Central America, the death penalty, affirmative action, the English-only movement, bilingual education, and abortion.

Finally, the LNPS asked each subgroup to assess its closeness to or distance from the other two Latino subgroups as well as other actors in the American political system. Respondents also evaluated the meaning of the terms "Latino" and "Hispanic."

Each of these components of the LNPS allows me to compare the Latino subgroups to learn the extent to which there is either a common Latino perception or a more mixed, yet equally "non-Anglo" approach.

This summary of the NLIS and LNPS highlights elements of the surveys that can be brought to bear on the question of current and future Latino political behavior and its effect on the national electorate. These surveys, particularly when viewed jointly, offer a rare opportunity for scholars to evaluate Latinos and the comparative experiences of the Latino national-origin groups from a national perspective.

Estimating the Size of the Naturalization-Eligible Noncitizen Population

In order to examine the potential impact of new electorate number 4, it is necessary to make several calculations. The first of these is in some ways the most difficult. It is necessary to estimate the denominator—the number of adult Latino noncitizens who are eligible for naturalization. This estimate is subject to much potential error. Nevertheless, it is a necessary exercise. This figure is a maximum possible Latino noncitizen new electorate. Based on this calculation, I develop several estimates in chapter 5 of realistic components of the Latino noncitizen population that have behaviorally or attitudinally initiated the process of becoming a U.S. citizen. Together these estimates will allow me to calculate the potential impact of the Recruits and the states where their votes could have the greatest impact.

The Latino non-U.S. citizen population includes many immigrants who have resided in the United States for the five-year period necessary to apply for U.S. citizenship. It also includes populations ineligible for naturalization, including recent arrivals, the undocumented, and recipients of legalization under the Immigration Reform and Control Act. Despite the importance to the polity of immigration and citizenship, there are no reliable estimates of the size of the naturalization-eligible immigrant populations. The unavailability of two sets of data prevents the calculation of estimates of this population based on immigration data. First, no records are kept of permanent residents who emigrate. Second, there is no source of data on mortality of permanent residents. So, it is not possible to develop an estimate based on a count of legal immigrants, subtracting those who have naturalized, emigrated, or died.

As a result, analysts must undertake a more complicated and potentially error-filled exercise—counting backward from the census count of noncitizen Latinos. This exercise is potentially error filled because the noncitizen figure includes three populations who are ineligible to naturalize: the undocumented, recent arrivals, and recipients of permanent status under the legalization and Special Agricultural Worker provisions of the Immigration Reform and Control Act of 1986. The noncitizen figure is also inaccurate because of a persistent undercount of Latinos by the census.

According to the Current Population Survey, Latino noncitizens numbered 5.9 million in 1992 (Census 1993a). To count backward from the number of noncitizens, I must subtract the ineligible and add those not counted:

| Latino Foreign Born | − | Undocumented | − | Recent Arrivals | − | IRCA/ SAW | + | Undercount | = | Eligible |

Of the three populations that must be subtracted, the most difficult to count are the undocumented. For obvious reasons, many undocumented immigrants fear discussing their status with Census Bureau enumerators. Thus, they probably disproportionately contribute to the high Census Bureau undercount of Latinos (Bailar 1988; Census 1991*b*). Among those counted in the decennial census and included in Current Population Survey estimates, the census makes no effort to determine the respondent's legal status. To cover their tracks further, many undocumented may be counted but report that they are U.S. citizens. So, they appear in the census, but not as the noncitizens they are.

Despite these complications, without an estimate of the undocumented Latino population, it is not possible to use census counts of the noncitizen population to estimate the pool of citizenship-eligible Latino immigrants. To date, there has not been any analysis of the number of Latino undocumented counted in the 1990 census. Passel and Woodrow (1984) estimated that approximately 2 million undocumented were counted in the 1980 census. As part of this estimate, they find undocumented immigration of between 100,000 and 300,000 per year in the years 1979–83, not all of whom were Latino (Passel and Woodrow 1985). Although dated, these are the most recent respectable estimates of the undocumented population counted in the census and annual undocumented migration. A more recent estimate found that 3.4 million undocumented immigrants resided in the United States in October 1992 (U.S. INS 1994: table O). This estimate, however, does not indicate how many of these undocumented immigrants were counted in the census.

On the basis of these estimates and several hypotheses, I estimate that the 5.9 million figure included between 1 and 1.5 million undocumented Latino immigrants (as of 1992). These hypotheses are:

1. Most pre-1982 immigrants benefited from legalization, starting the count at zero in that year.

2. After 1982, undocumented immigration continued at the same pace as 1979–83 until the implementation of employer sanctions in 1988.

3. Some of the undocumented immigrants from the 1982–87 period earned legal status under the SAW program.

4. Other undocumented immigrants from 1982 to the present have been able to regularize their status in other ways such as marrying a U.S. citizen or having an employer perform a labor certification.

5. Between 1987 and 1989, undocumented immigration remained at the low end of this range as potential immigrants tested the limits of the employer sanctions program (Crane et al. 1990).

6. Since approximately 1989, undocumented immigration has been at the high end of the 100,000 to 300,000 per year range (Passel, Bean, and Edmonston 1991).

7. Many post-1982 undocumented immigrants were sojourners and were not in the country by 1992.

Needless to say, this is a very rough approximation.

The second of the populations that are included in the 5.9 million, but who are currently ineligible for citizenship are the beneficiaries of legalization and the Special Agricultural Worker (SAW) program. Although they may have experienced some emigration and mortality, approximately 2.6 million Latinos qualified for one of these programs—1.5 million for the legalization program and 1.1 million SAWs (U.S. INS 1990). Some of these may subsequently have emigrated or died, so I use a range of SAW/Immigration Reform and Control Act (IRCA) applicants from 2.4 to 2.6 million. IRCA legalization applicants began to be eligible in late 1993 (the peak period of initial eligibility was December 1994). A handful of SAW applicants attained initial eligibility for U.S. citizenship in December 1994 with the remainder becoming eligible in December 1995.

The final ineligible population of Latino adults is the legal immigrant who has arrived within the past five years. While the numbers of these immigrants can be more accurately counted than can the undocumented, these estimates are also rendered inaccurate by emigration and mortality. Over the past five years, the number of Latino legal immigrants averaged about 200,000 per year (U.S. INS 1989, 1992). As many as one third of these could have emigrated (or will emigrate). Further, some of these may have been resident in the United States in another immigrant category prior to their legal immigration and, as a result, are counted twice here. Thus, between 500,000 and 800,000 of the noncitizens in the 5.9 million estimate are recent immigrants, ineligible for naturalization. Though currently ineligible, up to 160,000 immigrants join the pool of new potential citizens each year; these are the Latino permanent resident immigrants from five years before who have attained statutory naturalization eligibility.

Finally, the Census Bureau estimated the Latino undercount to be between 4.3 and 7.9 percent or between 1.0 and 1.9 million (1991b). When the Census Bureau released these figures, it did not discuss the immigrant status of the undercounted Latinos. Reasonably, the undercount could be argued to have been concentrated among those who did not want to be counted (the undocumented) and those in poorer areas who are simply hard to find (both urban and rural). These urban poor Latino areas are likely to have concentrations of noncitizens. Thus, the undercount could add between 1.0 and 1.5 million to the 5.9 million noncitizen Latinos. My final assumption is that if the number not counted is at the high end of the range, then there are a higher number of undocumented immigrants counted in the census.

With these limitations in mind, I estimate that of the 5.9 million Latino non-U.S. citizens enumerated in the 1992 current population survey, between 2.5 and 3.0 million are currently eligible for naturalization:

Latino Foreign Born	− Undocu- mented	− Recent Arrivals	− IRCA/ SAW	+ Undercount	= Eligible
High estimate:					
5,900,000	− 1,000,000	− 500,000	− 2,400,000	+ 1,000,000	= 3,000,000
Low estimate:					
5,900,000	− 1,500,000	− 800,000	− 2,600,000	+ 1,500,000	= 2,500,000

As I have indicated, these estimates are not static. They increase by as many as 160,000 each year through the natural growth in the population with five years of legal residence. Further, by the end of 1995, the legalization and SAW beneficiaries attained citizenship eligibility. Some of the 1.5 million Latino legalization applicants have already completed some of the tests necessary for naturalization.

Notes

Chapter 1: New Americans and New Voters

1. I limit my discussion to new electorates of this century. Clearly, the mobilization of new electorates is not just a twentieth-century phenomenon. Jacksonian democracy and the extension of the franchise to most white males between 1828 and 1840 presaged the eventual expansion of the franchise beyond the native white population. In order to compare like situations and comparable political environments, however, I limit my discussion here to the four examples of twentieth-century new electorates.

2. The temporal dimension of the potential effect of Latino electoral and political participation is murky because immigration from the Americas continues at very high rates. This is in contrast to the southern and eastern European immigration that had largely ended (first with World War I and immigration literacy tests [beginning in 1918] and then with the National Origins immigration quotas of the 1920s) when these immigrants and their children began to have a national impact at the polls.

Edmonston and Passel (1991) estimate that if current immigration and fertility patterns continue, Latinos will be 25 percent of the national population by the year 2090 and have a larger population than blacks and Asian Americans combined. The authors warn that demographic estimates of this length are highly risky; these data should be used only to estimate the magnitude of continued high levels of Latino immigration.

3. Many women and some 18- to 20-year-olds had the vote before the passage of the Constitutional amendment guaranteeing all the franchise. As early as the 1880s, some, mostly western, states granted women the vote. In the 1960s, Georgia, Kentucky, Alaska, and Hawaii granted the vote to 18- to 20-year-old residents.

4. Gamm (1986, chapter 1) questions the validity of Anderson's use of retrospective survey data. Specifically, he recommends that she needs to estimate the total number of eligible voters in each of her targeted communities.

5. Throughout the NLIS's development, I was a staff member of the NALEO Educational Fund, the organization that conducted the survey. I was involved in all aspects of the project, from drafting the first questionnaire and supervising the feasibility study through selecting the survey contractor and analyzing the survey findings for the media. My involvement with the LNPS has been more tangential. By the time I became involved, the survey was already being tested in the field. Since then, however, I have coordinated two subsidiary projects.

Chapter 3: The Latino Electorates: Current and Potential

1. With one recent exception (Verba et al. 1993), there has not been extensive study of nonelectoral political activity by Latinos. In the previous chapter, I reviewed the literature on Latino community organizations. The three most studied Latino social movements involved Mexican Americans and Mexican immigrants, the land claims in New Mexico (Weber 1973, part 5; Rosenbaum 1981, chapters 8–10), farmworker organization (Matthiessen 1969; Daniel 1981), and Alinsky-type church-based community organization (Rogers 1990; Skerry 1993).

2. These estimates of Latino registration and voting are based on Current Population Survey estimates of electoral participation which rely on self-reported citizenship, registration, and voting rates collected in the weeks after the election (see methodological note to table 3.1). As such, they overestimate registration and voting. Despite this overreporting, they are the only source of data on registration and turnout for race and ethnic groups at both the national and state levels. As importantly, they offer a benchmark for comparing electoral participation for each presidential and off-year election since 1964 for whites and blacks and since 1972 for Latinos.

3. In this discussion of census data on aggregate registration and voting, I present data from the most current national election (1992). Because the survey data discussed throughout this manuscript were collected between 1988 and 1990, it might make more sense to use census data on the 1988 election. I have chosen not to do this for two reasons. First, the 1992 data have a slightly lower rate of overestimation of voting (Census 1993a, table D). Second, I use these data only to illustrate the magnitude of different components of the Latino adult population and to compare Latinos with other populations. Hence, I believe there is value in using the most current data.

4. An indeterminate number of these non-U.S. citizens are undocumented residents of the United States, ineligible for naturalization. Later, I develop an estimate of the undocumented share of this non–U.S.-citizen population. For now, it is worth noting that half—or between 2.5 and 3.0 million—are legal permanent residents eligible to naturalize.

5. Even after the authors added controls for sociodemographic characteristics, on the other hand, Asian Americans remain less likely to vote. This indicates that cultural factors may influence Asian American voting in California.

6. State-level estimates of Latino turnout are subject to much higher sampling errors (Census 1993a). Hence estimates, particularly in the smaller states like Colorado, can fluctuate widely. To compensate for this fluctuation, I calculate these estimates on the average change in reported Latino voting from 1980 to 1984, 1984 to 1988, and 1988 to 1992.

Chapter 4: The Reticents and the Reluctants: What Keeps U.S.-Citizen Latinos from the Polls?

1. Although I do not explore it here, this phenomenon may be an example of the mutually depressing effects of high concentrations of noncitizens and low voter mobilization among the citizens. The presence of these factors limits the likelihood of outreach by candidates, campaigns, and political institutions. Thus, each becomes a mutually reinforcing negative force on Latino electoral mobilization. This is discussed in greater depth in de la Garza, Menchaca, and DeSipio (1994).

2. Unexpectedly, Cuban American citizens who were not registered had much higher family incomes than their coethnics who voted despite the fact that they were younger and slightly less educated. They differed in other areas as well. Although the majority of the Reluctants were Catholic, many more either were Protestant or had no religious affiliation than among the voters. They were also much more likely than the voters to be bilingual; the majority of the voters reported Spanish dominance while the majority of the nonregistered were bilingual. Perhaps most interestingly, the Cuban American Reluctants were much more likely to be native-born with foreign-born parents compared to the Cuban American voters. Over half of the Cuban American Reluctants were native-born (56.5 percent) compared to just 23.9 percent of the voters. I interpret the significance of these data carefully because the number of Cuban American Reluctants is quite small (n = 55). If these results represent a pattern for the future and not just an anomaly in a small sample, however, it could indicate a change in the future of Cuban American political participation: the most acculturated are the least likely to participate.

3. The high number of former voters highlights a dilemma for efforts at Latino empowerment. Many Latino voters have only recently begun to participate in electoral politics; with weaker ties to the process, they can lose interest and become disaffected more readily than can people with a longer history of participation and a greater sense of connection. If 1988 was an anomaly, this is of little concern. If, however, it becomes the norm, then Latinos may see a steadily deceasing role in electoral outcomes. While much of my discussion focuses on what Latinos and Latino leaders can do to strengthen the Latino political voice, I do not mean to present this as a unidirectional process. Candidates, campaigns, and electoral institutions bear some responsibility for speaking to Latinos and to Latino concerns.

Chapter 5: Naturalization and New Voters

1. The data on naturalization rates are limited by the absence of data on emigration and mortality among immigrants. As a result, no single measure of naturalization is used that is accepted by all immigration analysts. By any of several measures, Latinos are slow to naturalize and have a high share of their long-term foreign-born population who have not naturalized.

2. Among the entire pool of Latino immigrants statutorily eligible for naturalization, approximately one third (34.4 percent) had either naturalized themselves or became U.S. citizens through the naturalization of their parents, 37.4 percent had made no effort toward naturalization, and 28.2 percent had begun but not completed the process.

If I limit the pool to those who had *not* naturalized, 43 percent initiated the application process in some behavioral manner.

3. Because of the small number of naturalized Dominicans and the equally small numbers in the nonnaturalized stages, I am cautious about lending too much credence to these findings about Dominicans. Whatever the proper weight, they do go in the anticipated directions.

4. Throughout this analysis, I will calculate the state estimates on the lower range of possible voters (calculated from the 2.5 million low estimate of the potential maximum Latino immigrant population eligible for U.S. citizenship). My caution derives from a concern that these state calculations are estimates based on estimates. Further, neither survey was designed to be representative of the state-level Latino or Latino immigrant populations.

5. State-level estimates from the LNPS are skewed by the limitation of its sample to Mexican-, Puerto Rican-, and Cuban-ancestry populations. In New York, for example, the bulk of the Latino noncitizen population is non-Mexican and non-Cuban in origin. As a result, New York's numbers do not appear in estimates derived from the Latino National Political Survey.

Chapter 6: Including the Excluded: Strategies for Making Voters of Latino Non-U.S. Citizens

1. The Immigration Act of 1965 eliminated the national origins restrictions enacted in the 1920s, allowing large numbers of non-Europeans to immigrate. The 1965 act offers the starting point to the present wave of immigration.

2. The courts were not consistent in their approach to naturalization. In *In re Rodriguez* 81 Fed. Rep. 337 (de León 1979), the courts took an expansive view recognizing the right of Mexican immigrants to naturalize. Other courts, however, limited access to citizenship. In cases from the 1920s through the 1940s, the courts prevented the INS from releasing older applicants with long periods of residence in the United States from the English-speaking requirement. *Petition of Katz* 21 F.2d. 867 September 19, 1927; *In re Swenson* 61 F. Supp.

373, June 30, 1945. Similarly, before the enactment of the civics requirement, courts denied naturalization to applicants without this knowledge.

3. I have been a staff member of the NALEO Educational Fund through almost the entire history of the U.S. Citizenship project.

4. The number of noncitizen Cuban immigrants who were currently applying for citizenship was quite small ($n = 37$). Although I report the results for this group in the tables, I do not report on these results in my analysis.

Bibliography

Alba, Richard D. 1990. *Ethnic Identity: The Transformation of White America*. New Haven: Yale Univ. Press.

Allsup, Carl. 1982. *The American G.I. Forum: Origins and Evolution*. Austin: Univ. of Texas Press.

Allswang, John M. 1971. *A House for All Peoples: Ethnic Politics in Chicago 1890–1936*. Lexington: Univ. Press of Kentucky.

Altus, William D. 1949. "The American Mexican: The Survival of a Culture." *Journal of Social Psychology* 29 (May): 211–20.

Alvarez, Robert R. 1987. "A Profile of the Citizenship Process Among Hispanics in the United States." *International Migration Review* 21 (2) (Summer): 327–51.

Anders, Evan. 1979. *Boss Rule in South Texas: The Progressive Era*. Austin: Univ. of Texas Press.

Andersen, Kristi. 1979. *The Creation of a Democratic Majority 1928–1936*. Chicago: Univ. of Chicago Press.

Arian, Asher, Arthur S. Goldberg, John H. Mollenkopf, and Edward T. Rogowsky. 1991. *Changing New York City Politics*. New York: Routledge.

Bailar, Barbara. 1988. "Finding Those the Census Missed." *Technology Review* (May/June).

Baker, Ross K. 1993. "Sorting Out and Suiting Up: The Presidential Nominations." In *The Election of 1992: Reports and Interpretations*, ed. Gerald M. Pomper et al., pp. 39–73. Chatham, N.J.: Chatham House.

Balz, Daniel J. 1987. "Polling and the Latino Community: Does Anybody Have the Numbers?" In *Ignored Voices: Public Opinion Polls and the Latino Community*, ed. Rodolfo O. de la Garza, pp. 32–41. Austin: Univ. of Texas Press.

Barker, Lucius J., and Ronald W. Walters, eds. 1989. *Jesse Jackson's 1984 Presidential Campaign: Challenge and Change in American Politics*. Urbana: Univ. of Illinois Press.

Barnes, James A. 1992. "Voter Turnoff." *National Journal* (August 15): 1895–98.

Barrera, Mario. 1988. *Beyond Aztlán: Ethnic Autonomy in Comparative Perspective*. Notre Dame: Univ. of Notre Dame Press.

Baver, Sherrie. 1984. "Puerto Rican Politics in New York City: The Post–World War II Period." In *Puerto Rican Politics in Urban America*, ed. James Jennings and Monte Rivera, pp. 43–60. Westport, Conn.: Greenwood Press.

Bayes, Jane H. 1992. *Minority Politics and Ideologies in the United States*. Novato, Calif.: Chandler and Sharp.

Bean, Frank D., and Marta Tienda. 1990. *The Hispanic Population of the United States*. New York: Russell Sage Foundation.

Bernard, Richard, and Bradley R. Rice, eds. 1983. *Sunbelt Cities: Politics and Growth since World War II*. Austin: Univ. of Texas Press.

Betts, Katherine. 1988. *Ideology and Immigration: Australia 1976 to 1987*. Carlton, Victoria: Melbourne Univ. Press.

Black, Earl, and Merle Black. 1987. *Politics and Society in the South*. Cambridge: Harvard Univ. Press.

Bobo, Lawrence, and Franklin D. Gilliam, Jr. 1990. "Race, Sociopolitical Participation, and Black Empowerment." *American Political Science Review* 84 (2) (June): 377–93.

Bogardus, Emory S. 1934. *The Mexican in the United States*. Los Angeles: Univ. of Southern California Press.

Boswell, Thomas D., and James R. Curtis. 1984. *The Cuban-American Experience: Culture, Images, and Perspectives*. Totowa, N.J.: Rowman and Allanheld.

Bouvier, Leon F. 1992. *Peaceful Invasions: Immigration and Changing America*. Lanham, Md.: Univ. Press of America.

Branch, Taylor. 1988. *Parting the Waters: America in the King Years 1954–1963*. New York: Simon and Schuster.

Brischetto, Robert R. 1987. "Latinos in the 1984 Election Exit Polls: Some Findings and Some Methodological Lessons." In *Ignored Voices: Public Opinion Polls and the Latino Community*, ed. Rodolfo O. de la Garza, pp. 76–94. Austin: Univ. of Texas Press.

Brown, Ronald E. 1991. "Political Action." In *Life in Black America*, ed. James S. Jackson, pp. 254–63. Newbury Park, Calif.: Sage Publications.

Browning, Harley L., and Rodolfo O. de la Garza, eds. 1986. *Mexican Immigrants and Mexican Americans: An Evolving Relationship*. Austin: Univ. of Texas Press.

Browning, Rufus P., Dale Rogers Marshall, and David H. Tabb. 1984. *Protest Is Not Enough: The Struggle of Blacks and Hispanics for Equality in Urban Politics*. Berkeley and Los Angeles: Univ. of California Press.

Brubaker, William Rogers, ed. 1989a. *Immigration and the Politics of Citizenship in Europe and North America*. Lanham, Md.: Univ. Press of America.

———. 1989b. "Citizenship and Naturalization: Policies and Politics." In *Immigration and the Politics of Citizenship in Europe and North America*, ed. William Rogers Brubaker, pp. 99–128. Lanham, Md.: Univ. Press of America.

Bryce, James. 1921. *The American Commonwealth*, rev. ed. New York: Macmillan.

Burma, John H. 1954. *Spanish-Speaking Groups in the United States*. Durham: Duke Univ. Press.

Butler, R. E. "Rusty." 1986. "On Creating a Hispanic America: A Nation within a Nation?" Special Report. Washington, D.C.: Council for Inter-American Security.

Cain, Bruce, and D. Roderick Kiewiet. 1987. "Latinos and the 1984 Election: A Comparative Perspective." In *Ignored Voices: Public Opinion Polls and the Latino Community*, ed. Rodolfo O. de la Garza, pp. 47–62. Austin: Center for Mexican American Studies.

Calavita, Kitty. 1992. *Inside the State: The Bracero Program, Immigration, and the I.N.S.* New York: Routledge.

Calvo, Maria Antonia, and Steven J. Rosenstone. 1989. "Hispanic Political Participation." San Antonio: Southwest Voter Research Institute.

Campbell, Angus, Philip E. Converse, Warren Miller, and Donald Stokes. 1960. *The American Voter*. New York: Wiley.

Carpenter, N. 1927. *Immigrants and Their Children 1920*. New York: Arno Press.

Ceaser, James, and Andrew Busch. 1993. *Upside Down and Inside Out: The 1992 Elections and American Politics*. Lanham, Md.: Rowman and Littlefield.

Chan, Sucheng, ed. 1991. *Entry Denied: Exclusion and the Chinese Community in America, 1882–1943*. Philadelphia: Temple Univ. Press.

Chávez, Leo R., and Estevan T. Flores. 1988. "Undocumented Mexicans and Central Americans and the Immigration Reform and Control Act of 1986: A Reflection Based on Empirical [sic]." In *In Defense of the Alien*, ed. Lydio F. Tomasi, pp. 137–56. Staten Island, N.Y.: Center for Migration Studies.

Chávez, Leo R., Estevan T. Flores, and Marta Lopez-Garza. 1990. "Here Today, Gone Tomorrow? Undocumented Settlers and Immigration Reform." *Human Organization* 49 (3) (Fall): 193–205.

Chávez, Linda. 1991. *Out of the Barrio: Toward a New Politics of Hispanic Assimilation.* New York: Basic Books.

Cohen, Lizabeth. 1990. *Making a New Deal: Industrial Workers in Chicago 1919–1939.* New York: Cambridge Univ. Press.

Congressional Budget Office. 1987. *Cost Estimate for HR 3810 (Immigration Reform and Control Act of 1986).* Washington, D.C.: U.S. Government Printing Office (July 15).

Corwin, Arthur. 1978. "A Story of Ad Hoc Exemptions: American Immigration Policy Toward Mexico." In *Immigrants—and Immigration: Perspectives on Mexican Labor Migration to the United States,* ed. Arthur Corwin, pp. 136–75. Westport, Conn.: Greenwood Press.

———. 1982. "The Numbers Game: Estimates of Illegal Aliens in the United States, 1970–1981." *Law and Contemporary Problems* 45 (Spring).

Craig, Steven C. 1991. "Politics and Elections." In *Government and Politics in Florida,* ed. Robert J. Huckshorn, pp. 77–110. Gainesville: Univ. Press of Florida.

Crane, Keith, Beth J. Asch, Joanna Zorn Heilbrunn, and Danielle C. Cullinane. 1990. *The Effect of Employer Sanctions on the Flow of Undocumented Immigrants to the United States.* Washington, D.C.: The Urban Institute Press.

Cummings, Richard. 1971. *Grito! Reies Tijerina and the New Mexico Land Grant War of 1967.* New York: Harper and Row.

Daniel, Cletus E. 1981. *Bitter Harvest: A History of California Farmworkers 1870–1941.* Berkeley and Los Angeles: Univ. of California Press.

Davidson, Chandler. 1990. *Race and Class in Texas Politics.* Princeton: Princeton Univ. Press.

Davidson, Chandler, and Bernard Grofman, eds. 1994. *Quiet Revolution in the South: The Impact of the Voting Rights Act 1965–1990.* Princeton: Princeton Univ. Press.

DeCew, Judson M., Jr. 1980. "Hispanics." In *Florida's Politics and Government,* ed. Manning J. Dauer, pp. 321–30. Gainesville: Univ. Presses of Florida.

de la Garza, Rodolfo O. 1980. "Chicanos and U.S. Foreign Policy: The Future of Chicano-Mexican Relations." *Western Political Quarterly* 33 (4) (December): 571–82.

———. 1984. "'And Then There Were Some . . . ' Chicanos as National Political Actors, 1967–1980." *Aztlán* 15 (1): 1–24.

———. 1987. *Ignored Voices: Public Opinion Polls and the Latino Community.* Austin: Univ. of Texas Press.

———. 1989. "Mexico, Mexicans, and Mexican Americans in U.S.-Mexican Relations." Texas Papers on Mexico Number 89–02. Austin: Institute of Latin American Studies.

———. 1992. "From Rhetoric to Reality: Latinos and the 1988 Election in Review." In *From Rhetoric to Reality: Latino Politics in the 1988 Elections,* ed. Rodolfo O. de la Garza and Louis DeSipio, pp. 171–80. Boulder, Colo.: Westview Press.

———. 1993. "Researchers Must Heed New Realities When They Study Latinos." *Chronicle of Higher Education* (June 2).

de la Garza, Rodolfo O., and Louis DeSipio, eds. 1992. *From Rhetoric to Reality: Latino Politics in the 1988 Elections.* Boulder, Colo.: Westview Press.

———. 1993. "Save the Baby, Change the Bathwater, and Clean the Tub: Latino Electoral Participation after Seventeen Years of Voting Rights Act Coverage." *Univ. of Texas Law Review* (June).

———. 1996. *Ethnic Ironies: Latino Politics in the 1992 Elections.* Boulder, Colo.: Westview Press.

de la Garza, Rodolfo O., Louis DeSipio, F. Chris García, John A. García, and Angelo Falcón. 1992. *Latino Voices: Mexican, Puerto Rican, and Cuban Perspectives on American Politics.* Boulder, Colo.: Westview Press.

de la Garza, Rudolph O., Z. Anthony Kruszewski, and Tomás Arciniega. 1973. *Chicanos and Native Americans: The Territorial Minorities.* Englewood Cliffs, N.J.: Prentice-Hall.

de la Garza, Rodolfo O., Martha Menchaca, and Louis DeSipio, eds. 1994. *Barrio Ballots: Latino Politics in the 1990 Elections*. Boulder, Colo.: Westview Press.

de la Garza, Rodolfo O., and Armando Trujillo. 1991. "Latinos and the Official English Debate in the United States: Language Is Not the Issue." In *Language and the State: The Law and Politics of Identity*, ed. David Schneiderman, pp. 209–26. Cowansville, Quebec: Les Editions Yvon Blais.

de la Garza, Rodolfo O., and Claudio Vargas. 1992. "The Mexican-Origin Population of the United States as a Political Force in the Borderlands: From Paisanos to Pochos to Potential Political Allies." In *Changing Boundaries in the Americas: New Perspectives on the U.S.-Mexican, Central American, and South American Borders*, ed. Lawrence A. Herzog, pp. 89–112. San Diego: Center for U.S. Mexican Studies, University of California–San Diego.

de la Peña, Fernando. 1991. *Democracy or Babel? The Case for Official English*. Washington, D.C.: U.S. English.

de León, Arnoldo. 1979. *In Re Ricardo Rodríguez: Attempt at Chicano Disenfranchisement in San Antonio, 1896–1897*. San Antonio: Caravel Press.

————. 1989. *Ethnicity in the Sunbelt: A History of Mexican Americans in Houston*. Houston: Mexican American Studies Program, Univ. of Houston.

DeSipio, Louis. 1995a. "Immigrants, Denizens, and Citizens: Latin American Immigration and Settlement in the 1990s." *Current World Leaders* 38 (2) (April): 63–87.

————. 1995b. "Are We Incorporating the Next Generation? Citizenship and Naturalization Among U.S. Immigrants." Paper prepared for presentation at the Annual Meetings of the Western Political Science Association, Portland.

————. 1995c. "Making Citizens or Good Citizens? Naturalization as a Predictor of Organizational and Electoral Behavior among Latino Immigrants." Paper prepared for presentation at the annual meetings of the American Political Science Association, August.

DeSipio, Louis, and Rodolfo O. de la Garza. 1992a. "Making Them Us: The Political Incorporation of Culturally Distinct Immigrants and Non-immigrant Minorities in the United States." In *Nations of Immigrants: Australia, the United States and International Migration*, ed. Gary P. Freeman and James Jupp, pp. 202–16. Melbourne, Australia: Oxford Univ. Press.

————. 1992b. "Will Latino Votes Equal Political Clout? Core Voters, Swing Voters, and the Potential Vote." Paper prepared for presentation at the Annual Meetings of the American Political Science Association, Chicago. September.

DeSipio, Louis, and Harry P. Pachon. 1992. "Making Americans: Administrative Discretion and Americanization." *UCLA Chicano-Latino Law Review* 12 (Spring): 52–66.

DeSipio, Louis, Harry Pachon, Sonia Ospina, and Eric Popkin. 1994. "The Political Incorporation of 'New' Latino Populations: The Dominicans, Colombians, Salvadorans, and Guatemalans." Paper prepared for delivery at the American Political Science Association. New York (September 1–4).

DeSipio, Louis, and Gregory Rocha. 1992. "Latino Influence on National Elections: The Case of 1988." In *From Rhetoric to Reality: Latino Politics in the 1988 Elections*, ed. Rodolfo O. de la Garza and Louis DeSipio, pp. 3–22. Boulder, Colo.: Westview Press.

Deutsch, Sarah. 1987. *No Separate Refuge: Culture, Class, and Gender on an Anglo-Hispanic Frontier in the American Southwest, 1880–1940*. New York: Oxford Univ. Press.

Duarte, E. B. 1985. "Role of the INS in Naturalization Outreach." In NALEO Educational Fund. *Proceedings of the First National Conference on Citizenship and the Hispanic Community*, pp. 16–17. Washington, D.C.: NALEO Educational Fund.

Edmonston, Barry, and Jeffrey Passel. 1991. "The Future Immigrant Population of the United States." Paper prepared for presentation to a conference entitled "Immigration and Ethnicity" at the Urban Institute, Washington, D.C. (June 17–18).

Edsall, Thomas Byrne, and Mary D. Edsall. 1991. *Chain Reaction: The Impact of Race, Rights, and Taxes on American Politics.* New York: Norton.

Erie, Steven P. 1988. *Rainbow's End: Irish Americans and the Dilemmas of Urban Machine Politics, 1840–1985.* Berkeley and Los Angeles: Univ. of California Press.

Falcón, Angelo. 1984. "A History of Puerto Rican Politics in New York City: 1860s to 1945." In *Puerto Rican Politics in Urban America,* ed. James Jennings and Monte Rivera, pp. 15–42. Westport, Conn.: Greenwood Press.

Flores, Henry, and Robert Brischetto. 1992. "Texas Mexicans in the 1988 Election." In *From Rhetoric to Reality: Latino Politics in the 1988 Elections,* ed. Rodolfo O. de la Garza and Louis DeSipio, pp. 87–98. Boulder, Colo.: Westview Press.

Foster, Lois, and David Stockley. 1984. *Multiculturalism: The Changing Australian Paradigm.* Clevedon: Multilingual Matters.

Fraga, Luis Ricardo. 1992. "Prototype From the Midwest: Latinos in Illinois." In *From Rhetoric to Reality: Latino Politics in the 1988 Elections,* ed. Rodolfo O. de la Garza and Louis DeSipio, pp. 111–26. Boulder, Colo.: Westview Press.

Franklin, Frank G. 1906. *The Legislative History of Naturalization in the United States from the Revolutionary War to 1861.* Chicago: Univ. of Chicago Press.

Frankovic, Kathleen A. 1993. "Public Opinion in the 1992 Campaign." In *The Election of 1992: Reports and Interpretations,* ed. Gerald M. Pomper et al., pp. 110–31. Chatham, N.J.: Chatham House.

Fuchs, Lawrence H. 1990. *The American Kaleidoscope: Race, Ethnicity, and the Civic Culture.* Hanover, N.H.: Univ. Press of New England [for Wesleyan Univ. Press].

Gamm, Gerald H. 1986. *The Making of New Deal Democrats: Voting Behavior and Realignment in Boston, 1920–1940.* Chicago: Univ. of Chicago Press.

Gann, Lewis H., and Peter Duignan. 1986. *The Hispanics in the United States: A History.* Boulder, Colo.: Westview Press.

García, F. Chris, and Rudolph O. de la Garza. 1977. *The Chicano Political Experience: Three Perspectives.* North Scituate, Mass.: Duxbury Press.

García, F. Chris, Rodolfo O. de la Garza, John A. García, and Angelo Falcón. 1991. "Ethnicity and Ideology: Political Attitudes of Mexicans, Puerto Ricans, and Cubans." Paper presented at the Annual Meetings of the American Political Science Association, Washington, D.C. September.

García, F. Chris, John A. García, Rodolfo O. de la Garza, Angelo Falcón, and Cara J. Abeyta. 1991. *Latinos and Politics: A Select Research Bibliography.* Austin: Univ. of Texas Press.

García, F. Chris, John A. García, Angelo Falcón, and Rodolfo O. de la Garza. 1989. "Studying Latino Politics: The Development of the Latino National Political Survey." *PS: Political Science and Politics* 12 (4) (December): 848–52.

García, Ignacio M. 1989. *United We Win: The Rise and Fall of La Raza Unida Party.* Tucson: Mexican American Studies and Research Center, University of Arizona.

García, John A. 1981. "Political Integration of Mexican Immigrants: Explorations into the Naturalization Process." *International Migration Review* 15 (4): 608–25.

———. 1987. "The Political Integration of Mexican Immigrants: Examining Some Political Orientations." *International Migration Review* 21 (2): 372–89.

García, Mario T. 1989. *Mexican Americans.* New Haven: Yale Univ. Press.

García Passalacqua, Juan M. 1993. *The 1993 Plebiscite in Puerto Rico: The Story, the Results, and Their Implications.* New York: Institute for Puerto Rican Policy.

Garrow, David. 1978. *Protest at Selma.* New Haven: Yale Univ. Press.

Gavit, John Palmer. 1922. *Americans by Choice.* New York: Harper Brothers.

Gettys, Luella. 1934. *The Law of Citizenship in the United States.* Chicago: Univ. of Chicago Press.

Glazer, Nathan, and Daniel P. Moynihan. 1963. *Beyond the Melting Pot.* Cambridge: Harvard Univ. Press.

————, eds. 1975. *Ethnicity Theory and Experience.* Cambridge: Harvard Univ. Press.

Gómez-Quiñones, Juan. 1994. *Roots of Chicano Politics.* Albuquerque: Univ. of New Mexico Press.

Gonzalez, David, with Martin Gottlieb. 1993. "Power Built on Poverty: A New Yorker's Odyssey." *New York Times (National Edition)* (May 14): A14.

Gordon, Milton. 1964. *Assimilation in American Life.* New York: Oxford Univ. Press.

Grebler, Leo, Joan W. Moore, and Ralph C. Guzman. 1970. *The Mexican American People: The Nation's Second Largest Minority.* New York: The Free Press.

Greeley, Andrew M. 1974. *Ethnicity in the United States: A Preliminary Reconnaissance.* New York: John Wiley and Sons.

Grenier, Guillermo J. 1992. "The Cuban American Labor Movement in Dade County: An Emerging Immigrant Working Class." In *Miami Now! Immigration, Ethnicity and Social Change,* ed. Guillermo J. Grenier and Alex Stepik, III, pp. 133–59. Gainesville: Univ. Press of Florida.

Grenier, Guillermo J., with Fabiana Invernizzi, Linda Salup, and Jorge Schmidt. 1994. "Los Bravos de la Política: Politics and Cubans in Miami." In *Barrio Ballots: Latino Politics in the 1990 Elections,* ed. Rodolfo O. de la Garza, Martha Menchaca, and Louis DeSipio, pp. 161–96. Boulder, Colo.: Westview Press.

Grenier, Guillermo J., and Alex Stepik, III, eds. 1992. *Miami Now! Immigration, Ethnicity, and Social Change.* Gainesville: Univ. Press of Florida.

Grimshaw, William J. 1992. *Bitter Fruit: Black Politics and the Chicago Machine 1931–1991.* Chicago: Univ. of Chicago Press.

Griswold del Castillo, Richard. 1990. *The Treaty of Guadalupe Hidalgo: A Legacy of Conflict.* Norman: Univ. of Oklahoma Press.

Guerra, Fernando. 1992. "Conditions Not Met: California Elections and the Latino Community." In *From Rhetoric to Reality: Latino Politics in the 1988 Elections,* ed. Rodolfo O. de la Garza and Louis DeSipio, pp. 99–110. Boulder, Colo.: Westview Press.

Gurak, Douglas T. 1987. "Family Formation and Marital Selectivity among Colombian and Dominican Immigrants in New York City." *International Migration Review* 78 (21) (2) (Summer): 275–97.

Gutiérrez, David G. 1995. *Walls and Mirrors: Mexican Americans, Mexican Immigrants, and the Politics of Ethnicity.* Berkeley: Univ. of California Press.

Gutiérrez, José Angel. 1968. "*La Raza* and Revolution: The Empirical Conditions of Revolution in Four South Texas Counties." MA thesis, St. Mary's University, San Antonio, Tex.

Guzmán, Pablo. 1995. "The Young Lords Legacy: A Personal Account." *Crítica: A Journal of Puerto Rican Policy and Politics* 11–12 (April–May): 1, 5–6.

Hammerback, John C.; Richard J. Jensen; and José Angel Gutiérrez. 1985. *A War of Words: Chicano Protest in the 1960s and 1970s.* Westport, Conn.: Greenwood Press.

Handlin, Oscar. 1951. *The Uprooted.* Boston: Little Brown.

Hansen, Marcus Lee. [1937] 1987. *The Problem of the Third Generation Immigrant.* Rock Island, Ill.: Swenson Swedish Immigration Research Center and Augustana College Library.

Harles, John C. 1993. *Politics in the Lifeboat: Immigrants and the American Democratic Order.* Boulder, Colo.: Westview Press.

Hawkins, Freda. 1989. *Critical Years in Immigration: Canada and Australia Compared.* Montreal: McGill-Queens Univ. Press.

Hero, Rodney. 1987. "The Election of Hispanics in City Government: An Examination of the Election of Federico Peña as Mayor of Denver." *Western Political Quarterly* 40 (1) (March): 93–105.

————. 1992. *Latinos and the U.S. Political System: Two Tiered Pluralism.* Philadelphia: Temple Univ. Press.

————. 1996. "An Essential Vote: Latinos and the 1992 Elections in Colorado." In *Ethnic Ironies: Latino Politics in the 1992 Elections*, ed. Rodolfo O. de la Garza and Louis DeSipio. Boulder, Colo.: Westview Press.

Hero, Rodney E., and Kathleen M. Beatty. 1989. "The Elections of Federico Peña as Mayor of Denver: Analysis and Implications." *Social Science Quarterly* 70 (2) (June):93–106.

Higham, John. 1955. *Strangers in the Land: Patterns of American Nativism, 1860–1925*. New Brunswick: Rutgers Univ. Press.

Holmes, Jack E. 1967. *Politics in New Mexico*. Albuquerque: Univ. of New Mexico Press.

Horrowitz, Donald L. 1985. *Ethnic Groups in Conflict*. Berkeley and Los Angeles: Univ. of California Press.

Huckfeldt, Robert, and Carol Wetzel Kohfeld. 1989. *Race and the Decline of Class in American Politics*. Urbana: Univ. of Illinois Press.

Huddle, Donald L., Arthur F. Corwin, and Gordon J. MacDonald. 1985. *Illegal Immigration: Job Displacement and Social Costs*. Alexandria, Va.: American Immigration Control Foundation.

Isaacs, Harold R. 1975. *Idols of the Tribe: Group Identity and Political Change*. New York: Harper and Row.

Jackson, Bryan O., and Michael B. Preston, eds. 1991. *Racial and Ethnic Politics in California*. Berkeley, Calif.: Institute for Governmental Studies Press.

Jasso, Guillermina, and Mark R. Rosensweig. 1990. *The New Chosen People: Immigrants in the United States*. New York: Russell Sage Foundation.

Jennings, James. 1977. *Puerto Rican Politics in New York City*. Washington, D.C.: Univ. Press of America.

————. 1984*a*. "Introduction: The Emergence of Puerto Rican Electoral Activism in Urban America." In *Puerto Rican Politics in Urban America*, ed. James Jennings and Monte Rivera, pp. 3–12. Westport, Conn.: Greenwood Press.

————. 1984*b*. "Puerto Rican Politics in Two Cities: New York and Boston." In *Puerto Rican Politics in Urban America*, ed. James Jennings and Monte Rivera, pp. 75–98. Westport, Conn.: Greenwood Press.

Joint Center for Political and Economic Studies. 1991. *Black Elected Officials: A National Roster*. Washington, D.C.: Joint Center for Political and Economic Studies Press.

Kamasaki, Charles, and Raul Yzaguirre. 1991. "Black Hispanic Tensions: One Perspective." Prepared for delivery at the 1991 Annual Meeting of the American Political Science Association, Washington, D.C., August 29–September 1.

Kelley, Jr., Stanley, Richard E. Ayres, and William G. Bowen. 1967. "Registration and Voting: Putting First Things First." *American Political Science Review* 61 (June): 359–79.

Kettner, James H. 1978. *The Development of American Citizenship, 1607–1870*. Chapel Hill: Univ. of North Carolina Press.

Key, V. O. 1984 [1949]. *Southern Politics in State and Nation*. Knoxville: Univ. of Tennessee Press.

Kleppner, Paul, et al. 1981. *The Evolution of American Electoral Systems*. Westport, Conn.: Greenwood Press.

Kluger, Richard. 1976. *Simple Justice: The History of Brown v. Board of Education and Black America's Struggle for Equality*. New York: Knopf.

Kosmin, Barry A., and Sriela Keysar. 1992. "Party Political Preferences of U.S. Hispanics: The Varying Impact of Religion, Social Class and Demographic Factors." Revised version of a paper presented at the Annual Conference of the American Association for Public Opinion Research. New York: Berman Institute, City University of New York Graduate School and University Center.

Lawson, Steven F. 1976. *Black Ballots: Voting Rights in the South 1944–1969*. New York: Columbia Univ. Press.

————. 1991. *Running for Freedom: Civil Rights and Black Politics in America Since 1941.* Philadelphia: Temple Univ. Press.

Lesko Associates. 1975. "Final Report: Basic Data and Guidance Required to Implement a Major Illegal Alien Study During FY 1985." Prepared for the Office of Planning and Evaluation, Immigration and Naturalization Service.

Levinson, Sanford. 1988. *Constitutional Faith.* Princeton: Princeton Univ. Press.

Lubell, Samuel. 1952. *The Future of American Politics.* New York: Harper and Brothers.

Márquez, Benjamin. 1993. *LULAC: The Making of a Mexican American Political Organization.* Austin: Univ. of Texas Press.

Matthiessen, Peter. 1969. *Sal Si Puedes: César Chávez and the New American Revolution.* New York: Random House.

McCleskey, Clifton, and Bruce Merrill. 1973. "Mexican American Political Behavior in Texas." *Social Science Quarterly* 53 (4) (March): 785–98.

McCleskey, Clifton, and Dan Nimmo. 1968. "Differences Between Potential, Registered, and Actual Voters: The Houston Metropolitan Area in 1964." *Social Science Quarterly* 49: 103–14.

Merriam, Charles E., and Harold G. Gosnell. 1924. *Non-voting: Causes and Methods of Control.* Chicago: Univ. of Chicago Press.

Meyer, Gerald. 1989. *Vito Marcantonio Radical Politician: 1902–1954.* Albany: State Univ. of New York Press.

Monroy, Douglas. 1990. *Thrown among Strangers: The Making of Mexican Culture in Frontier California.* Berkeley and Los Angeles: Univ. of California Press.

Montejano, David. 1987. *Anglos and Mexicans in the Making of Texas, 1836–1986.* Austin: Univ. of Texas Press.

Moore, Joan, and Raquel Pinderhughes, eds. 1993. *In the Barrios: Latinos and the Underclass Debate.* New York: Russell Sage Foundation.

Moreno, Dario. 1994. "Cuban Americans and Miami Politics." Paper Presented at the Conference on Minority Relations, Wellesley College. Wellesley, Mass. (April).

Moreno, Dario, and Nicol Rae. 1992. "Ethnicity and Partisanship: The Eighteenth Congressional District in Miami." In *Miami Now! Immigration, Ethnicity and Social Change,* ed. Guillermo J. Grenier and Alex Stepik III, pp. 186–204. Gainesville: Univ. Press of Florida.

Moreno, Dario, and Christopher Warren. 1992. "The Conservative Enclave: Cubans in Florida." In *From Rhetoric to Reality: Latino Politics in the 1988 Elections,* ed. Rodolfo O. de la Garza and Louis DeSipio, pp. 127–46. Boulder, Colo.: Westview Press.

————. 1996. "The Conservative Enclave Revisited: Cuban Americans in Florida." In *Ethnic Ironies: Latino Politics in the 1992 Elections,* ed. Rodolfo O. de la Garza and Louis DeSipio. Boulder, Colo.: Westview Press.

Mormino, Gary R., and George Pozzetta. 1987. *The Immigrant World of Ybor City: Italians and Their Latin Neighbors in Tampa, 1885–1985.* Urbana: Univ. of Illinois Press.

Muñoz, Carlos, Jr. 1989. *Youth, Identity, Power: The Chicano Movement.* New York: Verso.

Muñoz, Carlos, Jr., and Charles P. Henry. 1990. "Coalition Politics in San Antonio and Denver: The Cisneros and Peña Mayoral Campaigns." In *Racial Politics in American Cities,* ed. Rufus P. Browning, Dale Rogers Marshall, and David H. Tabb, pp. 179–90. New York: Longman.

Myers, Gustavus. 1968 [1917]. *The History of Tammany Hall.* New York: Burt Franklin.

Nabakov, Peter. 1969. *Tijerina and the Court House Raid.* Albuquerque: Univ. of New Mexico Press.

NALEO Educational Fund. 1985. *Proceedings of the First National Conference on Citizenship and the Hispanic Community.* Washington, D.C.: NALEO Educational Fund.

————. 1988. *New Citizens in Limbo? One in Three Applicants Neither Pass Nor Fail.* NALEO Background Paper 8. Washington, D.C.: NALEO Educational Fund.

———. 1989. *The National Latino Immigrant Survey*. Washington, D.C.: NALEO Educational Fund.

———. 1991. *Rejection of U.S. Citizenship Applicants: One Out of Four Applicants Bureaucratically Rejected Annually*. NALEO Background Paper 17. Washington, D.C.: NALEO Educational Fund.

———. 1992. *The Latino Vote in 1992*. Washington, D.C.: The NALEO Educational Fund.

———. 1993a. *1992 National Roster of Hispanic Elected Officials*. Washington, D.C.: NALEO Educational Fund.

———. 1993b. "Review of Academic Studies of the Colombian, Dominican, Guatemalan, and Salvadoran Populations in the United States." Typescript. Los Angeles: NALEO Educational Fund.

———. 1994. *The Surge of Naturalization: Promise or Peril?* Proceedings of the 1993 NALEO Educational Fund U.S. Citizenship Conference. Los Angeles: NALEO Educational Fund.

National Academy of Public Administration. 1991. "Managerial Options for the Immigration and Naturalization Service." A report to the United States Department of Justice submitted in fulfillment of contract 1C-G-JMD-0033.

National Council of La Raza. 1991. *Unlocking the Golden Door: Hispanics and the Citizenship Process*. Washington, D.C.: National Council of La Raza Policy Analysis Center.

Nelson, B. A. 1984. *The Coming Triumph of Mexican Irredentism*. Monterey, Va.: The American Immigration Control Foundation.

Nelson, Dale C. 1993. "Latino Political Participation: An Analysis of the Literature on Chicanos, Cubans, and Puerto Ricans." Paper presented at the Annual Meeting of the Western Political Science Association, Pasadena, Calif., March 18–20.

North, David. 1985. *The Long Grey Welcome: A Study of the American Naturalization Program*. Washington, D.C.: The NALEO Educational Fund [abbreviated version in *International Migration Review* 21 (2) (Summer 1987): 311–26].

Novak, Michael. 1971. *The Rise of Unmeltable Ethnics: Politics and Culture in the 1970s*. New York: Macmillan.

Oboler, Suzanne. 1995. *Ethnic Labels, Latino Lives: Identity and the Politics of (Re)presentation in the United States*. Minneapolis: Univ. of Minnesota Press.

O'Connor, Karen, and Lee Epstein. 1985. "A Legal Voice for the Chicano Community: The Activities of the Mexican American Legal Defense and Education Fund, 1968–1982." In *The Mexican American Experience: An Interdisciplinary Anthology*, ed. Rodolfo O. de la Garza, Frank D. Bean, Charles M. Bonjean, Ricardo Romo, and Rodolfo Alvarez, pp. 282–92. Austin: Univ. of Texas Press.

Olzak, Susan, 1983. "Contemporary Ethnic Mobilization." *Annual Review of Sociology* 9: 355–74.

———. 1992. *The Dynamics of Ethnic Competition and Conflict*. Stanford: Stanford Univ. Press.

Omi, Michael, and Howard Winant. 1986. *Racial Formation in the United States from the 1960s to the 1980s*. New York: Routledge.

———. 1994. *Racial Formation in the United States: From the 1960s to the 1990s*. Second Edition. New York: Routledge.

"Opinion Roundup." 1989. *Public Opinion* (January/February).

Ornstein, Norman, Andrew Kohut, and Larry McCarthy. 1988. *The People, the Press and Politics: The Times Mirror Study of the American Electorate, Conducted by the Gallup Organization*. Reading, Mass.: Addison-Wesley.

Orozco, Cynthia. 1992. "The Origins of the League of United Latin American Citizens (LULAC) and the Mexican American Civil Rights Movement in Texas with an Analysis of Women's Political Participation in a Gendered Context, 1910–1929." Ph.D. dissertation, the University of California, Los Angeles.

Pachon, Harry P. 1987. "An Overview of Citizenship in the Hispanic Community." *International Migration Review* 21 (2) (Summer): 209–311.

———. 1991. "U.S. Citizenship and Latino Participation in California." In *Racial and Ethnic Politics in California*, ed. Byran O. Jackson and Michael B. Preston, pp. 71–88. Berkeley, Calif.: Institute of Governmental Studies Press.

Pachon, Harry P., and Lourdes Argüelles, with Rafael González. 1994. "Grass-Roots Politics in an East Los Angeles Barrio: A Political Ethnography of the 1990 General Election." In *Barrio Ballots: Latino Politics in the 1990 Elections*, ed. Rodolfo O. de la Garza, Martha Menchaca, and Louis DeSipio, pp. 115–60. Boulder, Colo.: Westview Press.

Pachon, Harry P., and Louis DeSipio. 1986. "The Attitudes of Citizenship Service Providers toward Low Rates of Citizenship in the Hispanic Community." Paper prepared for presentation at the Annual Meetings of the Western Political Science Association. Eugene, Ore. (March).

———. 1987. "Invisibility in the Data, Invisibility in the Policy: The Latino Family and Public Policy." *Family Resource Coalition Report* 6 (2): 3.

———. 1988. *The Latino Vote in 1988*. Washington, D.C.: NALEO Educational Fund.

———. 1990. "Latino Legislators and Latino Caucuses." Working Paper No. 11. Inter-Univ. Program for Latino Research and the Social Science Research Council. Austin, Tex.: Center for Mexican American Studies.

———. 1992a. "A Study of the Public Policy Information Sources and Methods Which Latino Elected Officials Utilize." Final Report to the Rockefeller Foundation. Los Angeles: NALEO Educational Fund.

———. 1992b. "Latino Elected Officials in the 1990s." *PS: Political Science and Politics* 25 (2) (June): 212–17.

———. 1994. *New Americans by Choice: Political Perspectives of Latino Immigrants*. Boulder, Colo.: Westview Press.

Pachon, Harry P., Louis DeSipio, and Jack Sullivan. 1991. "Americans by Choice: Factors That Distinguish Naturalizing from Non-naturalizing Immigrants." Paper prepared for presentation at the annual meeting of the American Political Science Association, Washington, D.C., August.

Padilla, Felix. 1985. *Latino Ethnic Consciousness: The Case of Mexican Americans and Puerto Ricans in Chicago*. Notre Dame: Univ. of Notre Dame Press.

Parenti, Michael. 1967. "Ethnic Politics and the Persistence of Ethnic Identification." *American Political Science Review* 61 (September): 717–26.

Parker, Frank R. 1990. *Black Votes Count: Political Empowerment in Mississippi after 1965*. Chapel Hill: Univ. of North Carolina Press.

Passel, Jeffrey. 1990. "Effects of Population Estimates on Voter Participation Rates." In U.S. Bureau of the Census. *Studies in the Measurement of Voter Turnout*, pp. 31–54. Current Population Reports, Population Characteristics Series P-23 No. 168. Washington, D.C.: U.S. Government Printing Office.

Passel, Jeffrey S., Frank D. Bean, and Barry Edmonston. 1991. "Assessing the Impact of Employer Sanctions on Undocumented Immigration to the United States." In *The Paper Curtain: Employer Sanctions' Implementation, Impact, and Reform*, ed. Michael Fix, pp. 193–214. Washington, D.C.: Urban Institute Press.

Passel, Jeffrey S., and Karen A. Woodrow. 1984. "Geographic Distribution of Undocumented Immigrants: Estimates of Undocumented Aliens Counted in the 1980 Census by State." *International Migration Review* 18 (3): 642–71.

———. 1985. "Growth of the Undocumented Alien Population in the United States, 1979–1983, as Counted in the Current Population Survey and the Decennial Census." Paper presented at the Population Association of America Meetings.

Paz, Octavio. 1961. *Labyrinth of Solitude*. New York: Grove Press.

Peel, Roy V. 1935. *The Political Clubs of New York City*. New York: G. P. Putnam's Sons.

Pérez, Lisandro. 1992. "Cuban Miami." In *Miami Now! Immigration, Ethnicity and Social Change*, ed. Guillermo J. Grenier and Alex Stepik, III, pp. 83–108. Gainesville: Univ. Press of Florida.

Pérez, Louis A., Jr. 1978. "Cubans in Tampa: From Exiles to Immigrants, 1892–1901." *Florida Historical Quarterly*: 129–40.

Pessar, Patricia R. 1987. "The Linkage between Household and Workplace of Dominican Women in the U.S." In *Caribbean Life in New York City: Sociocultural Dimensions*, ed. Constance R. Sutton and Elsa M. Chaney, pp. 253–77. Staten Island, N.Y.: Center for Migration Studies.

Petrocik, John R. 1981. *Party Coalitions: Realignment and the Decline of the New Deal Party System*. Chicago: Univ. of Chicago Press.

Pitt, Leonard. 1966. *The Decline of the Californios: A Social History of the Spanish-Speaking Californians, 1846–1890*. Berkeley and Los Angeles: Univ. of California Press.

Piven, Frances F., and Richard A. Cloward. 1988. *Why Americans Don't Vote*. New York: Pantheon Books.

Polinard, J. L., Robert D. Wrinkle, Tomás Longoria, and Norman E. Binder. 1994. *Electoral Structure and Urban Policy: The Impact on Mexican American Communities*. Armonk, N.Y.: M. E. Sharpe.

Pomper, Gerald M. 1993. "The Presidential Election." In *The Election of 1992: Reports and Interpretations*, ed. Gerald M. Pomper et al., pp. 132–56. Chatham, N.J.: Chatham House.

Portes, Alejandro, and John Curtis. 1987. "Changing Flags: Naturalization and Its Determinants among Mexican Immigrants." *International Migration Review* 21 (2) (Summer): 352–71.

Portes, Alejandro, and Rafael Mozo. 1985. "The Political Adaptation Process among Cubans and Other Ethnic Minorities in the United States: A Preliminary Analysis." *International Migration Review* 19 (2): 35–63.

Portes, Alejandro, and Alex Stepik. 1993. *City on the Edge: The Transformation of Miami*. Berkeley: Univ. of California Press.

Reed, Adolph L. 1986. *The Jesse Jackson Phenomenon: The Crisis of Purpose in Afro-American Politics*. New Haven: Yale Univ. Press.

Richmond, Anthony H. 1991. "Immigration and Multiculturalism in Canada and Australia: The Contradictions and Crises of the 1980s." *International Journal of Canadian Studies* (Spring): 87–110.

Rodríguez, Clara, Virginia Sánchez Korrol, and José Oscar Alers, eds. 1980. *The Puerto Rican Struggle: Essays on Survival in the United States*. New York: Puerto Rican Migration Research Consortium.

Rodríguez, Jeanette. 1994. *Our Lady of Guadalupe: Faith and Empowerment among Mexican American Women*. Austin: Univ. of Texas Press.

Rodríguez, Nestor P., Noelia Elizondo, David Mena, Ricardo Rojas, Adolfo Vásquez, and Frank Yeverino. 1994. "Political Mobilization in Houston's Magnolia." In *Barrio Ballots: Latino Politics in the 1990 Elections*, ed. Rodolfo O. de la Garza, Martha Menchaca, and Louis DeSipio, pp. 83–114. Boulder, Colo.: Westview Press.

Rogers, Mary Beth. 1990. *Cold Anger: A Story of Faith and Power Politics*. Denton: Univ. of North Texas Press.

Rosberg, Gerald M. 1977. "Aliens and Equal Protection: Why Not the Right to Vote." *Michigan Law Review* 75 (April–May): 1092–1136.

Rosen, Gerald Paul. 1975. *Political Ideology and the Chicano Movement: A Study of the Political Ideology of Activists in the Chicano Movement*. San Francisco: R and E Research Associates.

Rosenbaum, Robert J. 1981. *Mexican Resistance in the Southwest: "The Sacred Right of Self-Preservation."* Austin: Univ. of Texas Press.

Rothschild, Joseph. 1981. *Ethnopolitics: A Conceptual Framework.* New York: Columbia Univ. Press.

Rubel, Arthur J. 1966. *Across the Tracks: Mexican Americans in a Texas City.* Austin: Univ. of Texas Press.

Saiz, Martín. 1992. "Cohesion, Mobilization, and Latino Political Influence: Colorado in 1988." In *From Rhetoric to Reality: Latino Politics in the 1988 Elections,* ed. Rodolfo O. de la Garza and Louis DeSipio, pp. 69–76. Boulder, Colo.: Westview Press.

San Miguel, Guadalupe, Jr. 1987. *'Let All of Them Take Heed': Mexican Americans and the Campaign for Educational Equality in Texas, 1910–1981.* Austin: Univ. of Texas Press.

Sánchez, George. 1993. *Becoming Mexican American: Ethnicity, Culture and Identity in Chicano Los Angeles, 1900–1945.* New York: Oxford Univ. Press.

Sánchez Korrol, Virginia E. 1983. *From Colonia to Community: The History of Puerto Ricans in New York City, 1917–1948.* Westport, Conn.: Greenwood Press.

———. 1994. *From Colonia to Community: The History of Puerto Ricans in New York City, 1917–1948.* Revised Edition. Berkeley: Univ. of California Press.

Sandmeyer, Elmer Clarence. 1991 [1939]. *The Anti-Chinese Movement in California.* Urbana: Univ. of Illinois Press.

Sassen-Koob, Saskia. 1987. "Formal and Informal Associations: Dominicans and Colombians in New York." In *Caribbean Life in New York City: Sociocultural Dimensions,* ed. Constance R. Sutton and Elsa M. Chaney, pp. 278–96. Staten Island, N.Y.: Center for Migration Studies.

Shafer, Byron E., ed. 1991. *The End of Realignment? Interpreting American Electoral Eras.* Madison: Univ. of Wisconsin Press.

Schuck, Peter H., and Rogers M. Smith. 1985. *Citizenship without Consent: Illegal Aliens in the American Polity.* New Haven: Yale Univ. Press.

Shelton, Edgar Greer, Jr. 1946. "Political Conditions among Texas Mexicans along the Rio Grande." M.A. thesis, University of Texas (Austin).

Sierra, Christine Marie. 1983. "The Political Transformation of a Minority Organization: the Council of La Raza, 1965–1980." Ph.D. dissertation, Stanford University.

———. 1992. "Hispanos and the 1988 General Election in New Mexico." In *From Rhetoric to Reality: Latino Politics in the 1988 Elections,* ed. Rodolfo O. de la Garza and Louis DeSipio, pp. 43–68. Boulder, Colo.: Westview Press.

Sigelman, Lee and Susan Welch. 1991. *Black Americans' Views of Racial Inequality: The Dream Deferred.* New York: Cambridge Univ. Press.

Skerry, Peter. 1985. "The Ambiguity of Mexican American Politics." In *Clamor at the Gates: The New American Immigration,* ed. Nathan Glazer, pp. 241–57. San Francisco: Institute for Contemporary Studies.

———. 1993. *Mexican Americans: The Ambivalent Minority.* New York: Free Press.

Smith, Anthony. 1981. *The Ethnic Revival.* New York: Cambridge Univ. Press.

———. 1986. *The Ethnic Origins of Nations.* New York: Basil Blackwell.

Smith, Darrell Hevenor. 1926. *The Bureau of Naturalization, Its History, Activities, and Organization.* Baltimore: Johns Hopkins Univ. Press.

Southwest Voter Registration and Education Project. 1983. *National Hispanic Voter Registration Campaign.* San Antonio, Tex.: Southwest Voter Registration and Education Project.

Stowers, Genie N. L. 1990. "Political Participation, Ethnicity, and Class Status: The Case of Cubans in Miami." *Ethnic Groups* 8: 73–90.

Sullivan, John L., James E. Pierson, and George E. Marcus. 1978. "Ideological Constraint in the Mass Public: A Methodological Critique and Some New Findings." *American Journal of Political Science* 22 (May): 233–49.

Tarrance, Lance, Jr. 1987. "Hispanic Vote Behavior: Selected Findings from Past Research Conducted by Tarrance and Associates." In *Ignored Voices: Public Opinion Polls and the Latino Community*, ed. Rodolfo O. de la Garza, pp. 63–75. Austin: Univ. of Texas Press.

Tate, Katherine. 1993. *From Protest to Politics: The New Black Voters in American Elections.* Cambridge: Harvard Univ. Press.

Tarrance, Lance, Jr. 1987. "Hispanic Vote Behavior: Selected Findings from Past Research Conducted by Tarrance and Associates." In *Ignored Voices: Public Opinion Polls and the Latino Community*, ed. Rodolfo O. de la Garza, pp. 63–75. Austin: Univ. of Texas Press.

Teixeira, Ruy A. 1992. *The Disappearing American Voter.* Washington, D.C.: Brookings Institution.

Terborg-Penn, Rosalyn Marian. 1977. "Afro Americans in the Struggle for Women's Suffrage." Ph.D. dissertation, Howard Univ.

Tingsten, Herbert. 1963. *Political Behavior: Studies in Election Statistics.* Totowa, N.J.: Bedminster Press.

Thernstrom, Abigail M. 1987. *Whose Votes Count? Affirmative Action and Minority Voting Rights.* Cambridge: Harvard Univ. Press.

Tocqueville, Alexis de. 1981. *Democracy in America.* New York: Modern Library.

Tomás Rivera Center. 1995. "Reality and Rhetoric Clash over Latino Vote: California Latinos Turned Out in Record Numbers Despite Claims of Analysts and Pundits." Press Release. June 14.

Torres, Maria de los Angeles. 1988. "From Exiles to Minorities: The Politics of Cuban Americans." In *Latinos and the Political System*, ed. F. Chris García, pp. 81–98. Notre Dame: Univ. of Notre Dame Press.

Ueda, Reed. 1980. "Naturalization and Citizenship." In *Harvard Encyclopedia of American Ethnic Groups*, ed. Stephan Thernstrom. Cambridge: Harvard Univ. Press.

Uhlaner, Carole J., Bruce E. Cain, and D. Roderick Kiewiet. 1989. "Political Participation of Ethnic Minorities in the 1980s." *Political Behavior* 11 (3) (September): 195–232.

U.S. Bureau of the Census. 1973. *Voting and Registration in the Election of November 1972.* Current Population Reports, Population Characteristics. Series P-20 No. 253. Washington, D.C.: U.S. Government Printing Office.

———. 1988. *Popularly Elected Officials, 1987 (Advance Report).* GC87-2[P]. Washington, D.C.: U.S. Government Printing Office.

———. 1989. *Voting and Registration in the Election of November 1988.* Current Population Reports, Population Characteristics. Series P-20 No. 440. Washington, D.C.: U.S. Government Printing Office.

———. 1990. *Studies in the Measurement of Voter Turnout.* Current Population Reports, Population Characteristics Series P-23 No. 168. Washington, D.C.: U.S. Government Printing Office.

———. 1991a. *1990 Census Profile: Race and Hispanic Origin.* (June).

———. 1991b. "Census Releases Preliminary Coverage Estimates from the Post-enumeration Survey Demographic Analysis." Press Release (April 18).

———. 1993a. *Voting and Registration in the Election of November 1992.* Current Population Reports, Population Characteristics Series P-20 No. 466. Washington, D.C.: U.S. Government Printing Office.

———. 1993b. *The Foreign-Born Population by Race, Hispanic Origin, and Citizenship for the United States.* CPH-L-134. Washington, D.C.: U.S. Bureau of the Census, Population Division, Ethnic and Hispanic Branch.

———. 1993c. "Table 4A. Reported Voting and Registration by Race, Hispanic Origin, and Age, for States: November 1992." Unpublished data. Washington, D.C.: U.S. Bureau of the Census.

U.S. General Accounting Office. 1991. *Immigration Management: Strong Leadership and*

Management Reforms Needed to Address Serious Problems GAO/T-GGD-91-23. Washington, D.C.: U.S. Government Printing Office.

U.S. Immigration Commission. 1911. *Reports of the Immigration Commission.* Washington, D.C.: U.S. Government Printing Office.

U.S. Immigration and Naturalization Service. 1966. *Report of the Commissioner of Immigration and Naturalization for the Year Ending June 30, 1966.* Washington, D.C.: U.S. Government Printing Office.

———. 1989. *1988 Statistical Yearbook of the Immigration and Naturalization Service.* Washington, D.C.: U.S. Government Printing Office.

———. 1990. *1989 Statistical Yearbook of the Immigration and Naturalization Service.* Washington, D.C.: U.S. Government Printing Office.

———. 1992. *1991 Statistical Yearbook of the Immigration and Naturalization Service.* Washington, D.C.: National Technical Information Service.

———. 1994. *1993 Statistical Yearbook of the Immigration and Naturalization Service.* Washington, D.C.: National Technical Information Service.

U.S. Senate. 1980. *The History of the Immigration and Naturalization Service.* Report to the Committee on the Judiciary. Washington, D.C.: Congressional Research Service.

———. 1987. *Senate Report 100–182.* Washington, D.C.: U.S. Government Printing Office (revised by INS in 1988 based on requests for clarification from the committee).

Valadez, John. 1994. "Latino Politics in Chicago: Pilsen in the 1990 General Election." In *Barrio Ballots: Latino Politics in the 1990 Elections,* ed. Rodolfo O. de la Garza, Martha Menchaca, and Louis DeSipio, pp. 115–35. Boulder, Colo.: Westview Press.

Valdes y Tapia, Daniel. [1964] 1976. *Hispanos and American Politics.* New York: Arno Press.

Velásquez, William. 1983. "The Experience of the Southwest Voter Registration and Education Project in Mounting an Effective Voter Registration Drive." In National Puerto Rican Coalition. *Strategies for Increasing Voter Participation in Puerto Rican Communities in the Continental United States,* pp. 51–58. Alexandria, Va.: National Puerto Rican Coalition.

Verba, Sidney, and Norman H. Nie. 1972. *Participation in America: Political Democracy and Social Equality.* Chicago: Univ. of Chicago Press.

Verba, Sidney, Kay Lehman Schlozman, Henry Brady, and Norman H. Nie. 1993. "Race, Ethnicity, and Political Resources: Participation in the United States." *British Journal of Political Science* 23: 453–97.

Vigil, Charles S. 1976. "Spanish-Surnamed Americans in the First Hundred Years of Government." In *The Hispanic Contribution to the State of Colorado,* ed. José de Onís, pp. 183–89. Boulder, Colo.: Westview Press.

Villareal, Roberto E., and Norma Hernandez, eds. 1991. *Latinos and Political Coalitions: Political Empowerment for the 1990s.* New York: Praeger.

Warren, Robert, and Ellen Percy Kraly. 1985. *The Elusive Exodus: Emigration from the United States.* Population Trends and Public Policy Number Eight. Washington, D.C.: Population Reference Bureau.

Warren, Robert, and Jeffrey S. Passel. 1987. "A Count of the Uncountable: Estimates of Undocumented Aliens Counted in the 1980 United States Census." *Demography* 24 (3): 375–93.

Waters, Mary C. 1990. *Ethnic Options: Choosing Identities in America.* Berkeley and Los Angeles: Univ. of California Press.

Weber, David J. 1973. *Foreigners in Their Native Land: Historical Roots of the Mexican Americans.* Albuquerque: Univ. of New Mexico Press.

Weeks, O. Douglas. 1929. "The League of United Latin-American Citizens: A Texas-Mexican Civic Organization." *Southwestern Political and Social Science Quarterly* (December): 257–78.

————. 1930. "The Texas Mexican and the Politics of South Texas." *The American Political Science Review* 24 (August): 606–27.

Weiss, Nancy J. 1983. *Farewell to the Party of Lincoln*. Princeton: Princeton Univ. Press.

Welch, Susan, and Lee Sigelman. 1993. "The Politics of Hispanic Americans: Insights from National Surveys, 1980–1988." *Social Science Quarterly* 74 (1) (March): 76–94.

Werner, M. R. 1932. *Tammany Hall*. Garden City, N.Y.: Garden City Publishing Group.

Weyr, Thomas. 1988. *Hispanic U.S.A.: Breaking the Melting Pot*. New York: Harper and Row.

Wolfinger, Raymond, and Steven Rosenstone. 1980. *Who Votes?* New Haven: Yale Univ. Press.

Zamora, Emilio. 1993. *The World of the Mexican Worker in Texas*. College Station: Texas A & M Univ. Press.

Index

abortion issue, 81
affirmative action, 8, 80
affluence, and political affiliation, 29
AFL-CIO, 46
African Americans: and Civil Rights movement, 14, 15, 111, 114–16; and Democratic Party, 15; group political influence of, 168, 171; as new electorate, 14–16; political exclusion of, 7–8; political incorporation of, 1; registration in southern states, 112; registration rates of, 15; voter mobilization of, 111–17; voting participation of, 60–61; and Voting Rights Act, 7, 14, 112–13
age: and naturalization, 124–29, 157; among voters, 61, 93, 96, 97, 99
Alien and Sedition Acts, 7, 144
Allswang, John M., 19
American G.I. Forum, 34, 47
American Labor Party, 37
American Party, 7
ancestry, terminology of, 23–26
Anglo, definition of, 26–27
antisuffragist sentiment, 12
Arizona, and nonvoter impact, 91
Armenian immigrants, 152
ASPIRA, 45–46
assimilationist advocacy, 33, 42–43
Australia, immigrant policies of, 6
Aztlán, romantic notion of, 47, 153

Babbitt, Bruce, 77
Barrera, Mario, 42–43
bilingual education, 44, 46, 81
blacks. *See* African Americans
Boston, during New Deal, 18
Brown, Ronald E., 114
Buchanan, Patrick, 81
bureaucracy, and naturalization, 149–50
Bureau of Naturalization, 145, 146
Bush, George: on civil rights issue, 38; and Cuban Americans, 83–84; and former voters, 108; "kinder, gentler America" of, 80; and Latino vote, 74–77; nonvoter support of, 100, 103, 109; swing

votes for, 83–84; and voter malaise, 88; and voter mobilization, 71
Bush Democrats, 83–85

California: and former voters, 108; and informed nonvoters, 106; Latino voting declines in, 69–70; mobilization strategies for, 109; naturalization strategies for, 137–38; and nonvoters, 91, 98; and Proposition 187, 73, 182
Campbell, Ben Nighthorse, 78
Canada, immigrant policies of, 6
Canadian immigrants, 130
capital punishment issue, 55, 162
Castro, Fidel, 38, 47, 82
Central America: immigrants from, 121; policy issue of, 55, 81, 102–3, 162
Chávez, Linda, 6, 42–43
Chicano movement: and Aztlán ideal, 47, 153; ideologies of, 34–35; and naturalization, 153; radicalism of, 40; and Raza Unida, 115–16; and separatism, 42
Chinese Americans: discrimination against, 8; political incorporation of, 8
Chinese Exclusion Act (1882), 144
citizenship: by birth, 120, 144; preparation for, 123; of Puerto Ricans, 181; service centers for, 154–55; treaty-based, 2, 35; among voters, 61
citizenship milieus, 126–29
civics knowledge, and naturalization, 145
civil rights, 38, 44–45
Civil Rights movement, 132; and African Americans, 14, 15, 111, 114–16; as model for Latinos, 175–76; and naturalization, 132
class: in Cuban American politics, 62; and political affiliation, 29
Clinton, Bill: and Latino vote, 75, 84; and voter mobilization, 70–71, 73
Cohen, Lizabeth, 18–19
Colombians, ideologies of, 39–40
Colorado: Latino voting declines in, 69–70; and nonvoter impact, 90–91; and po-

Race, Ethnicity, and Politics

Counting on the Latino Vote
LATINOS AS A NEW ELECTORATE
Louis DeSipio

Imagining Miami
ETHNIC POLITICS IN A POSTMODERN WORLD
Sheila L. Croucher